C000162787

A Pilgrim's Guide to The Grief Journey

The Vale of Tears

Experiencing Growth through Loss

Robert Weston

New Wine Press

New Wine Ministries
PO Box 17
Chichester
West Sussex
United Kingdom
PO19 2AW

ISBN 978-1-905991-20-4
Typeset by Ruach Breath of Life Ministries
www.ruachministries.org

Printed in Malta

The Vale of Tears

Cultivating an eternal Perspective

Commendations

Having experienced the inexplicable nocturnal death of our eleven year old son, we can personally attest to the accuracy of Robert's explanations, the Holy Spirit's anointing on his prayers, and the authority of his life-giving council. This important book will help you in and through grief and, beyond any other resource we are aware of, will prepare you to minister to others. Thanks, Robert, for an exceptionally hard job extremely well done."

Paul and Gretel Haglin,
(Resurrection Christian Ministries)

In the book you have in your hands, Robert shines warm light on the difficult and dark experience of loss – which can affect any one of us at any time. Liberally peppering his compassionate writing with vivid illustrations, quotes and moving stories – many from his own journey – he provides us with deep understanding of what is happening, as well as pointing us towards strategies for finding "treasures" in the darkness.

As he says, "this book is all about preparing our hearts for times when it feels as though the bottom has fallen out of the world." Robert helps us equally to come sensitively alongside others in their loss, to help them cast their burden on the Lord.

Rather than ploughing on relentlessly, Robert invites the reader to pause frequently and reflect. To this end he has provided a series of succinct yet striking prayers. Apart from the Bible, which Robert frequently quotes and illuminates, I can think of no better book to help turn loss and grief into the growth experience God intends.

Mike Field,
(Jersey Evangelical Alliance)

Grief is like a rocky valley with sharp dark sides. This comprehensive introduction to the grief journey offers the grieving

– and those who travel with them – wise and compassionate insight into widely differing kinds of loss. Robert examines the threats that loss poses in the Valley of the Shadow, and shows us how we can find healing and wholeness, eventually emerging into green refreshing pastures.

Revd. David Woodhouse,
(Editor, "Trauma and Abuse")

When do we learn to drive? Is it before we own a car, in anticipation of owning one soon? Or is it after we have bought a car that we decide it might be a good idea to learn how to drive it? We might ask the same question about grief. Do we learn about grief and the process of grieving before or after encountering it – either in our own life, or in the life of a friend or relative?

Robert's book makes the sensible assumption that it is better to prepare ourselves beforehand for what will inevitably come our way in the course of life. Unlike many books on grief, he does not just deal with bereavement, but considers grief that is caused by all sorts of other events: loss of friends or job, loss of vision, or ambition, divorce or retirement and so on.

In the practical and Biblically-based way that has typified his earlier books, Robert writes about the emotional and spiritual forces involved in the grief process. Whether you are suffering yourself, or anticipate consoling others, his wisdom, experience and examples offer insight, foresight and perspectives that cannot fail to prepare you.

Even in the midst of grief it is not too late to read this book. The many themes that Robert explores will enable you to home in on just what you are experiencing to provide the help you need most. There are no quick fixes to grief, let alone any easy triumphalism, but Robert shows us that it is possible to advance along the grief journey courageously, and to avoid many of the pitfalls on it. I commend it.

David Barratt,
(Author of "C. S. Lewis and his World")

We have known Robert Weston for twenty five years and have stayed in close touch throughout that time. We have shared each other's joys and trials, and Robert has had his share of these. It is from this background that he addresses the great problem of Grief and the last Taboo of our society: Death. The pages of this book take the reader through the many aspects of grieving including the loss not just of loved ones but jobs, dreams and aspirations. It pulls no punches and is full of honest advice both practical and spiritual on how to cope with our worst fears. A must for those who are going through avenues of pain, or who are involved in helping others who are.

Peter and Mac Tompsett,
(Image Consultants)

May I say how impressed I am by your ability to pull together so many thoughts, quotes and stories, as well as research? Your heart, combined with your wisdom and long ministry experience is a stunning combination. This book is going to actively minister to many!

Laurie Klein,
(Author, and composer of the song "I love you Lord")

Note about References

To save putting long web addresses at the end of each chapter, I have posted useful links on our web site. See www.ruachministries.org/valeoftears/refs.htm for specific references, and www.ruachministries.org for our main site.

Acknowledgements

Rather as bees gather nectar from many flowers, I have benefited from the input of many friends and publications during the demanding process of completing this book. I would particularly like to thank Sally Mowbray for walking this journey with me from the beginning. You have provided valuable spiritual insight, as well as showing enormous patience in helping to edit the numerous drafts of this book.

Laurie Klein – your perceptive suggestions have greatly helped to shape the text, drawing on your experience both as a writer and as one who has received help with past abuse.

As surely as I am grateful to *King* David for the many biblical quotes I have incorporated, I would also like to thank two other Davids: David Barratt, for your clarity in suggesting structural changes during an early drafts, and David Woodhouse, for your contributions from your many years of ministry in this field.

Linda Louisa – your insights into the grief process are life-proven and poignant. It is always a joy to work with you. Thanks to you, Dad, for once again coming up with many timely suggestions, not to mention essential help with the formatting. Rona Scott – for the anecdotes you have contributed; Mike Field – for your help with proofreading; Peter and Mac Tompsett and Jane Carmichael – for reading the manuscript through; Tony and Brid Browne – for allowing me to reproduce several of your daughter's poems. Alison wrote her moving poems, knowing that she did not have long to live.

Special thanks too to Elisabeth Harding for reading the manuscript through several times. Your long involvement in caring for the grieving, as well as your literary experience in your editorial capacity with New Wine Ministries, combined to make your comments sharp and perceptive. Each of you have blessed me with your thoughtful suggestions. I dedicate this labour of love above all to Rosalind, who has walked with me through many griefs as well as joys during the twenty five years that I have had the privilege of being married to her.

Robert Weston © 2008 Canterbury

Author's Preface

C.S. Lewis once wrote that he was "pregnant with book." Books have a habit of changing shape as they develop. The first draft of *Vale of Tears* was a straightforward "manual" to accompany a workshop on grief. The volume served its purpose, but I sensed that the Lord was looking for something more prayerful and more creative – something that would both identify the inner workings of grief *and* reveal more of God's own heart.

I started again from scratch, setting out this time to write something that would be both factually accurate but also spiritually inspiring. Even though it covers most of the issues often associated with loss and grief, *Vale of Tears* is much more than a "textbook:" it is also a call to draw closer to God's heart.

Whatever else changes in society, the human heart remains the same. I asked for this book to be published with a hard cover in order to preserve its shelf life. My prayer is that it will be as relevant for you if loss comes your way in ten or twenty years time as it will hopefully prove to be concerning griefs that happened long ago – and that you will be equipped to cope with it for having taken the time to explore the subject now.

Together we will unmask the many faces of grief, and examine strategies that will help us to work our way through those times when it feels as though the bottom has fallen out of our world. As we explore the underlying causes of sorrow, we will find ourselves gaining greater confidence to befriend, pastor and counsel those who are walking their own grief journey, and to pour balm into bruised and hurting hearts.

Woven into the text are numerous references to the chequered experiences of Israel's shepherd king – for who better than David to show us how to handle the numerous griefs that punctuate life's pilgrimage?

The extensive Contents and Index pages will help you to track down specific issues you may wish to follow up. The quotes I have included from writers and counsellors well-versed in the grief process are worth savouring too, and will bring much wisdom.

Throughout the book you are sure to find yourself customising the material according to whether you are primarily grieving yourself, or reaching out to support someone else. To bind these viewpoints together, and to make the reading of this book a truly spiritual experience, may I encourage you to pause at the end of each section and make good use of the prayers of reflection?

It is my prayer that the Lord Jesus, who is intimately acquainted with grief in all its forms (Isaiah 53:3), will refresh your spirit and lift grief and trauma from your heart as you read these pages. May He guide you step by step through whatever valley you may be passing through, and restore you to a place of trust in the love that flows from His heart.

A Starting Prayer

Trail-Blazer and Lord of Hope,
by the rising of your Son
You have removed for all time
the veil between Your world and ours.
Friend and Comforter,
Who alone knows every pain
that torments the human soul,
by the power of Your Holy Spirit,
guide us through this Vale of Tears
until we are filled with the fullness of Your presence
in Jesus' love,
Amen.

Part One

The Valley of the Shadow

Save me, O God, for the floodwaters are up to my neck.
Deeper and deeper I sink into the mire;
I cant find a foothold to stand on. I
I am in deep water and the floods overwhelm me.
I am exhausted from crying for help . . .
My eyes are swollen with weeping,
waiting for my God to help me.

Psalm 69:1-3

MORE AND MORE I am meeting people whose world has fallen apart. Loved ones leave or die, marriages unravel, friendships tear apart, and even seemingly vibrant ministries lose their cutting edge, and people find themselves as shocked and dismayed as David was as he wrestled with many pressures and losses.

Events that cause us to experience the valley of the shadow of grief can strike any of us unexpectedly at any time. One moment King David was sitting securely on his throne overseeing his far-flung empire. The next he was on the run for life in a barren wilderness.

When we go through times of extreme mental anguish, we will find ourselves gravitating towards the psalms of David, for they blend the heart cry of our human pain with a profound longing to see God move on our behalf. It is not so much our faith as the the Lord's faithfulness that supports us through the often long-drawn out process during which we struggle to accept what has happened, and to adjust to the changes that are now called for.

Fully aware of the effect His death would have on those He left behind, the Lord Jesus prophesied to His disciples,

> *I tell you the truth, you will weep and mourn while the world rejoices. You will grieve, but your grief will turn to joy . . . Now is the time of your grief, but I will see you again and you will rejoice, and no one will take away your joy.*
>
> *John 16:20, 22*

In Psalm 84, the poet pictures a group of pilgrims wending their way to Jerusalem through the Valley of Baca – a phrase variously translated as "a dry valley," or "the valley of weeping." Most explorers find their strength diminishing in proportion to the length of their journey and the ruggedness of the terrain they are passing through, but the psalmist promises here a very different outcome, that *we will go from strength to strength* (Psalm 84:7). God anticipates the hardest times we must pass through, and sends special help and comfort to see us through.

When the psalmist speaks of the autumn rains gathering in pools, the image is of our tears mingling with the Lord's comfort to provide a balm that can transform even savage wildernesses into a place of renewed hope. It is only unresolved grief, or grief that has developed complications, which leaves people brittle and embittered, weighed down by ancient scars that remain achingly close to the surface, crushing all flicker of hope.

By the grace of God, it is entirely possible that we will emerge from such times with renewed hope and fresh goals, but there may be a considerable journey to experience first. If even swallows and sparrows make their dwelling close to the altar of the Lord, then how much more welcome are we? We cry out with David, *Be to me a protecting rock of safety, where I am always welcome (Psalm 71:3).*

As surely as the young man David emerged beyond his griefs and losses as a man of God, so we can also see that many of the world's most caring ministers, and our most brilliant artists, musicians and scientists, have only emerged in their full anointing and creativity on the far side of profound loss.

Far from permitting their suffering to crush them, these people have found ways to "cooperate" with God's mysterious purposes through the grief process, *using* their loss to strengthen their spirits.

If I may dare to speak of such a thing, their ongoing surrender to God has permitted suffering to accomplish in them its highest redemptive work. We come away from spending time with such people feeling cleansed and refreshed.

In this opening section, therefore, we are going to examine some of the most common reactions people experience when loss strikes and grief comes their way.

Reflect and Pray

Lord, You have been my dwelling place,
ever since I put my trust in You.
As I embark on this journey of grief,
thank You that You know all about grief in all its forms.
You desire nothing but my good,
and will be with me every step of the way.
Even though this path is leading me
far from familiar landmarks,
You are taking me towards the future
that You have already prepared.

Patterns of Grief

No one ever told me that grief felt so like fear. I am not afraid, but the sensation is like being afraid. The same fluttering in the stomach, the same restlessness, and yawning, I keep on swallowing.

C. S. Lewis, A Grief Observed

Although every grief experience is unique, we can distinguish certain features that are common in almost all of them. Elizabeth Kubler-Ross's seminal work *On Death and Dying* identified five stages associated with the grief process: denial, anger, bargaining, and depression, before finally reaching a place of acceptance. These have been widely accepted in grief and bereavement counselling, and they hold true for any form of loss – redundancy, retirement, loss of status, change of physical or emotional circumstances, and a host of other conditions.

These stages do not follow one another in an orderly progression, but are rather cyclical, often overlap with each other. It is quite possible to progress beyond one of these stages, only to fall back into it again later on. Thus we find David expressing the highs and lows of his pilgrimage within a single couplet:

> *When I was prosperous, I said, "Nothing can stop me now!"*
> *Your favour, O Lord, made me as secure as a mountain.*
> *Then You turned away from me and I was shattered.*
>
> *Psalm 30:6-7*

Like David, we find ourselves crying out to God to deliver us from our pressing problems. This is important psychologically as well as spiritually, for it means that we are expressing our grief as near as possible to the event that occasioned it, and are doing the very best thing possible in taking it to the Lord. There are many things that only He can sort out.

Our first and most important step, therefore, is to recognise when we need to grieve. This may not be quite as automatic as it sounds. Apart from anything else, grief is such an untidy emotion that it is hardly surprising that many of us – those who are in any form of leadership especially – may be tempted to put on a mask and pretend that all is well. Perhaps we are afraid it would indicate some lack of faith on our part were we to give voice to it. If so, the Psalms of David show us a very different pattern!

Every one of us needs grace to adjust our priorities and perspectives when cherished people, positions, health or possessions are taken from us – especially if the loss occurs suddenly. Each of us process life's setbacks in different ways, however, and although there is no virtue in trying to jump start anyone into making responses they are not yet ready to embrace, it is as well to be aware that to sidestep embarking on the grief journey risks making the long-term cost higher.

Life

I have wandered many worlds unknown to you.
I have watched the tears for life's sorrows slowly brew.
I have tasted the fruits of joy,
and the bitter seeds of hate.
I have seen the paths of life laid out for me.
The towering mountains of trouble,
to be toiled with and slowly climbed –
battled with step by step until I reach the summit:
the many different forms and turnings.
Which way will I turn?
Which path will I follow?
The smooth or the rough?
The selfish or the selfless?
Which is which?
Will I be forced or tempted and take the wrong path?

Alison Browne (aged 13)[1]

Embarking on the Journey

O Lord, I come to You for protection;
Don't let me be put to shame.
Rescue me, for You always do what is right.
Bend down and listen to me;
Rescue me quickly.
Be for me a great rock of safety,
A fortress where my enemies cannot reach me . . .
For the honour of Your name, lead me out of this peril.
I entrust my spirit into Your hand.

Psalm 31:1-5

While we were still engaged, Rosalind and I visited a man of God called Alex Buchanan. Over the years, we have been given many wonderful words of prophecy, but on this occasion we received something altogether more sobering:

"When I think of the trials you two are going to go through," Alex declared, "I shudder!"

This was not *quite* the encouragement we had been hoping for(!) but at least God was telling us straight how things would be. The Scriptures tell us that we are destined to enter the kingdom through many hardships and tribulations,[2] but it is important not to underestimate the psychological effects such trials can have on us.

As surely as some would regard moving house or changing church as an adventure rather than a trauma, others need to allow themselves more space and grace in which to adjust and mourn when friends move away, children leave home, and other shocks come their way.

It is by no means a sign of unbelief or immaturity to mourn when precious seasons coming to an end, and to recognise that certain things may never be the same again. Bland reassurances that "time heals everything" often prove misleading.[3]

When extreme grief comes our way, time often seems to all but stand still. Perhaps the African concept of "Time coming" provides a more helpful perspective than our agonising western preoccupation with time passing so quickly. As Rosemary Green reminds us,

> *Time only really brings healing when the resentment at the source of the infection has been cleaned. A wound may heal on the surface but it will go septic if the dirt remains inside.[4]*

The one thing time does serve to do is to put distance between us as we are today and grief events that have happened in the past. By definition, even the most acute memories fade with the passing of time, albeit it with occasional sharp reprises. The more willing we are to work our grief through, the less likely we are to end up harbouring emotional time-bombs.

It is comforting to reflect that the Lord has all eternity to make up for our troubles in this life. An elderly missionary couple entering New York harbour on board a liner were rather ruefully watching the great crowds that had assembled to welcome the celebrities as they disembarked from the ship.

"Nobody's putting on a party to welcome me," lamented the husband, sad and somewhat afraid lest his decades of faithful service had passed unnoticed. Seeing how upset he was, his wife encouraged him to pray about the matter. He did so, and the Lord spoke clearly to him: "But this isn't your homecoming yet!"[5]

Reflect and Pray

When you go through deep waters and great trouble, I will be with you. When you go through rivers of difficulty, you will not drown . . . I am the Lord your God.

Isaiah 43:1-3

Lord, give us the grace to ride
grief's white-knuckle rapids.
and to find You on the journey.
Land us at last on safer kinder shores,
Enriched and not diminished.
In Jesus' name, Amen.

The Disorientation Loss Brings

How small and selfish sorrow is – but it bangs one about until one is senseless.

Queen Elizabeth, the Queen Mother[6]

Because grief is like a physical blow, none of us knows for sure how we will cope when it comes our way. Some who normally crumple at the slightest setback surprise us by their robustness, whilst others, renowned for their resilience, find themselves all but paralysed by sorrow.

Selwyn Hughes, a well known Bible teacher, was so disorientated when his wife finally died after a long illness that he stood for ages at a service station, unable to remember how to fill his tank with petrol. Another newly widowed person told me that she felt as vulnerable walking the aisles in a supermarket as if she had been crossing a minefield!

Like a damaged CD randomly skipping tracks, the grief-stricken mind performs erratically. There is nothing in the least bit unusual about a bereaved person absentmindedly pouring a cup of tea for someone who is no longer there.

As the grief and tension go round and round in search of relief, why be surprised if symptoms such as muscular pains, excessive fatigue and difficulty in breathing develop?[7] Or if headaches, dizziness, digestive problems, rapid weight loss, embarrassing forgetfulness and an almost overwhelming desire to sigh and groan combine with a greatly reduced ability to concentrate?

Bereavement especially can leave us feeling as though we have suffered an amputation. After all, when someone loses a spouse, they lose a lover, friend and confidante all rolled into one. No wonder, then, if they feel less than half a person without the child, spouse, friend, parent or even the role in life that has meant so much to them. Writing candidly about his reaction when his wife died, C. S. Lewis protested,

> Meanwhile, where is God?
> This is one of the most disquieting symptoms.
> When you are happy,
> if you . . . turn to Him with gratitude and praise,
> you will be – or so it feels – welcomed with open arms.
> But go to Him when your need is desperate,
> when all other help is in vain, and what do you find?
> A door slammed in your face,
> and a sound of bolting and double bolting on the inside.
> After that, silence.
>
> C. S. Lewis, A Grief Observed

Elsewhere, Lewis observed that, "Her absence is like the sky, spread over everything." If we are one in spirit with our partner, how can we not feel as though our heart has been torn in two? As we shall see in the next section, some of us do experience a special sense of being "carried" in the immediate aftermath of a major loss, but others are too distraught to be able to discern much if anything of the Lord's presence at such times. When his brother died, St Ambrose wrote:

> Not all weeping proceeds from unbelief or weakness.
> Natural grief is one thing; distrustful sadness is another.

We should not judge our relationship with the Lord by how we feel during those terrible days when the thought of reading the Bible appals us, and prayer feels altogether too painful to contemplate. The Lord has not turned against us. This is what one friend wrote to me after going through such a time:

> After my husband left me, I had a real feeling of being abandoned by God. The pain was so great that when I fell into bed I called out to Jesus, "Lord, I keep looking up to see You, but You just aren't there. I can't see You!" One night I heard these words clearly: "The everlasting arms of the Lord are underneath you." The comfort that came with these words was immense. I felt like I was being rocked in the Father's arms. My despair was never as great again after that experience.

Reflect and Pray

They say, "God has abandoned him . . .
There is no one to help him now."
O God, don't stay away; please hurry to help me . . .
I will keep on hoping for You to help me;
                    Psalm 31:11,12,14

Lord, at this time of profound disorientation,
we entrust into Your safekeeping
the person or thing we miss most of all –
or most fear losing.
In Jesus' name, transform even these fears and regrets
into something meaningful. Amen.

The Divine Anaesthetic

Like a child, I was taken over and "managed." It was as if,
at the time of Peter's death, I literally stepped into the
radiant Kingdom of God on Earth.
                    Catherine Marshall, To Live Again [8]

In the aftermath of the shock of her preacher husband suffering a fatal heart attack, Catherine Marshall experienced a generous measure of what I can only call a "divine anaesthetic." Along with a series of detailed instructions that she was quite sure came straight from God, she received a deep inner strengthening during those vital first few days, which enabled her to care for other people's spiritual and emotional needs, as well as to attend to the host of practical matters that needed dealing with.[9]

Not everyone understands the value of this divine safe-guard that protects us from being paralysed by grief and anxiety. Adopting an overly robust attitude, some feel it their duty to shake people out of what looks to them suspiciously like denial. We cannot state too strongly that trying too soon to make people face their new realities can seriously weaken, and even puncture, the protection this God-given anaesthetic provides.

Other people are inclined to make well-intentioned but utterly unhelpful observations such as, "Well, at least you survived. You ought to be grateful!" Or, "The fact that you've got other children must surely cushion the pain for you!" As one friend put it, after coming through a particularly compli-cated divorce,

> Such remarks compress the sufferer's shock and pain, and cause the person to remain in limbo: a sort of frozen state of shock. When the anaesthetic wears off, the person will still be in shock, but much more uncomfortable and disori-ented because of people's failure to empathise.

One of the fastest ways to jeopardise the covering this "divine anaesthetic" provides is to try to respond in the way that other people are expecting of us. We can end up using the greater part of what little energy we still have trying do this – only to discover that our best efforts still fall well short of whatever it was that they were looking for. Sooner or later, we have no choice but to face this issue head-on if we are to develop new patterns successfully.

May the Lord give those of us who are watching and caring grace not to push too hard. There will be a time when people will need to let go of the person, position, place or possession they have lost, but until they are ready to do so it may be wiser just to stand alongside them, loving and praying for them while the divine anaesthetic continues its precious work.

Reflect and Pray

Father,
I realise that the sweetness You are giving me
may only last season,
but let me profit from it for as long as possible.
When the tide of grief returns in full spate,
help me lean into the pain,
and, like a skilful surfer,
ride each wave in prayer.

Searching and Pining

In the natural word, graylag geese become desperately distressed if they are separated from each other. The goose moves about restlessly by day and night, flying great distances and visiting places where the partner might be found, continuously making its penetrating, tri-syllabic, long-distance call . . . The searching expeditions are extended farther and farther, and quite often the searcher itself gets lost, or succumbs to an accident.

Lorenz[10]

You may never have compared yourself to a goose, but if you have lost a precious friend or partner, the chances are that you will relate to the distress geese go through when deprived of their mate. Intense yearning in the aftermath of loss is an integral part of our quest to make sense of life as we now experience it. Colin Murray Parkes defines pining as,

A persistent and obtrusive wish for the person who is gone;
a preoccupation with thoughts that can only give pain.[11]

So many of our thoughts and feelings, as well as our actions, have been mentally directed to or around a particular person, and if they are no longer there to receive them, it is hardly surprising that we should feel like a ship that has been holed beneath the waterline, and that has been cast adrift on an uncertain sea.

Since we are unable to do what we most want to do, which is to spend time with the person we most want to be with, why be surprised if our subconscious continues to pine, as if the very intensity of our emotions could somehow rewrite reality. Grief is, as C. S. Lewis described it, a "suspense:" from the first hint that something is wrong through all that lies beyond.

This phase of searching and pining may well last a year or more. In its early stages, we are likely to experience many sharp "peaks" of grief, followed by an almost overwhelming series of rolling "waves." These *will* decrease with the passing of time – though often very slowly.

Tempted though we may be to feel "past hope, past cure and past help" (to quote Alexander Pope's trenchant words) it is always wise to direct our "searching" upwards to the Lord, rather than constantly backwards to what we have lost. Although nobody can ever fully replace the person or project we have lost, there is no reason, God willing, why we should not eventually experience what the truth of John Ruskin's comment that "When the Lord closes a door, He opens a window."

Reflect and Pray

Lord Jesus, as I measure the full extent of my loss,
increase my heart's hunger for You.
Lead me safely through
this phase of intense searching and pining,
and on to the people, places and positions
You have in mind for me to find.
In Jesus' name, Amen.

Sadness and Sorrow

Most, if not all . . . intense episodes of sadness are elicited by the loss, or expected loss, either of a loved person, or else of familiar and loved places and social roles. A sad person knows who or what he has lost and yearns for his (or its) return.

John Bowlby[12]

When we finally begin to accept that all our searching to recover what we had once enjoyed cannot succeed, we are likely to move into a gray but flatter phase in which we may well feel all but completely becalmed. Very different from the turbulent peaks and troughs of earlier days, this "sea" lies beyond the divine anaesthetic, and the most intense of our initial outbursts of anger and disbelief. It is marked above all by a profound, and potentially prolonged, sadness – a word that derives from an old English word that means "weary," for this is precisely what grief is.

I shall be referring on several occasions in this book to Robbie Davis-Floyd's beautifully written but deeply harrowing account of life in the aftermath of her daughter's tragic death. This is how her story begins.[13]

It has been two and a half years since I was invited to write this article, and I have been unable to face it until this moment – 1 a.m., as I rise from my unrestful rest to put fingers to computer keys . . .

I have been happy all my life, living out of a deep wellspring of joy bubbling up within me. When Peyton died, I lost that deep bubbling happiness – it comes back now only in fleeting moments all the more precious for their scarcity. I have a wonderful son, many friends, and a fulfilling career. But I have lost the very most precious thing in my life, and no platitudes about how I will see her again in Heaven, or that we will be united past this life, or she is always with me in spirit (which I know to be true) can alleviate for more than a little while the exquisite agony I always feel about her death. I thought I knew the meaning of suffering before she died – I had already experienced a good deal of pain and loss in my life – but I had absolutely no clue what real suffering was . . .

Peyton's death put a knife in my heart – a big fat butcher knife that tapered down to a fine point. Not to mention the five or so daggers sticking into my back. I was astonished. I honestly don't think it would have hurt more if there had been a solidly physical knife in my heart. I walked around for months pressing my hand to my heart, doubled over in pain.

As in the pains of labour, there were breaks. When I laughed with friends, when I wrote an article, when I taught class, when I gave talks, the butcher knife would slide out till only the tip was still sticking in. But when the laughter ended, or I stood up from the computer, the knife would slam right back into my heart up to the hilt, and I would gasp and double over again.

Many of us will identify with these feelings. Grief is so profoundly wearying that the journey requires immense physical energy as well as mental courage. We should not, however, mistake even the most intense sadness for full-blown clinical depression.

In depression, self-esteem collapses, either through some chemical imbalance in the brain, or as the result of an apparently irresolvable conflict or dilemma. Depression usually requires much more time, and specialised input to recover from, whereas sadness can fade away as better times come our way.

Reflect and Pray

My work seems so useless! I have spent my strength for nothing and to no purpose.

Isaiah 49:4

Have we not all cried out in such ways from the depths of our grief and despair? But remember how that verse continues: *Yet I leave it all in the Lord's hand. I will trust God for my reward!*

Whilst feelings of condemnation are to be shunned like the plague, sadness, like godly sorrow itself,[14] can actually draw us closer to God's heart. How else will we discover that the Lord Jesus Himself is, *A man of sorrows, acquainted with grief* (Isaiah 53:3)?

On the South Pacific island of Ifaluk, inhabitants use the term *fago* – a word that embraces love, compassion and sadness, all rolled into one.[15] These are qualities dear to the

Lord's own heart, for it is as we experience more of His compassion love and sadness that we pray more earnestly and become much more spiritually alive and authentic.

Breaking Grief's Isolation

An odd by-product of my loss is that I'm aware of being an embarrassment to everyone I meet. Perhaps the bereaved ought to be isolated in special settlements like lepers!
                                       C. S. Lewis, *A Grief Observed*

About the time the divine anaesthetic starts to wear off, the sense of isolation may begin to bite more keenly. If this coincides with the phone and doorbell ringing less often, new and most unwelcome challenges come our way. We realise with a fresh intensity that we are no longer card-carrying members of the 'fit and well' brigade!

All forms of grief are top heavy not only with sorrow but also with embarrassment.[16] It is so important not to despair when people show us less than no understanding. I have seen people rush to cross the road rather than stop to talk to someone who has recently suffered a loss. This is how one friend set about coping with such disorientating experiences:

I came to terms with this by realising that these people were unable to put their own feelings to one side to minister to the grieving. Effectively, they had not died to self. This helped me so much because I ceased to be the problem.

The more complicated our circumstances, the more of a misfit we are likely to feel. No wonder people pour out their lonely agonies in poems and personal journals – like the beautiful Japanese poetess Ono no Kamachi, over a thousand years ago, who wrote:

So lonely am I,
my body is a floating weed severed at the roots.
Were there water to entice me,
I would follow it, I think.

The intense imagery in this stanza from a first century Tamil poetess conveys a similar message.

I grow lean in loneliness
Like a water lily gnawed by a beetle.

The imagery of having one's roots severed, and finding oneself at the mercy of moving water, perfectly reflects the isolation that the grief process induces – even though these poems contain no pointers to the help the Lord is both able and willing to provide. It is that above all which prevents our sense of isolation from "petrifying" – that is, from turning to stone.

In our shock and grief, we may feel tempted to withdraw from fellowship. Necessary though this may be in the short term, we dare not separate ourselves far from our life-stream, lest we isolate ourselves still further and make a shrine to what we have lost.

Too much time on our own risks causing us to lose touch with our place in the world and our worth as individuals. This is when we start making decisions in the light of our *imagined* version of what is happening.

When we are obliged to spend much time on our own, we will find the isolation easier to bear if we can view it as "solitude" – which is, at best, a positive and sought out quality – rather than the loneliness that we dread.

As we give God the great swathes of time that now lie ahead, and seek to take such opportunities as He sets before us, who knows what He will do? We may yet end up more fully integrated in His Body and His purposes than we would ever have dared to believe when we were first afflicted.[17]

Reflect and Pray

Lord, this is a real-life drama
that You have caused me to be living!
Even though You have allowed episodes and scenes
that I would much rather have cut out,
You know exactly how this story will unfurl.

Scriptwriter Supreme and Peerless Director,
break the grip of Grief's isolation,
and link me to the people and places

who will further Your purposes for my life.
May neither my embarrassment,
nor other people's indifference,
cause me to miss Your purposes for my life.

Where fellowship is not coming my way,
grant me the energy to reach out to others,
and not lose heart on this flat becalmed sea
In Jesus' Name, Amen.

Living under the Shadow of His Wings

The challenge is not how to escape death, but how to sanctify life.

Rabbi Sherwin

The quicker we are to accept that some situations really have changed for ever, the more rapidly we will move through the grief process. Unless we are dealing with a literal bereavement, however, it is by no means always obvious whether the loss we are experiencing will prove to be permanent.

The chaplain of a local hospital asked David Woodhouse to visit the parents of a seventeen-year-old boy, who had been involved in a severe traffic accident. The doctors were planning to withdraw the young man's life support, as David recalls.

My head was in a spin – what was I going to say or do? On the short journey to the house, I prayed in tongues and the Lord gave me a verse. On arrival I met the parents and a grandmother, who informed me that as they were leaving the hospital, one of the doctors had told them they had just run a further brain scan which detected life at the lowest level. So far as I was concerned, that just made my situation worse! Were we to pray for a peaceful death, a full recovery or risk a vegetative state with all its tragic consequences? These were the verses the Lord gave me:

No good thing will the Lord withhold from those who walk uprightly. O Lord of hosts, happy is everyone who trust in You.

Psalm 84:11-12

We saw the latest scan result as a positive and decided that we could trust the Lord for the best outcome. We stood in the centre of the room with our arms on each other's shoulders and prayed together. That afternoon I went to the ICU and prayed in tongues at the boy's bedside. Four days later the lad was on a general ward and none the worse for his accident!

Such outcomes may be rare, but they are such an encouragement! Sometimes, however, the Lord flags up that a season of suffering lies ahead.[18] Thus it was, just days after Jesus was born, that Simeon, by the power of the Holy Spirit, warned Mary of the suffering she would experience as a result of what people would do to her Son.

> *This child is destined to cause many in Israel to fall, but He will be a joy to many others. He has been sent as a sign from God, but many will oppose Him. As a result, the deepest thoughts of many hearts will be revealed. And a sword will pierce your very soul.*   Luke 2:34, 35

During all the years when Jesus was growing up, Mary lived with this awareness of what lay ahead. Jesus Himself intimated clearly to both Peter and Paul the extent of the sufferings they would experience in the course of fulfilling their respective ministries.[19] He told His followers that they were to take heart precisely because He has overcome the worst this world can throw at Him. Even when it appears as though we are all but completely overwhelmed, He is careful not to take us anywhere His power cannot sustain us.[20]

Reflect and Pray

What does living under the shadow of His wings mean to you? It is surely far more than some passive concept of "God up there taking care of matters while I remain groping around in the dark." It is rather a matter of having the determination to keep seeking the Lord, despite the grief and uncertainties, and trusting Him to be at work, even when you cannot begin to see how He can possibly turn some impossible situation around.

Lord, how priceless is your unfailing low
Both high and low among men
find refuge in the shadow of your wings.
Keep me as the apple of your eye;
hide me in the shadow of your wings
Because you are my help,
I sing in the shadow of your wings.
Psalm 36:7;17:8, 63:7

Beyond the Sequence of Losses

Every parting gives a foretaste of death, every reunion a
hint of the resurrection.

Arthur Schopenhauer

Losses, like the proverbial buses, often arrive in clusters, leaving us feeling pinned against the ropes. One thing I have repeatedly observed is that many of the experiences I am inclined to label at the time as "horrendous" turn out later to be the matrix by which the Lord brings about great blessings. Just look at how many of the Lord's finest servants went through staggering losses, only to rise to positions of great influence.

Where would Israel be had Moses not been forced to flee his privileged position in Pharaoh's palace and serve for long decades as a shepherd in the back of beyond? Although he must long since have given up all thought of ever seeing the Hebrew people rescued from Pharaoh's grasp, the time came when the bush blazed and the Lord sent forth His extraordinary summons. The rest, as we know, is history – "His story!" As for the life of Israel's greatest king, we have seen already that it was interspersed from start to finish with a sequence of immense losses.

If we could catch sight of him on the run, bedraggled and hunted like an outlaw, which of us would have dared to discern in that ramshackle existence the training ground for Israel's most successful king? Yet here was a man so exquisitely sensitive to the Holy Spirit that his prayers and poems have fed the souls of countless millions to a depth that no other writings have even begun to do. None of this would have occurred had David enjoyed a straightforward succession to Saul's throne, with Jonathan selflessly making way for him, and the nation rejoicing in his far flung military successes.

From the moment we leave the protection of the womb and enter this physically and emotionally more challenging environment, life consists of a series of "mini" deaths and losses as we embark on life's journey and engage with the wider world. Many factors determine whether or not we relish these new experiences, but it is critically important to remember that the Lord's unfailing love remains the one constant in our lives. If our faith does not remain on top of everything else, we risk becoming a chronic Puddleglum![21]

Like David, who was neither too proud to acknowledge his agony, nor too stoical to give voice to his complaint, we may often have cause to lament loud and long as we express the agony we are experiencing. Provided that we, like David, call on God to deliver us, He will surely find ways to go on turning one grief-laden situation after another around for His glory.[22]

Reflect and Pray

Righteous people face many troubles,
but You come to their rescue every time.
Psalm 34:19

From your earliest days onward, you may have experienced the pain and frustration of material things breaking, precious relationships turning sour and promising opportunities failing to lead where you had once hoped.

Take time to ponder the losses you have sustained, and to mourn if need be those that have involved emotional or financial loss. Only may the Lord help you to grieve "into" Him, rather than cursing yourself for being one of life's losers – for that can only lead to more disappointment and frustration.

Take time, too, to recall how the Lord has helped you when certain phases of your life have come to a close. Have other things not opened up in their place?

God of sharp distinctions,
I give you my strong contradictions –
my longings, lapses,
and many backwards glances.
I give you what You most desire –
a heart that is set on reaching out to You.
In your name I throw off
all loss that weights my spirit down,
all shackles that make my heart dumb.
I turn right round to seek Your face,
and to embrace the new, the now, the next,
in the fullness that comes from Heaven above.

References

1 Allie's Song. Alison Browne. Copyright Tony and Brid Browne (1999). Herne Bay, Kent. A collection of poems and writings by Allie, who knew at the age of thirteen that an early death awaited her from cystic fibrosis.

2 Acts 14:22

3 In the wider community, people feel grieved when "houses with memories" are sold or knocked down, and churches, businesses and enterprises that have meant a lot to them are closed. Neither does it help when green areas are paved over to provide new housing to point out that nobody has been hurt in the process. It can still feel as though something of a person's own identity has been affected – and it is quite alright to grieve.

4 Rosemary Green. *God's Catalyst.* Christina Press (1997)

5 See www.ruachministries.org/valeoftears/refs.htm

6 Following the death of her husband, George VI in 1952.

7 e.g. Psalms 6:2-3, 31:10, 42:10, 102:3-5, cf Proverbs. 3:8, 12:4.

8 Catherine Marshall, *To Live Again.* Chosen Books (2001)

9 As above

10 Lorenz, K. 1991. *Here am I – Where are you? The Behaviour of the Graylag Goose.* New York, and San Diego: A Helen and

Kurt Wolff Book. Harcourt Brace Jovanovich.

11 Parkes, C. Bereavement, Studies of Grief in Adult Life, Tavistock Publications.

12 Bowlby, J. *The Making and Breaking of Affectional Bonds.* Routledge (2005)

13 Davis-Floyd, R. *Windows in Space and Time: A personal Perspective on Birth and Death. Birth: Issues in Perinatal Care. Vol. 30 (4):272-277. Dec. 2003.* Robbie is a distinguished anthropologist whom Ros has met at various conferences around the world. She has kindly given permission for people to reproduce her material.

14 2 Corinthians 7:10-11

15 Lutz, C. *Unnatural emotions: Everyday Sentiments on a Micronesian Atoll and their Challenge to Western Theory.* University of Chicago Press (1998)

16 Parents of children with ADD (Attention Deficit Disorder) grow used to this when bystanders, who know nothing of their true condition, urge them to keep their children under better control. It is no wonder if these parents learn to cope by "burying " their grief beneath the sheer weight of getting on with day-to-day practicalities rather than facing up to their own personal needs.

17 Many Scriptures point to the truth of this, for instance Psalm 119:67,71

18 One aspect amongst many of the gift of prophecy is to reveal such things. E.g. Acts 11:28; 21:10-11

19 John 21:18-19, Acts 9:16

20 John 16:33

21 Puddleglum was the Marshwiggle in C.S. Lewis', *Chronicles of Narnia* who always considered it wisest to look on the gloomy side of things. Collins (2001) The Lord says to His people through Isaiah, *If you do not stand firm in your faith, you will not stand at all (Isaiah 7:9).*

22 See for example Psalms 18:6, 50:15, 86:7

Part Two

Facing the Reality of Grief

I F THERE IS ONE PHRASE in particular that stands out to me from the messages that God sends to the seven churches at the start of the book of Revelation, it is this: that the Lord Jesus *knows* what we are going through – and what He intends to do about it.

Just as broken bones can become stronger than they originally were if they are properly reset, we too can emerge at the far end of our grief journey stronger in the Lord, despite – perhaps even because of – the ordeals we have been through. This is hard to believe when are overwhelmed with shock and grief – especially for those who have put off making a serious commitment to God until a more convenient moment.

Since grief episodes are never "convenient," I have started this chapter with a section for any who feel uncertain of their relationship with the Lord. Before we look in more detail at the *effects* on grief on our lives, the most important thing is to entrust ourselves to His care and leading. The principle remains as true in times of grief as at any other part of our pilgrimage: that it is as we seek first the Kingdom of God that He attends to our needs too.

Knowing God

Christianity has not been tried and found wanting, it has been found hard and left untried.

G.K. Chesterton

When grief overtakes us, the smattering of wise sayings and psychological truisms most of us have picked up here and there are rarely enough to sustain our souls. Surely it is not so much good advice that we need as a living relationship with the Lord Jesus, who is Lord of this world and the next.

The writer of the Letter to the Hebrew Christians asks a question that virtually every man and woman who has ever lived has asked at one time or another: *What is man that you are mindful of him, and the son of man that You should care for him* (Hebrews 2:5)? The remarkable answer is that we are God's highest creation, and His crowning achievement. He has made us only a little lower than the angels, and capable of achieving extraordinary exploits.

The fact that He is *mindful* of us means that He is always thinking about what He can do to help and care for us. He *wants* to share the riches of His presence, and the purposes of His Kingdom with us.[1]

If ninety-nine per cent of our life lies ahead of us in eternity, surely our time on Earth is essential preparation for this? It takes courage to make the first all-important step to open our hearts to the Lord, and to embark on this relationship, but also many repeated choices and decisions whenever we are tempted to turn back and trust in our own resources.

If failing to attend to our financial matters can make life difficult for survivors, how much more important is it for us to consider the fate of our eternal soul? The teaching of Scripture is clear: Heaven is reserved for those who consciously respond to God's generous offer of eternal life through Jesus Christ, and who seek to make Him Lord of their lives.

If we have been mentally putting off any thought of getting right with God until our final hours, we are forgetting that there is no guarantee that we will be in any mental or physical condition at that most intense of times to make such a choice coherently. God has not placed us here on Earth to scrape a pass into Heaven at the last minute – He wants us to live each day in vital union with Himself.[2]

We are not used to considering such things however. Whereas life after death was a major preoccupation in previous generations, ours is more concerned with finding meaning and direction, relationships that satisfy and overcoming boredom at all costs. This is precisely what Jesus offers. At the same time He promises that those who receive His saving grace in this life will have resurrected bodies in the next, and will no longer be confined to their present physical and spiritual limitations.

If no one has explained to you what it means to open your heart to His love in this way – or fear and grief have held you back from embarking on such a relationship, may I urge you to invite Christ into your heart? Don't let your present pain or confusion keep you from the Lord who wants to share His Heaven with you!

Reflect and Pray

Lord Jesus,
You did not die on the cross to leave us uncertain of Your
goodness towards us –
or for us to remain at a safe distance from You.
You want to be fully involved in our lives.
I want to respond to You now
by bringing as much of myself as I can
to as much of You as I understand.
Forgive my many sins and make me Your child.
May I have the joy of serving You
and may You have the joy of leading me –
all the days of this life,
and on into eternity.
In Your Name, I pray, Amen.

Faith or Presumption?

Asking Jesus to be Lord of our lives and embarking on a journey of faith brings the direction we had been longing for, but it by no means guarantees that we will miraculously be spared life's griefs and losses. Such pummellings are common to saint and sinner alike: the difference is that Jesus is with us as we go through them.

We heard a wonderful story recently of how God miraculously restored the liver of a former alcoholic in Shetland. He is now going round the islands, sharing his testimony at every opportunity. The fact that God *can* give the alcohol dependent person a new liver (or the abusive person a reformed character) is a source of profound hope and inspiration, but on some occasions, it can cause us to put our hope in outcomes that God has not promised to endorse.

Most of us have discovered that the boundary between genuine faith and mere presumption can be surprisingly thin. Faith proceeds from taking a stand and following a course of action that we believe to be in line with God's revealed word. Presumption sets in only when we expect – one might almost say *demand* – that God implements *our* longings and assumptions. Fine tuning our spirits to the point where we can tell the difference between what is truly of God and what are only "our" wishes is a considerable test of maturity – and we should not expect to always get it right.

If there is any trace of spiritual pride in our make-up, we are likely to become increasingly shrill in our insistence that God is going to "come through" for us in a particular way. God is always willing to work on our behalf, but He is not honour-bound to grant the outcome we would ideally like in the way or timescale that we expect. Wisdom lies in knowing when to "press on" in faith, when to wait, and when to "draw the line" and hand some particular longing or situation back to Him.

These are not easy issues to grapple with at any time, but can be particularly disturbing especially when grief is tugging our emotions in all directions. Close friends and mentors can sometimes be more clear sighted as to whether what we are feeling represents God's true leading, or whether we are merely indulging hopes that have no real substance.

We have walked the journey recently with a much loved pastor, whose wife developed an aggressive cancer. Waves of prayer swept in for her from around the world, without making any apparent impact on the tumours. The prophetic call on her life was strong, but it was clearly not destined to find its full outworking on Earth, as she and her husband came to realise during their last few months together. The vision she had certainly did not include leaving her husband and five children on their own at this time. The practical and emotional ramifications are enormous. We are praying not only for the immediate family, but also that none in the wider Body of Christ look on her homecoming as a "failure," or lose the courage to exercise faith for healing in other situations. Her mission will undoubtedly continue, albeit now from the vantage point of Heaven.

Reflect and Pray

Tightly closed hands are not in a position to receive anything – not even comfort. It matters little whether they are hands clenched in rebellion or just piteously trying to clutch the past.

Catherine Marshall[3]

Is there a shadow over your life at the moment? The best way to handle it is to continually hand it back to the Lord – and to press on and attend to Kingdom matters.[4] Since none of us can pass through Heaven's waiting door without stooping lower, the more fully we let go, the better we will fare. You simply cannot lose out, therefore, by praying the following prayer. There may even be eternal consequences bound up in it!

Lord, all that I am, all that I have,
all whom I love, and all that I am hoping for,
I yield to You now.
I ask You to turn this intense grief,
and this immense disappointment,
around for good,
and bring glory to Your name as only You can.
In Jesus' name, Amen.

The Shock of Severed Hopes and Shattered Dreams

Break, break, break,
On thy cold gray stones, O Sea!

And I would that my tongue could utter
  The thoughts that arise in me.
O, well for the fisherman's boy,
  That he shouts with his sister at play!
O, well for the sailor lad,
  That he sings in his boat on the bay!

And the stately ships go on
  To their haven under the hill;
But O for the touch of a vanished hand,
  And the sound of a voice that is still!

Break, break, break,
  At the foot of thy crags, O Sea!
But the tender grace of a day that is dead
  Will never come back to me.
                    Alfred Lord Tennyson

Long-term hopes and treasured dreams provide comfort as well as direction for our lives. When circumstances appear to thwart them, however, or our own shortcomings hinder them from being fulfilled, the sense of shock and loss can be enormous. Tennyson illustrates this acutely in this grief-laden poem about bitter and unrecompensed loss. He contrasts the joy and serenity of life around him – symbolised by happy children and ships sailing on their regular journeys – with his own intense inner grief, expressed by the sea, whose waves break continually on the detached and disinterested rocks.

In times of grief and loss, everyone seems to know their role and place in life, while you are left "looking in" on it from the outside. This is the terrifying and alienating feeling of being a "non person" which Robbie Davis-Floyd experienced during the traumatic months that followed her daughter's death.

The first year, I was in total shock. The intensity of pain and loss was everywhere around me. One day at a time? Impossible to contemplate. I could only live one second at a time: now I am climbing the stairs, now I am sitting down at the computer, now I am turning it on. People say shock wears off in a few months, but that was not my experience. Coming out of shock means accepting that your child is dead. Do you have any idea how many millions of new neural networks, new synaptic connections, your brain needs to create to accommodate that information? The death of a child means that everything you took for granted about life is shaken, in question. The world is upside down. Nothing makes any kind of sense, especially that you should be alive when your child is not. It takes lots of time and enormous energy simply to accept the fact of the death.

It took me one solid year to begin to accept the possibility that she was really dead, even though I had stayed with her in that hospital room for five hours, had begged her with all my might to live, had realized with my body that no one was there in hers to beg or who could respond. That helped, but it wasn't enough for my mind to get it. I spent much of that first year bargaining with God: "Who wrote this screenplay? Can't we write another one?" "Can't we press rewind on the DVD and watch a different movie?" "I have her hair and her baby teeth – couldn't we clone her?"

"Irrevocable" is not something we accept easily in a society where we can change so much through technology – hasn't there got to be a way to change this? One year I spent in that process of denial and bargaining, even though my dead daughter's ashes sat on the altar I had made for her in my bedroom. My poor brain just could not encompass this terrible truth.

And what did I gain when finally, near the first anniversary of her death, I "got it" that she had died, and no amount of bargaining would alter that? Utter despair and the complete loss of hope. Irrational as it was, the hope I gained from bargaining had been sustaining me. When I accepted the finality of her death, and let go of my hope that somehow I could have her back, I gained truth but I lost myself. If the pain of death had lasted even only 365 times as long as the pain of birth, I could have stood it without drugs. I did stand it for one year.

And then I couldn't stand it any more. Around the first anniversary of her death, just when I thought I was supposed to be feeling better (integrating, accepting, and all that), I cratered into depression. If you haven't been there, you can't imagine what it's like. The simplest act – putting on my socks, going to the kitchen to heat up some soup – is like struggling inch-by-inch through thick black mud.

People told me I had to "do something." So I gritted my teeth and found a wonderful bereavement counsellor. I collapsed in tears when she said to me during our first session,

"I bet everyone is telling you that you should be all better now that the first year is past. Let me just tell you how it really is: the first year you are in shock, and you still nurture hope. The second year you give up hope, you are left with despair, looking at the reality of the rest of your life without your child, and you have to fight back from that. So the second year is always the hardest."

I have never felt so understood. Her words did not magically make me well, but they did reassure me that I was not going crazy. Seven months of hell went by before I began to stabilize. Things were looking up – maybe I could survive this after all. Maybe I could even be happy again, for more than a few moments at a time.

When the unthinkable happens, we, like Robbie, may experience such strong shock waves that they all but take us over. Why be surprised if it takes time for our trust levels to recover? It need by no means automatically be the case that we are just heaping up empty words in vain repetition[5] if we find ourselves praying the same thing over and over again. We may *need* to do this in order to bring God's peace to the deeply shocked and hurting parts of our heart – and to remind ourselves that God's purposes will still work out, even though the person or vision we had set our heart may no longer play any part in our future.

If we do not allow ourselves to go through this cathartic process, there is every chance that our emotions will ricochet wildly when the cocoon of the divine anaesthetic lifts. One moment we are hoping against hope that we can find a way to solve our problem, the next we are trembling at how we are going to cope if we do not.

We hate feeling so helpless, but there is nothing wrong with this provided that we continue to bring our helplessness to the God who is always willing to help. Not all our hopes and dreams may be fulfilled on Earth, but Jesus is still our Friend and Saviour – even if the substance of our prayer for the moment consists of little more than repeated cries for help. He can always pick us up one more time than we can fail or fall – and when we and He are both ready, He will move again on our behalf.

Reflect and Pray

When He sees all that is accomplished by the anguish of His soul, He will be satisfied.

Isaiah 53:11

Lord, moment by moment,
minister to the shock that is shredding my heart apart.
Calm the racing thoughts,
and restore my poise, my posture and my trust.
In Jesus' name, Amen.

Broken Relationships

He who loses wealth loses much; he who loses a friend loses more; but he that loses his courage loses all.

Cervantes

"There is no pain equal to that which two lovers can inflict on one another," Cyril Connelly declared. He was probably right, but fallouts between friends can come a close second. What can be more painful than to lose the friendship of someone we had assumed we would be walking with all the days of our life?

It is an enormous relief if reconciliation can be achieved, but realistically we have to accept that there are times when "all the king's horses and all the king's men cannot put Humpty together again," to quote the nursery rhyme. It makes one feel marginally better to know that even Paul and Barnabas had such a sharp disagreement that they too parted company!⁶

If you have been abandoned or severely slandered by someone you once walked closely with, you will know how just how deep such shocks can go. Instead of enjoying unlimited access to their thoughts and feelings, you find yourself obliged to guard yourself against them. How devastating is that for your whole sense of well-being?

The more closely bonded we are to people or projects, the more likely we are to suffer an acute reaction if they are taken away from us. In extreme cases, such relationship breakdowns can provoke identity crises that plunge us into profound anxiety and depression. The great danger then is that we lose that most precious of all qualities – our courage. Nothing of lasting value is accomplished in the Kingdom without faith and courage.

Relationship breakdowns can be equally painful whether they are brought about through other people's shortcomings, or as the result of our own foolishness. It may only be much later – if ever – that we are able to unravel all the dynamics that were at work, and to begin to make sense of what has happened.

It is wise to be on the alert, for spirits of division are ever on the prowl to drive wedges between believers. We are often slow to recognise flash points building up, hoping perhaps that they will dissolve of their own accord.

Sometimes we need to rouse ourselves to action. When people started putting their trust in the bronze serpent that Moses had lifted up in the wilderness, King Hezekiah realised that something was profoundly wrong in the heart of his nation. Recognising that what had once been a God-given means of salvation had now become a snare and idol,⁷ Hezekiah proceeded with immense courage to cut down the no-longer-useful-but-actually-positively-dangerous idol.

There are times when we may need to be equally as decisive in dealing with anything that is leading our hearts astray.[8] The Lord is *jealous* for our time and attention. It grieves Him when we allow our energies and affections to be diverted in some other direction and become inward-looking and exclusive. More than we are likely to realise at the time, it is a kindness if the Lord shoulders His axe and lays it to the root of our idolatry and wrong priorities in order to bring us back into line with His best purposes for our lives.

When I was sixteen, I was delighted to be going out with a young lady called Jean. When I returned from a week's holiday, I discovered to my intense distress that her affections had switched to someone else. I was devastated! It took me the best part of two years to recover. But in retrospect, God was already thinking far ahead.

Shortly after I became a Christian, the Lord asked me to pray for Jean regularly. Years went by without any contact or sign of encouragement, but one night I had a dream. I turned to Ros and said, "I can't believe this: Jean's become a Christian!" Two days later I received my first letter from her in over a decade. "I thought you would like to know that I have just become a Christian and been filled with the Spirit. I've led a couple of people in my village to the Lord already!"

I had only been praying for one person, but the Lord was thinking of all the people He would one day be reaching through her!

Reflect and Pray

If you have experienced, perhaps many times over, the sadness of long-term relationships breaking down, may the Lord break the cycle and lead you into new and richer ones, where your support and constancy will be truly appreciated.

Father, where relationships have frayed or broken asunder,
forgive every part I have played in the process.
Heal all that has been crushed or dented,

and bless me in long-term relationships
that will not be broken asunder.
In Jesus' name, Amen.

When the Grief is all our Own Fault

Won't you look and see how upset I am, o Lord?
My stomach is in knots and my heart is broken
because I let You down.

Lamentations 1:20[9]

Many times in the Psalms, we hear David praying that God will not abandon him. During times of stress and grief, we will doubtless echo his words many times over, but the reality is that it is we who let the Lord down rather than He who deserts us.

Back in 1981 the Lord called me to start a prayer and worship organization that would draw people together from across the denominations. We made it our aim from the outset to pray for wider matters, trusting that the Lord would take care of our needs as we did so.

We soon reaped the benefit of this. Many were healed, filled with the Spirit and commissioned for new seasons of ministry without much need on our part to "push" conventional ministry. Beneath the surface, however, a crisis was brewing. The Lord insists on heart unity amongst His people, but there were underlying tensions within the original team, combined with mistaken emphases, for which I, as the leader, must take the lion's share of the blame. The time came when the Lord judged that we were no longer honouring each other sufficiently – and He determined to do something about it.

I often find that the Lord speaks to me in the twilight moments between sleep and waking. One morning in early 1985, however, the Lord told me something that I did not in the least want to hear: that the ministry team I had founded was going to unravel – and that I was going to find this hard to cope with.

The day before we held a "make-or-break meeting" with the man who oversaw our ministry team, I was acutely aware that the signs were pointing firmly to it being more "break" than "make." I was in the local swimming pool, when the Lord suddenly overwhelmed me with a strong sense of His presence. I can remember that enveloping sense of warmth even now. For a moment I resisted it: "Are you giving me this lovely sense of Your presence, Lord, because things are going to go wrong tomorrow?" I asked suspiciously.

The special Presence lifted somewhat. "What happens tomorrow is for tomorrow," the Lord replied; "but I want you to enjoy today!" I realised, of course, that He had by no means given me any reassurance that things would be resolved – which is hardly surprising in light of the fact that the meeting hastened the parting of our ways as a ministry team.

How right the Lord had been when He said that I would find His decision hard to cope with! Shocked to the core of my being that there had been no last minute resolution, I ended up taking many long walks through the lovely Cheshire countryside that spring, pouring out my hurt and insecurities to the Lord.

I remained in a state of shock for the next few months. A major part of the problem was that I could not in all conscientiousness take any comfort in laying the blame for what had happened elsewhere. The truth was that we *had* become over intense, and carried away with our own visions, albeit with every possible desire to serve and honour the Lord (which I am sure He took into account). Nevertheless, the Lord could see further ahead down the road we were advancing along and judged it best to bring matters to (what felt to me at the time) a brutal closure.

When we know that we have brought the greater part of our suffering on ourselves, it is easy for our thoughts to become circular. Even hindsight risks becoming an enemy as we go over and over events in our minds: "If only I had realised what I was doing, I would never have . . ." But this of course merely induces still more stress in our body, mind and emotions.

Shafts of condemnation stung me repeatedly, until I felt like I was scything my way through a nettle patch. Along with bucket loads of unhelpful remorse came genuine Holy Spirit conviction: we really had become too intense for our own good! The path to restoration usually lies by embracing a path that at first sight appears decidedly gritty rather than motor-way-smooth: the Royal Road of Repentance.

By God's grace, our errors were primarily examples of overeagerness and mistaken emphases. They were certainly not in the same league as King David, who committed adultery and, worst of all, was responsible for taking another man's life. For the sake of his psychological well-being as well as his spiritual restoration, it was vital that David faced up to these things. As for so many of us who have blind spots, he needed help to do see his faults, which is why the Lord sent the prophet Nathan, first to expose his sin and then to warn him of its consequences.

To his credit, David faced the challenge head on – at which point Nathan reassured him that although the fallout would be serious, it did not mean that God would no longer be with him.[10] After all, coming to our senses is, for many of us, just the starting point for living in the clean and authentic fear of the Lord.

The experience left David chastened and humbled. Less complacent now than when he had first declared, "I will never be shaken," subsequent events make one inclined to feel that he sometimes wondered if God really would continue to intervene on his behalf when major challenges came his way. The way he responded to the threats posed by Shimei and Absalom, for example, hint at the extent to which his sins had scarred and undermined his soul.[11]

By God's mercy, David's illicit relationship with Bathshe-ba was no more the end of the story for him than it was for us once we realised our mistaken emphases. This is such an important point that it is worth exploring it further. The Lord does not wish us to live bowed down by the weight of mistakes we have made in the past – but it is wise to realise that they may be pointing to a fault line in our make-up. The Lord finds many ways to initiate new beginnings out of the seed of our failures – provided we do not slip back into old ways when times get easier and the pressure is off.

Two thoughts are going through my head as I write these words. Firstly, I would almost certainly not be writing this book now had I not been through so many griefs and failures myself. Secondly, the Lord *has* fulfilled many of the things I believed He promised us at that time – but in a completely different way from how I imagined. It was my striving to reach that place ahead of time that caused the problems. Effectively, I fell into the trap of making the vision more important than anything else – like honouring each other.

When the Lord discerns soul disease in the "tree" of our life, He may choose to perform the equivalent of a "Nebuchadnezzar" experience, and cut it right down. There is nothing cruel or capricious about this, but rather immense love and wisdom. Although we may not realise it at the time, He may graciously leave a stump in the ground, from which, new and better seeds will sprout in due time.[12] When the axe falls, however, it is easy to convince ourselves that "all is lost" when, in reality, it only *feels* as though everything is falling apart.

Sadly, the reverse can also be the case. It is much harder for the Lord to rebuild and restore our lives if we harden our hearts and insist that we "were in the right," for the simple reason that we never reach the starting gate of repentance. *A man who remains stiff-necked after many rebukes will suddenly be destroyed without remedy* (Proverbs 29:1).

It seemed incredible to me that all the plans we had envisioned together had suddenly fallen into the ground. When you firmly believe that God Himself had given these plans, the shock is doubly great. Questions pounded through my mind; would the Lord somehow put everything right even beyond the eleventh hour? Or was He enforcing this "break-up" for His own reasons?

To put this another way round, there is no way that I could have escaped the Lord's discipline by holding up the promises He had given me, and by exercising more "faith" in them. There are times when the Lord prunes unflinchingly – but He is always on the watch for those signs of repentance that will enable Him to intervene in mercy.

O God, You know how foolish I am;
My sins cannot be hidden from You.
Don't let those who trust in You
Stumble because of me . . .
Against you, and you alone, have I sinned;
I have done what is evil in your sight.
You will be proved right in what you say,
and your judgment against me is just.
                              Psalm 69:5-6, 51:4

Restored to Refresh

But as for me, my feet were nearly slipping.
                              Psalm 73:2

Child, you came within an inch of a mile
of losing the gift I put within your grasp;
but with a millisecond thrust of My perfect timing
I swept to your aid and cushioned your fall.
Reproved, restored, refreshed, revived –
with an edge of wisdom not there before –
and a dash of pride-resistant humility.
Fence-mender and hope-restorer,
you now exude My peace,
and bring My special grace to those
who roam and rove from safety moorings,
and stray to the lip of the bottomless drop.

Shrinking Horizons

Some time later the brook dried up because there had been
no rain in the land.
                              1 Kings 17:7

As surely as many in the Body of Christ are feeling overwhelmed by what they are going through, there are at least as many who are feeling decidedly *under*whelmed. The pain of hopes being raised only to see them being dashed again can be a source of the most profound and paralysing grief. This is roughly what I experienced in the aftermath of the break-up of our team.

Sometimes it is our expectations that make it hard for us to endure such discipline. If we have been led to believe that everything we do for the Lord ought to grow and expand, we are almost certain to experience considerable desolation when everything appears to go into reverse. Will we still trust the Lord when the very opposite of all that we had hoped for appears to be happening?

I named one of the chapters in *Ravens and the Prophet* "Shrinking Brooks," after Elijah's extraordinary sojourn in the Cherith ravine. As the drought he had called into being took effect and bit ever more deeply, the prophet had the unnerving experience of watching the water levels of the brook that sustained him dwindling from day to day. But have you not noticed how the Lord often seems to allows us to watch a particular source drying up before He shows us what He is going to do next? Before God sends His deliverance, we need to have the crisis first! As Mike Breen explains,

> *If you want to get to a high mountaintop, you have to be prepared for a journey that takes you through a deep valley first. Watch for leaders who walk with a limp!*[13]

Before she became a well known author, Catherine Marshall describes the immense difficulties she had in adjusting to full-time bed rest during her battle with tuberculosis.

> *The first three months were the worst. Every muscle in my body ached in protest against too much bed rest. The minutes held their breath; the hours dragged their feet. Every inner resource available had to be mustered to fill those days . . . All of life looks different when viewed from the horizontal position.*[14]

Catherine went on to describe how the Lord helped her to use the time profitably. As others have discovered, however, she found it equally as challenging when the time came to reintegrate back into vertically upright life again!

Many of us share the grief of our loved ones as their bodily functions decline, and little by little the frontiers of their world shrink. Since nobody relishes the thought of no longer being self-sufficient, why be surprised if they react with frustration when they find themselves unable to do certain things any longer?

Quite apart from reduced physical abilities, much of the grief associated with the aging process stems from the lack of interest people show in their wisdom and experience. If fewer opportunities come their way – or they lack the wherewithal to respond to those that do, it takes a generous and unselfish spirit to respond graciously and prayerfully.

Mike Field tells me that when Eva Parker, a seasoned missionary, returned home from China with terminal cancer she found the pain was so intense that she was often more aware of the absence of God than of His presence. Despite this, she wrote,

> *Concentrated reality is a potent challenge as horizons start coming closer, but David expresses his response – "by my God I can leap over a wall" . . .*

> *The God of eternity and the singing springing spaces ask us to leap, by faith, into the broader realms of His reality; mortality is merely the necessary springboard for that leap.*

> *Physical death is just a hinge or a hiccough; a door labelled "greater opportunities" and "more adventure"; a breaking through at last of the tantalisingly thin curtain which has hitherto kept "there" from "here". . .*

Reflect and Pray

F. B. Meyer was one of the most popular conference speakers of his era. The time came when Meyer's followers flocked to listen to a new young preacher: Campbell Morgan. Many ministers would feel grieved at being thus superseded.

Instead of succumbing to disappointment and resentment, however, Meyer resolved to spend as much of his spare time as he could praying for the success of the other man's ministry. I can think of no finer response to the challenge of shrinking horizons and changing roles!

> *Lord, these are the areas*
> *where I am facing shrinking horizons . . .*
> *I name them before You now . . .*
> *Help me to be both flexible and courageous*
> *during this transition that*
> *I, or others I am close to, are having to make.*
> *Help us to trust that You are in this "shrinking"*
> *just as You were in the expanding. Amen.*

Changing Roles

> *Elijah was afraid and ran for his life.*
>
> 1 Kings 19:3

One moment Elijah was a prophet to the nation; the next an outlaw on the run for his life. It takes grace and fortitude to adjust to such immense changes. If you find yourself a leader one moment and a nobody the next, (as I did back in 1985) – or a wife or husband one moment, and a "single" again the next, then, although it may sound attractive to rush out to find some suitable role or vision to latch onto, it may actually not be the wisest move.

After all, many of our problems may have stemmed from being "vision-centred" rather than Christ-focused in the first place – in which case the Lord will be most interested in bringing our souls back into balance. Taking time out to be with Him is essential, therefore, for our long-term well-being.

Many of us also experience a profound sense of anticlimax when we *reach* the goals we have worked so long and hard to achieve. Suddenly we are left wondering what it is we should be aiming for next.

It is much the same for the hefty percentage of parents who experience the pangs of "empty nest syndrome." They have spent so many years investing time and energy – along with other stuff that having kids entails – but what comes next when they have finally left home?

Rather than remaining devastated because we have "lost" our child, we will find it easier if we can look on this as a jumping off point for ourselves as well as for them. In fits and starts, and with many a missed flap of their wings, our sons and daughters have long been en route to becoming fully fledged adults in their own right. Is this not what we have been working and praying towards?

To be sure, they may still be far from fully safe and stable, but the whole nature of our relationship with them has been changing throughout their growing years. All roles and relationships are loaned to us in life, and when their season is complete, we must hand them back. It does not mean that we have suddenly ceased to be their parents.

If you are blessed to still have a partner, this is time given back to rediscover that sense of purpose and "chemistry" you once shared as a couple before you had children, but which may have become somewhat stale with the passing of years.

If the opportunity is there, start now, before the children have left. There is no surer way to avoid the fate so many fall prey to in mid-life, who do little more than co-exist together.

Reflect and Pray

Although many untowards events happen in the course of our life, the Lord is so skilful at re-stranding the threads that, in one sense, there can never be a "second-best." He puts every that we go through to good use, so long as we give Him all the pieces – including every trace of resentfulness, bitterness and regret.

Lord, You know why this particular window has closed.
May no hurt or disappointment
prevent me from embarking on new initiatives,
no weariness or shock keep me from starting out again.
In the name of the One Who goes ahead
to open brand new doors for us, Amen.

Shock and Guilt in the Aftermath of Loss (i)

Jacob said to his sons, "You have deprived me of my children. Joseph is no more and Simeon is no more, and now you want to take Benjamin. Everything is going against me!"

Genesis 42:36

Have you ever lain awake at night, or woken early in the morning, echoing Jacob's words in your heart and feeling that everything is against you?

Deep down you know that it is not unusual for God's children to go through times of extreme loss, from Jacob's day right through to people like Corrie Ten Boom, who lost her entire family to the cruelty of the Nazi war machine. Nevertheless, you struggle to understand why so much suffering has come your way, and find yourself working hard not to let anxiety hold you back from proper risk taking. Or you find yourself going to the opposite extreme and becoming reckless, caring too little what happens to you.

Those who have experienced rape, burglary, assault, or some other physical or verbal threat, know only too well how the memory of these shocks can dominate not only your waking moments but surface again in your dream life. Wherever there is any crack in your spiritual or psychological armour, fear will attempt to slither though – and once fear takes root in the soul, the ramifications are enormous. You dread going out, the door being left open, the phone or doorbell ringing, the post arriving . . . No part of life remains untouched.

The Lord can give you grace to handle your "real" fears, as well as to cope with the underlying insecurities that make you susceptible to allowing a foothold to anxiety. If some generational sin or weakness has opened the way for your fears to "attract" dark powers, then by far the best response is to seek appropriate prayer from someone experienced in this field. As quickly as possible!

Reflect and Pray

I mentioned the example of Corrie Ten Boom a moment ago. She alone of her family survived the horrors of Belsen concentration camp, from which she was mercifully released – by a clerical error(!) – just days before she was scheduled to be killed. How easily she could have breathed a sigh of relief and settled down to rebuild her life in the aftermath of such intense trauma.

Instead, inspired by the vision her sister had received before she died in the camp, Corrie set out to minister to people who were suffering acutely, to tell them what Jesus can do for broken people. Only eternity will reveal how many people owe their salvation to Corrie rising to the challenge of such a sacrificial lifestyle, rather than pulling down the shutters and leading a safe and spinsterly existence.

> *Lord, inspire us with this same determination*
> *to fulfil the vision that You have given us.*
> *Use even the shocks we have experienced*
> *to propel us into more of Your purposes,*
> *In Jesus' Name, Amen.*

Shock and Guilt in the Aftermath of Loss (ii)

> *When I consider how my light is spent*
>   *Ere half my days in this dark world and wide,*
>   *And that one talent which is death to hide*
>   *Lodg'd with me useless, though my soul more bent*
> *To serve therewith my Maker, and present*
>   *My true account, lest he returning chide,*
>   *"Doth God exact day-labour, light denied?"*
>   *I fondly ask. But Patience, to prevent*
> *That murmur, soon replies: "God doth not need*
>   *Either man's work or his own gifts: who best*
>   *Bear his mild yoke, they serve him best. His state*
> *Is kingly; thousands at his bidding speed*
>   *And post o'er land and ocean without rest:*
>   *They also serve who only stand and wait."*
>   *John Milton, On his Blindness*

The huge number of people who live with some form of disability is one more good reason for taking the time to understand the grief process more fully – as well as for giving people time and space in which to mourn the things they can no longer do. People who suffer strokes or develop disabilities mourn the many things which we so easily take for granted but which they can no longer do: the freedom to drive, for example, or to applaud with both hands.

The more abruptly loss comes, the more grace we need to adjust, and to cope with the trail of unfinished business that it is sure to leave in its wake. Many struggled to come to terms with events in the summer of 2007, when flash flooding devastated whole communities in central and northern England. Few of us certainly are as phlegmatic as the nineteenth century senator Thomas Benton who declared, while watching his house burn down, "It makes dying easier. There is so much less to leave!"

Possessions can be replaced in a way that people cannot, but they still represent a considerable part of our livelihood. Quite apart from structural damage to houses, the one item that most people wish to preserve is the family photograph album, because it recalls events more precisely than memories alone can do. It is by no means a sign that we are "unspiritual" if it takes us a long time to recover from such losses. They truly are irreplaceable in the sense that we are no longer able to take our past in that particular form into our future,[15]

If I may take a rather small personal episode to illustrate how God can be "in" the losses that come our way, we were startled awake in the small hours of the summer solstice night of 2006 by members of the police and fire-brigade banging on our door. A man many times over the legal limit for alcohol had crashed into our car, which was parked outside our house.

As we peered blearily out, the twisted wreckage of two cars lay strewn across a road floodlit by arc lights, the flashing blue lights of fire, police and ambulance vehicles adding to the confusion. Two thoughts went simultaneously through my mind: the predictable one that "This is the work of the enemy," (who is always destroying things!) but also a more surprising one, that "The Lord is in this somewhere!"

I was very attached to that car, and experienced more than a twinge of grief at losing it (not least because I knew we would get very little from the insurers for our nine-year-old jalopy)! I had been aware for some time, however, that it would by no means be ideal for the city we were about to relocate to. The car we replaced it with has proved infinitely better suited to our present requirements: a small automatic that threads its way through Canterbury's heavily congested streets.

You can probably call to mind similar testimonies from your own experience, quite possibly concerning far more serious issues. For a considerable proportion of the world's Christians, the verses below have an extreme poignancy:

> *You sympathized with those in prison and joyfully accepted the confiscation of your property, because you knew that you yourselves had better and lasting possessions.*
>
> *Hebrews 10:34*

Reflect and Pray

God chose the weak things of the world to shame the strong. He chose the lowly things of this world and the despised things – and the things that are not – to nullify the things that are, so that no one may boast before Him . . . That is why, for Christ's sake, I delight in weaknesses, in insults, in hardships, in persecutions, in difficulties. For when I am weak, then I am strong.

1 Corinthians 1:27-28; 2 Corinthians 12:10

If, as many believe, Paul's thorn in the flesh was a person rather than the eye disease he mentions elsewhere, who can blame him for wanting the Lord to take the problem away? All too often, human and demonic adversaries conspire to hound and oppose everything that certain strategic leaders are setting out to do – even to the point of misrepresenting their best efforts.

If this is true for you, or for some leader you know about – there may be little you can do except to pray until God moves to vindicate and deliver. In the meantime, may the Lord help you to make the best of these "grace growers," as Graham Cooke calls them, and to let them make the best of you.

No Pit so Deep

There is no pit so deep that Jesus is not deeper yet.

Corrie Ten Boom

Whether grief comes as the consequence of physical death, or through the difficult circumstances that come our way, all loss spreads emotional ripples far and wide. "Untimely" deaths, especially those of young people, affect everyone concerned, from siblings to grandparents, and often leave bystanders afraid in case something similar happens to them. The fact that neither they nor anybody else was able to prevent the calamity from happening may leave them feeling acutely vulnerable.

If you are currently feeling that this latest shock is one too many to bear, never underestimate the Lord's ability to help you adapt. Most of you will be familiar with the story of how Joni Eareckson was paralysed for life as the result of a diving accident. The way God enabled her to rise above this most daunting of physical conditions, and the intense depression she went through in the aftermath, is one of the most powerful testimonies of our time.

My mind goes back to Amy Carmichael, who compassionately nurtured girls who would otherwise have been doomed to the most miserable of existences. During the fifty years she spent in India, she rescued more than a thousand children from abuse and exploitation. In the autumn of 1931, at a time when she was greatly exercised by a severe financial challenge, she prayed, "Do anything, Lord, that will fit me to serve Thee and help my beloveds."

Later that same day she fell into a newly dug pit and crushed her spine – an accident that left her bedridden for the rest of her life. Instead of bemoaning the frustration of her confinement, she used this enclosed time to pen pearls of immense wisdom.

Through her many books, Amy spread the gospel to far more people than ever she could have reached by any other means. Many who read them were inspired to set out for the mission field, and the money that accrued from their sales made all the difference to the fellowship at Dohnavur. Truly, God is not thwarted by our limitations.

In *Sparkling Gems from the Greek,*[16] a truly inspiring resource tool, Rick Renner asks why it is that Jesus healed some people outright, whereas others, such as the two blind beggars, had to cry out long and loud for Him to turn towards them.[17] He comes to the conclusion that although Jesus may not have been aware of any particular anointing being present for healing at the time, their faith and persistence *attracted* His attention.

When we are in extreme shock, therefore, we need to do as Amy Carmichael did in her time of financial crisis. We must cry out with all that is within us for the Lord to move by the power of His Spirit to bring about whatever Red Sea deliverance is needed.

Reflect and Pray

Lord, now it appears that the possibility
of fulfilling my dreams has been taken away,
use even these changed circumstances for Your glory.
God of the impossible, reweave my dreams,
yet still fulfil all that You can own,
and that You have called me to.

I call myself an artist,
and yet I have lost the use of my hands;
let me, like Joni, paint with my toes –
or learn to coach and encourage others.
I cannot broadcast to the nation,

but let my voice resound though Your megaphone.
Above all, keep the shadows of disillusionment
away from my heart,
So that I can express more of Yours.
In Jesus' name, Amen.

Eleventh Hour Miracle?

If we are thrown into the blazing furnace, the God whom
we serve is able to save us. He will rescue us from your
power, Your Majesty. But even if He doesn't, Your Majesty
can be sure that we will never serve your gods or worship
the gold statue you have set up.

Daniel 3:17-18

Many of us have seen the Lord intervene so many times at the last moment to turn situations round that we may almost come to regard this as being "normal." What we cannot afford to do is to make a doctrine out of our experiences. There is nothing automatic about the Lord's intervention. Mark Stibbe reminds us that Daniel's brave young friends had four things to say about the Lord's ability to rescue them:

> We declare that You can
> We believe that You will
> We recognise that know You might not – but
> We pray that You do![18]

As we hold these paradoxes in balance, pray along these lines for people who are facing a "fiery furnace."

Lord, we declare that nothing is too hard for You;
You have the power to heal and the power to rescue.
We pray right now that You would touch and release . . .
(Name the person who comes to mind)
Should You choose not to, help them
to keep worshipping You.
May they be so covered in the glory of Your presence
that they experience Your Heavenly comfort today.
In Jesus' name, Amen.

Removing Trauma

Lord, take away, melt away, rend away grief,
hide away, steer our days through,
drip-feeding, deep-cleansing,
all the dagger wounds left behind.
Fire away, every way
steer our days through.

After our ministry team broke up in 1985, the Lord confirmed to Ros that I was going to find this hard to handle because I had "never experienced failure before." How right He was! Not only was I profoundly shocked by seeing the ministry team going their separate ways, I felt traumatized that I had let the Lord down by getting a central part of our vision wrong, and by the fact that God had chosen not to restore the team once we had woken up to where we had been going wrong.

So far as I was concerned, confessing our mistakes to God and each other, and learning from them, was all it should have taken to retrieve the situation. But that was not how the Lord allowed events to turn out.

I was familiar with the idea that the Lord might, if need be, do what shepherds occasionally did in biblical days to sheep who insisted on going their own way. First they would break their leg, and then they would carry them around with them until they were healed. Not only were such sheep "cured" of their tendency to run wild – they often became trustworthy leaders of the flock.

Even though I had always assumed a profound trust in the sovereignty of God, it had never occurred to me that the Lord would allow me to go through anything as intense as this. It would have saved me a great deal of anxiety had I known then what I do now about the need to lift off the effects of shock and trauma. It is important to be aware that whereas grief is a process that takes as long as it takes to recover from, trauma and shock need to be actively resisted and lifted off in prayer.

Trauma comes as the result of intense emotional shocks and woundings. It induces such an overwhelming sense of fear and powerlessness that it can cause immense psychological distress to the soul, overpowering people's ability to cope with their grief symptoms, and drawing them vividly and intrusively back to the event that triggered the trauma. If this in turn makes them feel that their role and place in life is under threat, they may find themselves responding with alarm to any fresh challenge. In other words, once anxiety obtains a foothold, it can spread in all directions like cracks in a pane of glass.

When someone is grieving, they may wish that such and such had not happened. When they are traumatized, however, they may well be inclined to feel that everything is their fault – and that things are bound to go on getting worse for them. In other words, having gnawed away at their trust levels, trauma now attacks their central identity. That it is why it is important to lift it off as quickly as possible through prayer and counsel.

Throughout his long pastoral ministry, David Woodhouse prayed with many people to set them free from the effects of fear, shock and trauma. His wife often prayed in the same way for him to be protected from post-operative trauma whenever he came round from one of the numerous and lengthy operations his state of health required him to undergo. Sometimes the medical staff heard her praying, and, realising that such trauma can be life threatening, commended the practice highly. It also led to some of them identifying themselves as Christians.

There are many routes by which trauma can assail the soul: the sudden onset of illness (or its prolonged continuation); for instance accidents; intimidation at work; abuse at home; contact with evil in any of its many manifestations (especially violent crime); as well as unexpected demands and unfair constraints. No wonder the emotionally sensitive sometimes wonder if they are going crazy, and experience panic attacks in the aftermath of a grief episode![19]

Some of you may also be experiencing "secondary" traumatization, as the result of working in situations of extreme poverty or danger, of the kind that members of the Fire, Police and Ambulance Services regularly face, not to mention social workers in our own country and aid workers in developing countries. If this is true for you, may the Lord lift the shock of each traumatic episode from you, and enable you to continue the work that God has called you to do.

Road accidents are particularly shock inducing because of the suddenness of the impact, and the fact that there is nothing we can do to prepare ourselves. May the Lord grant special grace to lift the trauma from those who have friends and family members who have been killed or injured in this way – as well as those who are fighting the fear of ever getting back into a car again.

For many of us, however, the roots of our trauma lie in cumulative pressures rather than in single episodes. It is when further grief episodes come our way that the underlying grief risks exploding into total trauma.

Telling the truth about traumatic events is considered crucial for full healing to occur, but this is complicated by the fact that trauma is a seedbed that fosters secrets. When we deliberately suppress all reference to certain events or vital facts, we develop "walls" in our hearts. This in turn is likely to have a negative impact on other key relationships, as our trust levels swing and dip.

It is not that we are to rake up unpleasant facts from the past for the sake of it, let alone to drag in others who need have no awareness of the issues involved. We are blessed, however, if we can find someone trustworthy to share our traumas with. If they are *not* trustworthy, the consequences can be far-reaching. As Sir Thomas Browne wrote, "Let him have the key to thy heart who hath the lock to his own."

If we find our concentration levels and our decision making capabilities seriously impaired, it may be a sign that trauma is pushing us beyond the boundaries of "normal" grief into a major depressive disorder. In these instances, we almost certainly ought to consider seeking professional help from doctors, pastors or counsellors. As these people provide us with a secure environment to talk and pray issues through, trauma is often minimised, or even removed altogether. We shall have important things to say about a highly effective way of removing trauma in the section "The Power of Writing to Heal." It is a blessing beyond words when the ground underfoot begins to feel "solid," and we are again able to sense the Lord's peace and presence!

Reflect and Pray

Like all the "starter" prayers in this book, the following is intended purely as a launch pad for going deeper into the Lord's presence in order to find His strength and comfort.

Father of Comfort,
cleanse and release my soul now
from all shock and trauma.
Remove each shaft and shard,
so that none remain trapped inside.
In Jesus' name, Amen.

Never too Late to Grieve

Two wounds touching start to bleed again.
Rachel Hadas (Fix It)

At certain level crossings in rural France, signs can be seen warning that one train can conceal another: "Un train peut en cacher un autre." In much the same way, any loss we experience has the potential to release other losses that we never allowed ourselves to grieve about at the time.

Other people's grief can also serve as a catalyst for releasing our own. A number of people who watched *Shadowlands,* the film about C. S. Lewis' extreme reaction to the death of his wife wrote to the actor who played the part of the grieving Lewis, to tell him about grief and losses that they had never previously mentioned to anyone. They had been stirred by Anthony Hopkins' sensitive portrayal of Lewis' grief – and it brought their own to the surface.

When people back off, and bury their grief, or become disproportionately fearful or angry, it is often because something from earlier in their life (or from their family's history) is being in someway re-enacted. Understanding this goes a long way towards explaining why people sometimes demonstrate significantly more grief than a situation appears to warrant.

A typical example is when someone shows more emotion over the loss of a pet than they did for the death of some primary person in their life. It is as though they are giving themselves permission to grieve the *one* death now in turn releases buried layers of unexpressed griefs.

We should certainly not underestimate the effect that the death a pet can have on us.[20] Considering the pleasure we take in their companionship, to say nothing of the memories we accumulate around them (and the positive impact they can have on our blood pressure!) it is no wonder many of us grieve deeply when they are taken from us.

Two years after the loss of our faithful collie dog, Ros and I were still experiencing severe canine withdrawal symptoms. In a dozen different ways we found ourselves missing our deeply affectionate if somewhat behaviourally challenged four-footed friend. Another couple might have gone out the following week to chose another one, but it took us two full years before we felt ready to take on another dog – a delightful though elderly chocolate-brown Labrador, who had spent six long months in a rescue centre. He is delighted to have found a welcoming family – and we love him to bits![21]

Reflect and Pray

Father, if there is any buried grief in my heart,
that would be better off out than in,
I ask You first to expose it
and then to remove it.
In Jesus' name, Amen.

Yielded Hearts and altered Perspectives

All the days ordained for me were written in Your book
before one of them came to be. How precious to me are
Your thoughts, O God. How vast is the sum of them!
                                        Psalm 139:16-17

The premise I am following throughout this book is that the more willing we are to face our grief, the more we will see the Lord turning things that initially bring us much distress into blessings further along our pilgrimage – although we may only be able to appreciate this when we look back on it later.

This applies right across the board from the seemingly mundane to the really serious. When she was a young girl, Amy Carmichael used to look into the mirror and pray that the Lord would change her brown eyes into sparkling blue ones. She was very upset when this did not happen – but many years later she was grateful that she had brown eyes, because they made it so much easier for her to integrate into the Indian culture.

After completing his medical training, Dennis Burkitt found himself unable to obtain a surgical post in the UK because of the result of an injury, which had left him with only one eye. After all, who would want to employ a one-eyed surgeon? Far from allowing this disappointment to crush him, he followed the Lord's leading and went to Africa, where he became famous for describing what became known as Burkitt's lymphoma (the most common cancer amongst children in sub-Saharan Africa), and for discovering the importance of fibre in our diet. The example of this outstanding surgeon and missionary doctor reminds us of God's challenge to Moses to understand how sovereign He is over all our affairs.

Who makes a person's mouth?
Who decides whether people speak or do not speak,
hear or do not hear, see or do not see?
Is it not I, the Lord?
Now go! I will be with you as you speak,
and I will instruct you in what to say.   Exodus 4:11-12

Depending on how secure we are as people, how far advanced we are along the path towards grief resolution, and perhaps also on how confident we are in God's sovereignty over the situations we find ourselves in, we are likely to respond in very different ways when major difficulties come our way.

Some of us find it relatively easy to trust, while others are inclined to object and put up a fight: "Lord, I couldn't possibly do that," we protest – although our arguments usually fail to impress anyone except ourselves. Even Moses only got so far when he pleaded with the Lord to send someone else![22]

It is profoundly reassuring to remember that the Lord knows all about our physical, spiritual and emotional limitations. So far from putting Him off, He almost seems to *prefer* doing His greatest work despite our weakness. Best of all, He starts in enough time to get us to His destination. He even takes our "detours" into account!

Reflect and Pray

When the angel brought Mary the amazing news that she was going to be with child despite being a virgin, her initial reaction was very much what yours or mine would have been: *"How can this happen?"* (Luke 1:34). Are you facing one of those "how can this happen" moments? If so, you can do no better than to respond as Mary did: *Let it be to me according to Your Word.* Nothing is impossible to Him.

Father, the more I yield to Your call,
and accept that You have made me the way that I am,
the better I will cope –
and the more glory You will have.

Come, Holy Spirit,
lover of my soul,
lead me by Your Spirit,
and work in me the works of Heaven.
In Jesus' Name, Amen.

The Power of Letting Go

Oh my God . . . You had something far better for me than that I should waste my life in enjoyment – and repent though eternity. But at first I could not understand that and could not do it, and so force had to be used, just as one puts splints on a broken leg. The education consisted in leading me to be able to do freely what at first I had to be compelled to do.

Real renunciation, yes the delight of renunciation, is simply a lover's understanding with God. Truth obliges me to admit that it was God who gave the hint. I had not dreamed of it, neither had I believed myself capable of it. But it was as though God had whispered the secret to me: renunciation is a higher relation to God; it is really a love-relationship, and for me, at least, an enchantment was spread over renunciation – I have never been so enchanted.

Søren Kierkegaard

Writing from her own unique standpoint, this is how Robbie Davis-Floyd concludes her article:

Just as even obstetricians cannot explain the mystery of birth (they still don't know what initiates labour), I can't explain the mystery of this death/near-death/rebirthing process that is still taking place in me . . . I can give you no facile explanations or easy answers, only perhaps the sense that in fact, everything is as it should be. Certainly it is as it must be. As with labour, we can either surrender to the truth of death, or fight it till the effort kills us.

When I gave birth to my son at home, I learned the power of surrender to the tremendous force of life. Now I am learning the power of surrender to the tremendous reality of death.

May these two kinds of surrender balance and sustain me, teach me to let go of my fight to understand, and embrace the paradoxes my life encompasses. Like a mother who has just had the courage to give birth without knowing who her child will become, I am here, not knowing who I will become, but open, cracked wide open, to whatever life may bring.

I subtitled this book, *Experiencing spiritual growth through loss* because the Scriptures have much to say along these paradoxical lines. In his first letter to the Corinthians, Paul teaches that: *What we sow does not come to life unless it dies* (1 Corinthians 15:36).

This verse points us to a remarkable truth that usually lies hidden from our eyes until something happens to bring it to the fore. Somewhere in the course of our pilgrimage, the Lord brings us to the point where the seeds we sow, the visions we pursue, and even the promises He gives us must fall into the ground and die before they can reproduce exponentially.

Just as Jesus entrusted Himself to death on a cross, so Paul, when he "enlisted" in the service of the risen Christ, was obliged to lay down his hard-won reputation as a scholar and a leading Pharisee – and with it, all forms of earthly security.

At the heart of God's finest works and ministries lie occasions (usually out of the public eye) where men and women of God reach the end of themselves, and are obliged to hand their most cherished hopes and dreams back to the King of Kings. This may sound radical, but can you imagine anything worse than having bits of your life that are "yours" rather than "His?"

Catherine Marshall writes powerfully about what she calls the "prayer of relinquishment" in *Something More*. She testifies that yielding is the "golden key" that enables God's purposes to prosper without any of the glory "sticking" to the group or individual concerned.[23]

The Lord is so gracious that even when He takes something precious from us, He finds ways to bless the outcome as much as if we had handed it back to Him of our own free will! It was certainly like that for us in the way in which the Lord developed a new and broader-based team in time for the 1987 Message For Our Times Conference in Malvern, which did so much to launch our ministry wider.

It is an awesome moment when the Lord fans smouldering coals back into life again. It was here that we joined forces with a wide range of exceptionally gifted musicians, pastors and teachers.

As surely as there is blessing when we yield to the Lord's will, there is nothing but grief and frustration when we run away from it. Think of the desperate plight the Israelites found themselves in when the Lord told them that He had finally had enough of their prevaricating, and was no longer prepared to go up with them to the Promised Land. With the notable exceptions of Joshua and Caleb, the whole of that generation perished in the wildernesses.

Faced with such a dire sentence, the people immediately put it to the test, much as we might check the strength of a door we suddenly found ourselves confined behind. Hurling themselves against their enemy, they were soundly defeated, and left with no choice but to accept the terrible consequences that come when we push the Lord too far.[24]

Some of us hang on too tightly, as though everything depended on us. Yet all the time He is wooing our hearts to let go of all that tethers us, and to venture further out on the sea of trust – even when He leads us into waters we would not have chosen to sail in.

> *I tell you the truth, unless a kernel of wheat falls to the ground and dies, it remains only a single seed. But if it dies, it produces many seeds. The man who loves his life will lose it, while the man who hates his life in this world will keep it for eternal life. Whoever serves Me must follow Me; and where I am, My servant also will be. My Father will honour the one who serves Me.*
>
> *John 12:24-26*

There is one exception to this. Jesus speaks in John 10 about the devil coming as a thief, a murderer and a destroyer. Like a skilled pick-pocket, the enemy is forever trying to steal things from us. He achieves most when his work goes undetected.

Not content with taking what is rightfully ours, the powers of darkness aim to dispirit us to the point where we "give up" on the rest. (This is the actual meaning of the word "murder" here). Subtly, they may even try to make this destructive temptation sound like "holy yielding."

Let us be under no illusion: if the Lord is *not* asking for something back, giving it up might be part of the devil's strategy for our life – in which case we need to respond with with resilience rather than surrender. God can send the grace we need, despite the darkness and the opposition.

Reflect and Pray

God of unique distribution,
and faithful intervention,
Since nothing exists without Your will,
God of the "no accident"
I bow my knee to Your singular choosing, and
pray for grace to embrace this new found vista.

A Pilgrim Restored

By way of illustrating the power of yielding in the right way, I would like to introduce you to Leo Tolstoy's moving story about Martin the Cobbler. One freezing cold day, this ailing man is standing at his bench, forlornly plying his trade. When his hale and hearty friend Vladimir walks past and invites him to join him in gathering wood for the winter festival, Martin angrily rejects his advances. Obsessed with the loss of his cherished young wife and his only child – just as the boy was reaching the age to have been of real help and companionship – the cobbler has no time for such frivolity.

One day a pilgrim calls, asking him to rebind his Bible. Martin is despondent, but honest with him, for in truth he blames God for leaving him with so little. "I am without hope," he declares. "All I want of God is that I may die."

The pilgrim looks at him kindly but keenly. "You are in despair, Martin, because you live only for yourself. Read the book; perhaps it may help." With that he leaves, promising to pick it up when he returns from his journey.

That night, Martin dreams that the Lord speaks to him, telling him that He is going to visit him, and urges him to look out the window the following day. Martin works extra hard that day, but often takes the time to peer expectantly out of the window. He sees an aged street sweeper freezing in the cold and brings him indoors to feed and care for him. Later, he sees a young mother shivering in the cold and struggling to feed her baby. He brings them into the warmth, and when he discovers that she has pawned her shawl for food he takes a garment he has long treasured, his own wife's shawl, and tenderly drapes it around her.

Others enter and leave the cobbler's shop that day, and he helps them all, but still he sees no sign of the Lord. The old despair rises again. Why hasn't He come? That is when the cobbler's weary eyes are drawn to a verse in the pilgrim's Bible: "Whatever you do to the least of these brothers and sisters, you are doing unto Me."

In a flash of insight, Martin recognises that Christ has come – in the form of each person he has met and helped that day: the street sweeper, the mother and child, and all the others. When his friend Vladimir passes by again, the cobbler can't wait to go out and join him. Healed of his grumpiness and despair, Martin has moved beyond his own grief and is ready to play his full part in the life of his community.[25]

Reflect and Pray

Tolstoy regarded this short story as perhaps his most important because it demonstrated how God uses people with love in their heart to restore hope and life to those who have lost it.

If you find yourself in the grip of unexpected loss, may I encourage you to remember how many intimate moments you have shared with Him? He will not fail to send you help, and to heal every trauma as you call on His name.

You are my servant. I have chosen you and have not rejected you. So do not fear, for I am with you; do not be dismayed, for I am your God. I will strengthen you and help you; I will uphold you with my righteous right hand.
Isaiah 41:9-10

Lord, You say in Your word, "Fear not."
I speak these powerful precious words now
to each area of my life that is gripped by fear.
Anchor of my soul, enable me
to weather the waves of anxiety by trusting You.
In Jesus' name, Amen.

Angelic Assistance

Last night an angel of the God whose I am and whom I
serve stood beside me and said, "Do not be afraid, Paul.
You must stand trial before Caesar; and God has gracious-
ly given you the lives of all who sail with you." So keep up
your courage, men, for I have faith in God that it will
happen just as He told me. Nevertheless, we must run
aground on some island.   *Acts 27:23-26*

No overview of the way the Lord guides His people through
difficult times would be complete without referring to the
help that angels bring praying saints at crucial moments.
From the angel of the Lord who found Hagar destitute and
desolate by the side of the road,[26] to the angel who guided the
children of Israel to safety through the wilderness, they guide,
they guard, and they provide God's people with invaluable
direction.[27]

May I share the story of how I believe an angel strengthened me recently when we were going through a most disturbing time?Rosalind and I went to bed late one night,
eagerly anticipating our early morning departure for a much
needed Easter holiday across the Channel in France. During
the night, a strange muscle spasm jolted Ros awake. For
nearly a minute, it immobilised her right hand, leg and foot.
She said nothing about it in the morning, hoping it would ease.

We drove across north France and spent the night in a
retreat house run by some friends of ours. Ros was strangely
subdued, and, to tell the truth, looked decidedly unwell. That
night she had two further spasms, which left me to do all the
driving to the mobile home we had hired.

The holiday was both special and strange. Special because
it was the south of France, and warmth and beauty surrounded

us. Strange because the after effects of her nightly attacks left Ros unable to venture further than the decking of the mobile home for the whole fortnight. Little did we know that these crippling spasms would continue, night after night, with ever growing intensity for the next ten weeks, each attack leaving her brain feeling increasingly slugged in its aftermath.

Overnight, our entire future was thrown into question. What did these repeated seizures portend? Would Ros be able to continue the work she loved mentoring the next generation of midwives? More to the point, how would we cope if she did not? I went quickly down the road of fearing the worst. Questions swirled through my mind, later to be echoed by puzzled doctors. Was she having a series of strokes? Or epilepsy? Or, Heaven forbid, was this the onset of multiple sclerosis?

After speaking to a French doctor, we agreed together that there was no point in embarking on lengthy tests which would need to be duplicated as soon as we returned to Britain. The spring was warm and peaceful, yet inwardly chilled by the shadow that was hanging over us. By the time we returned home, Ros was having difficulty remembering the alphabet.

We all react to setbacks in different ways. Some of us are only too ready to assume imminent doom, whilst others are inclined to minimise issues. If we can do our best to put to one side questions to which there are, as yet, no answers – without straying into denial – then this is surely the wisest approach to take – but it did not come readily to me on this occasion.

As soon as we returned home we kick-started the process of obtaining medical tests. Interminable waiting for appointments with a surprisingly surly consultant, further delays before receiving results that would only trigger further tests – many of you will be only too familiar with the whole frustrating process. Like Job so long ago, I felt profoundly shaken, with my heart weighed down by concern for Ros and for our decidedly Mum-centred seven-year-old son.[28]

I made several sorties into the beautiful French countryside – on my own, of course, because Ros did not feel well enough

to leave our holiday home. On one of these outings, I suddenly became aware that I was not on my own. I strongly sensed
there was a "Presence" in the car with me.

When a representative of the Host of Heaven comes close,
there is often an immense sense of spiritual uplift (but by no
means always, for angels are often sent in the most ordinary
of guises). This is less euphoria than a profound awareness of
the sovereignty of God over the minutest of affairs. The angel
spoke to me about things back home that I would somehow
not have expected a "French" angel to have been aware of.

I know enough about such encounters to realise that they
are decreed and appointed by the Father – but *why* was He
granting this experience? Being just that touch neurotic, as
well as extremely concerned about what was happening to
Ros, I soon began to wonder if the Lord had not sent this
wonderful strengthening precisely because things were about
to get a great deal *worse*.

On many of the occasions when angels appear to people in
Scripture, they begin by saying, "Fear not" – at which point
the person they are addressing faints from fear. I did not do
that, but I did lose some of the benefit I could otherwise have
enjoyed by indulging in some uncalled for worrying. There
was nothing but love behind this visitation. Even so, it is as
well to be aware that the day will come when the angel of the
Lord will come again to lead both Ros and I on our final
journey – though whether he will speak in French or English
remains to be seen!

Reflect and Pray

Are not all angels ministering spirits
sent to serve those who will inherit salvation?

Hebrews 1:7,14

The Treasures of Darkness

And I will give you treasures hidden in the darkness –
secret riches. I will do this so you may know that I am the
Lord, the God of Israel, the one who calls you by name.

Isaiah 45:3

For the first few weeks after Ros was convulsed by spasms, I found, as so many people do in times of crisis, that the Lord sent special strength. Friends leapt to action-stations in prayer, adrenaline flowed and the Lord's presence hovered like an overshadowing cloud, while I put this enclosed time to good use by completing the next draft of this book.

There is evidence in Scripture to suggest that the Lord quite enjoys a "rough and tumble," but I wasn't tempted to try and make any "bargains" with Him.[29] Over the course of my life, with a few notable exceptions, I have preferred to focus on the fact that He is much better placed than I am to make the key choices for my life.

Beyond a certain increased proneness to irritability, (every diabetic's perfect excuse!) anger wasn't particularly an issue either – which only goes to show that by no means all of us automatically experience all five of the classic grief stages.

Ros and I often see things differently. Most of the time we compliment each other well, but on this occasion I thought she might be straying into denial. In reality, she was just trying to make the time in France as sheltered and "cocooned" as possible under the circumstances. In other words, this was less denial than common sense, combined with a hint of "divine anaesthetic" to tide her over.

The one thing I was not short of, as a result of being well advanced with drafting this book was an understanding of the grief symptoms I could expect to experience! Was I experiencing sharp pangs of grief as the initial numbness wore off? Yes, an abundance of the darned things.

We knew we had been overworking – but how could we have done otherwise with Ros preparing her lectures for the first time as well as having to complete her Master's degree? Neither of us were inclined to indulge in prolonged "if only" regrets, and I think this protected us from many of the feelings of shame, guilt and depression which so often accompany the grief process.

Shakespeare termed sleep the "sole comforter of minds with grief oppressed," and loss of it is common in almost all grief episodes. No wonder sleep deprivation ranks as such an effective method of brainwashing and torture. Most of us can cope with almost anything, providing that we get enough rest! We were certainly "nocturnally challenged," both because of the increased frequency of the attacks, and the implications that they raised.

Engulfed by a sensation that I am sure many of you will be entirely familiar with, I felt alarmingly powerless. These feelings of helplessness became a cause of further grief themselves, leaving me prone to bouts of anxiety. My phone bill shot up as friends received phone calls at surprisingly early hours of the morning. (We were on holiday in rural France, you will recall, far from our usual support structure).

The fact that we have helped many others through times of anxiety undoubtedly went some way towards helping us to cope. We knew that it is usually best to skip the tricky questions in the initial stages of grief. After all, the Hebrew word for "why" doubles as the symbol for "chaos!"

For the time being, we could no more answer the inevitable questions going round our heads than we could appreciate a painting by standing with our noses pressed against it. We knew that it would only be when we were able to stand back that we would gain a better perspective.

Standing back is difficult, however, when every part of you is longing to find a solution. I sensed that if I could *cooperate* with this surging and unpredictable current I would have more chance of emerging intact from the experience. Being anything but level-headed when it comes to the health of my wife, however, my grasp on that particular perspective wavered from hour to hour, let alone from day to day.

Life proved complicated when we returned home. Like so many couples, our lifestyle affords little slack for emergencies, and shouldering all the transportation posed predictable problems for a two-driver family. Simon and Maria Redman took Dominic to school for us, and lovingly "soaked" Ros in the Lord's presence. A group of leaders came to our house to pray (at extreme decibel pitch) for the problem to shift.

All of these were vital stages along the way, yet every time people prayed seriously for Ros, the spasms invariably seemed to worsen afterwards. That itself, of course, was a clue. A condition that reacts so intensely against prayer is more than likely to be carrying the stench of sulphur.

A few weeks before Ros's first spasm I had gone for a walk with Rob Grinsell, a friend in the ministry. Suddenly, Rob threw his cap on the ground: "The gauntlet has been thrown down, and a challenge has gone out!" he declared theatrically. "Satan is challenging and God has accepted it." He was alluding, of course, to the passage in Job 2:3 in which the Lord challenges Satan concerning one of His own servants. There is a New Testament parallel to this when Satan asks permission to "sift" Peter. In that instance, as surely for our own, Jesus promised that His own prayers would bring Peter though this testing period.[30]

The Scriptures are clear: *Resist the devil and he will flee from you.*[31] By the time Ros had suffered well over one hundred of these dreadful attacks, we were desperate. Rather as military advances traditionally begin by laying down a heavy artillery barrage, I organised a major prayer push, mustering as many praying friends as we could to pray at a specifically arranged time, either with us or at a distance.

It was this day of prayer that proved to be the turning point. Even then there was a crocodile lash of the tail. As we drew to the end of an incredibly special time of prayer, Ros had one of her most violent ever attacks – and another one a few hours that night. Had our prayers not prevailed?

The following morning, as Ralph and Sarah Deakin laid hands on Ros and "soaked" her in prayer, the Lord showed Ralph a vision of an angel plying a microscopic needle and thread, gently "suturing" her nerve endings together. To our immense relief, the attacks receded in strength immediately and, within three or four days ceased altogether.

I discovered long ago that the same word is used in both Greek and Hebrew for to *tempt,* to *test* and to *try.* In other words, while the devil is *tempting*, God is also *testing*, and our soul is being *tried!* By God's mercy, this proved to be a test and an attack rather than a final chapter.

Rob Grinsell had also pointed out to me that "tunnels" are often God's fastest way of taking us through particular obstacles in order to reach an entirely different landscape beyond. As it turned out, the Lord had an entirely new appointment for me the moment this particular trauma had passed. In all probability, however, your situation may be an ongoing one, which is why we are going to turn our attention now to more serious forms of grief.

References

1 Study passages such as John 3:18, 5:24; cf 1 Thess. 4:13-14; 2 Thess. 1:8-10, 1 Cor. 15:20, 2 Cor. 5:1-5, and let their truth direct your days.

2 See, for example, *Man Alive*, by Michael Green, Inter-Varsity Press (1967) and *Who Moved the Stone?* (2006) by Frank Morrison, Authentic Media – useful books that examine the historical facts concerning the central tenets of our faith.

3 Marshall, C. "Open Hands," in *To Live Again.* (2002) Chosen Books.

4 The people in Haggai's day were profoundly grieved by the rampant inflation and other difficulties they were facing, but the prophet challenged them to realise that their lack of seeking God was a major cause of this. When they truly put the Lord first again, God was swift to promise His blessing. (Haggai 1:4-11; 2:18-19).

5 Matthew 6:5-8

6 Acts 15:36-40

7 2 Kings 18:14

8 Read Proverbs 6:1-5 on this matter!

9 Literally "betrayed You."

10 2 Samuel 12:1-14

11 2 Samuel 16:5-13

12 See Daniel 4:10-27

13 Notes from a conference for Cluster Leaders at Ashburnham Place, Sussex, October 2007.

14 Marshall, C. As above.

15 See Bright, R. *Grief and Powerlessness.* (1996) p. 64. Jessica Kingsley Publishers.

16 Available from www.amazon.co.uk

17 Matthew 9:27-30

18 Mark Stibbe. Copyright. December 2006 Used with permission.

19 Reid Wilson explores these themes in greater detail in *Don't Panic!* (1996) Harper Perennial.

20 Zunin has helpful things to say about this in *The Art of Condolence.* pp. 130-136. Harper Collins.

21 David Woodhouse writes that when an elderly woman lost her husband suddenly through an aneurism, she remembered a baby she had miscarried many years before. She contacted the hospital concenred, who arranged for the chaplaincy team to hold a service for her. One grief had triggered the previous pain, which, in those days, it was less customary to speak about. This service brought her peace concerning both losses. The hospital commented that it is not unusual for older people to want to bring such sad memories to a closure.

David adds that many Crematoria hold quarterly Services of Remembrance run by the local "Churches Together" groups for those whose loved ones had their service there. They have found this to be a great pastoral opportunity after the daze of the initial grief had lifted somewhat, and the bereaved are more able to receive the good news of hope and comfort. David's own Church invitates the bereaved family each year to attend a special service.

22 Exodus 4:13

23 Marshall, C. *Something More.* Chosen Books.

24 Numbers 14:26-45

25 Tolstoy wrote a similar piece called "Papa Panov's Special Christmas." See www.ruachministries.org/valeoftears/refs.htm

26 Genesis 31:11, Exodus. 14:19-20

27 cf Exodus 23:20-22 Acts 12:5-11 A new book on the subject has been published in the *Thinking Clearly* Series: Woolmer, J. *Angels.* Kregel (2003).

28 "In the past you have encouraged many people; you have strengthened those who were weak. Your words have supported those who were falling; you encouraged those with shaky knees. But now when trouble strikes, you lose heart. You are terrified when it touches you". (Job 4:3-4)

29 Genesis 18:22-23; 32:24-30; Exodus 32:11-13

30 Luke 22:31

31 James 4:7, cf 1 Peter 5:8-9.a

Part Three

Approaching the Final Transition

WESTERN SOCIETY is more understanding than it used to be, but many families and communities continue to send out unspoken signals to preserve self-control and decorum at all costs. This can leave us people in more emotionally turmoil than in supposedly less developed societies that encourage a more open expression of grief. I have looked at various issues related to death from a practical point of view in Appendix Three, but in this section, we will be exploring some of the spiritual aspects associated with it.

Eternal Homecomings

> *We look at death from the wrong point of view. We think of how much we're missing the one going home. We're not looking at it from God's point of view: a child's coming home, and Heaven is excited!*
>
> *Ruth Bell Graham*

Most of us warm to the quote above, not least because it comes from one of God's elder stateswomen when she was on the point of entering the glories of Heaven. It takes more grace to accept the fact that some people's earthly lives are, quite simply, a great deal shorter than others.[1]

Death probes our convictions and intensifies what we believe about this life and the next. In ultimate terms, death represents the drawing together of the strands by which the Lord has lovingly led us, and is therefore the prelude to an infinitely richer phase of our life. Just as the Lord has been good to us in this world, He will be no less so in the next.

For most of us who love the Lord Jesus, therefore, it is less a matter of death itself holding any terrors so much as our concern for those who are left behind, and our fear of the process of dying – hardly surprising, perhaps, in the light of all the stories of neglect and mistreatment we hear about these days.

Differentiating between death the "last and greatest foe," which the Lord Jesus has overcome for us, and death the "gateway to everlasting life"[2] can be a source of great tension. There are undoubtedly times when we are called to resist the "angel of death" – that is, the enemy's attempt to take us home prematurely. It is entirely appropriate then to pray with both urgency and authority against precious lives being snatched away before their time. In his pen-portrait of Jesus' ministry, Luke reminds us that,

> *God anointed Jesus of Nazareth with the Holy Spirit and with power. Jesus went around doing good and healing all who were oppressed by the devil, for God was with Him.*
>
> *Acts 10:38[3]*

At the other end of the scale, there is no shame whatsoever in recognising that there are other occasions when God is calling someone home – in which case it is right to bless and even speed them on their way through our prayers. May the Lord give us the discernment to know which response is most appropriate.

Reflect and Pray

> *When Jesus appears, we shall be like Him, for we shall see Him as He is . . . Love is made complete among us so that we will have confidence on the day of judgement, because in this world we are like Him.*
>
> *1 John 3:2 4:17*

Anticipatory Grief – The Gift of Tears

> *Heaven knows we need never be ashamed of our tears, for they are rain upon the blinding dust of earth, overlying our hard hearts.*
>
> *Charles Dickens, Great Expectations*

"Tears," Spurgeon once declared, "are liquid prayer." Sitting on a plane twelve years ago, returning from a ten-week sabbatical in America, I found myself engulfed in tears at the prospect of a particular person dying. As it turned out, he lived for well over another decade, but I knew that this "grief ahead of time" was the result of a heavenly prompting. There need be nothing morbid about such anticipatory grief: rather, it can be clean and purifying.

In the summer of 2005, our forty-two month sojourn on the Shetland Islands came to an abrupt end. There were two main reasons for this; the immense grief and pressure Ros was experiencing at work, and the fact that the Lord had told me through a variety of prophets that once the prayer conference I had been sent to organise had taken place, my time there would be complete.

A few weeks before we left, three thousand athletes made their way to the islands to participate in the Inter-Island Games. As we watched my friends in the table tennis team giving their all against players from around the world, I found myself dissolving repeatedly into floods of tears.

By the end of the week there were no more tears to shed, and I knew that my grief over leaving this unique phase of our lives in those amazing islands had been resolved. As a result, I was able to make the most of my remaining time on the island. It proved much harder for Ros, who had less opportunity to prepare herself for the transition. She loves the people of Shetland more than any other people-group or community we have ever been part of. She continued to fill up with tears for nearly two years every time she thought of the place and the people who meant so much to her.

Ros finally obtained release when Chris and Vicky Pemberton came round to pray for her. With a delightful combination of compassion and spiritual authority they set her free from the grief which had been locked up inside her for so long

Ros had left the islands "greeting" (which means "weeping" in the Shetland dialect). Six months after this time of prayer, we enjoyed a delightful return trip to Shetland, in which the Lord took Ros from "greeting" to a deep and welcoming "greeting".

Reflect and Pray

Record my lament; list my tears on your scroll –
are they not in your record?

Psalm 56:8

Lord, if Your Spirit leads,
give us grace to grieve ahead of time
for people, places and opportunities
that will soon no longer be there –
not in faithless fear
but in the true love
which pillows our heart against Yours.
In Jesus name, Amen.

Anticipatory Grief – Saying Goodbye ahead of Time

Well God, I'm in your hands.
I'll do everything I can,
and then all I can do is trust in You.

Alison Brown[4]

Many stories have come down to us concerning faithful Celtic saints like Columba, who were aware of the precise moment when the Lord would send His angel to gather them to their heavenly home. Some in our own day have been privileged to know this too. All of us who love the Lord can look forward to the moment when, inspired by the Spirit, the body releases a signal to the other parts of our being to initiate the "transition" process that will usher us into the presence of the Great Shepherd of our souls.

May the realisation that the Lord is watching over this final journey sustain us in the face of the anxiety that so many associate with the dying process – especially if it proves to be a long drawn out experience. Praise God for welcoming hospices which provide warm and loving environments for those who are no longer expected to recover. Here, at least, death is not seen as the ultimate failure of the health care team.

In countries where life expectancy is shorter – as indeed it was in our own nation until recent advances in environmental health and medicine radically altered our expectations – people learned from childhood how to grieve together. For most people today, however, death is something that happens in hospitals or hospices, surrounded by people who are specially trained to deal with it.

Blessed though we are to enjoy increased life expectancy today, this can also lead to complex and grief-laden complications. Certain forms of modern medical care undoubtedly militate against natural progression.

The fact that a goodly percentage of us face the possibility of being caught up in a prolonged "dying before death" phase is therefore another reason why there is a place for grieving ahead of time. Saying goodbye in this way is less an attempt to shut a relationship down than an important step to help us enjoy our remaining time together. Such leave-taking is neither "a denial of hope nor an acceptance of despair."[5] It can help us to make necessary emotional and practical adjustments, and to accept that grief often sets in from the very moment we realize that something precious is coming to an end.

Another advantage of saying the "big goodbyes" ahead of time is that we can do so before we, (or a loved one), become incapacitated. Degenerative conditions such as Alzheimer's tend to make us forget how people were in the prime of their life. It is often only if some remission occurs, or, after they have died, that happier memories resurface.

The challenge is to remain sensitive to how the dying person is feeling at a time when we ourselves may be in much need of grace to cope. Dying can be such an intense process that it encompasses every shade of human emotion, in which case it is a kindness to enable people to have whatever measure of control it is in our power to bestow, rather than rushing to take away their independence. As Kenneth and Sarah le Vaux remind us:

The dying need more intensive loving care than a plethora of charts and monitor screens, where privacy is at a premium and there are few facilities for friends and family. The message needs to be spelt out: it's all about people – not machines! "Touch time," and, above all, attentive listening are, as ever, the vital ingredients.[6]

Reflect and Pray

Four-year old Corrie Ten Boom looked up searchingly into her father's eyes. "What is it like to die, Daddy?" she asked. "When we go into Amsterdam," replied her wise and godly Father, "when do we buy the tickets?" "Just before we get on the train, of course," she replied. "Then in just the same way, the Lord will give us what we need when we need it."

Well before we reach the "last lap" it makes sense to give God any feelings of grief we may still be carrying. If we are approaching the climax of our earthly life without having seen the fulfilment of all we have been hoping for, many of us may be left wondering whether it is we who have missed the boat, or circumstances that have made the realisation of our dreams impossible. Or we come to realise that the Lord *has* fulfilled what He promised, but by a very different route from how we had originally expected.

Just as it was Joshua rather than Moses who finally led the Israelites into the Promised Land, and Solomon who built the Temple rather than David, so it may fall to another to complete what we have begun.

Moses and David could easily have succumbed to grief and resentment at finding themselves unable to fulfil what they had set their hearts on. To their credit, both men devoted themselves to doing all they could to ease the way for their successors. Is there anything the Lord would have you do in terms of making practical or emotional preparations to bless those who will take on your work and mantle?

Making a good Death

"Some day," D. L. Moody used to say, "you will read in the papers that D. L. Moody of East Northfield is dead. Don't believe a word of it! At that moment I shall be more alive than I am now!"

Watching someone approaching the end of their days with faith and equanimity is one of the most sacred experiences in life. Heaven is close at hand as they await their homecoming to a glory that will far surpass even one of Shetland's amazing sunsets. In those northern climes there are days in mid-summer when you can watch the sun slip beneath the crest of a hill in the west, and then glimpse the first flares of the rising sun a few moments later in the east. As the sun sets on one phase of our life, so it will emerge again in another, better place.

A long-term friend of ours has recently gone to be with her Lord. After fighting her way bravely through many years of struggles and anxieties, a deep peace settled on her when incurable lymphoid cancer set in. Sally's main concern was for her unsaved elderly mother, who would not be able to care for herself. With unmatchable precision the Lord drew all the threads together. Her mother went to be with the Lord just four days after making a commitment to Him – and Sally followed her almost immediately afterwards.

Following the first death in his mission, Rees Howells declared at her funeral,

> "Have you ever heard of a person who is dying shaking hands with everyone, as though she was going on a journey?" The heavens opened and the victory was such that they all started waving their handkerchiefs – even the mourners had to join in . . . The sad grave was turned to be the gate of heaven, and from that funeral we had the beginning of resurrection life in the mission.[7]

All too many in our fear-bound society lack the benefit of such a spiritual perspective – something that was epitomised by the ignominy a mother of a still-born baby had to endure when an insensitive health professional called back over her shoulder as she swept the body away, "It's not as if you knew her, is it?" How anyone can make such callous remarks to a woman who has just spent nine months cherishing a precious life within their womb is quite beyond me.

At the same time as challenging such insensitivity, it is honouring to recognise good models of care. Many hospitals have effective pastoral support for bereaved parents. As far back as the 1980's, Blackburn Infirmary used to call David Woodhouse, in order to provide pastoral care for the parents of still-born babies. This enabled them to hold their baby and to take photographs to record the event.

People who are unable to be present in the aftermath of the death of family members often require additional prayer and support. The fact that they missed the moment of transition can cause them such intense grief that it threatens to over-whelm the memory of all the good times they enjoyed togeth-er over the years. If this applies to you, read on: we have an insight that will minister to you!

We often noticed how pregnant mothers who were particu-larly eager to have Rosalind as their midwife managed to "hang on" until she was free to attend the birth of their baby. At the opposite end of life, many people (from newborn babes to the oldest great-grandparent) choose to slip away when they are on their own – even during the interludes when loved ones leave the room to eat or sleep.

Rona Scott sent me an account along these lines after the husband of one of her friends was admitted to hospital with terminal stomach cancer.

> *Unable to find any peace so long as his wife remained with him, the nurse suggested that my friend step outside to give him some space to calm down. He died almost immediately and very peacefully. My friend was convinced that, just as he had looked after her in life, he wanted to do the same now, not wanting her to see him die.*

If you "missed the moment" when your parent(s), child(ren) or partner passed into the next world, there is no need to spend the rest of your life plagued by regrets. What has happened may well be less a failure on your part than due to the fact that your spirits were so strongly united that it was not your presence but rather your *absence* that was required to complete the transition. I pray this insight will bring you great comfort.

Where it is possible, you may find it valuable to take time to be with your loved ones in the hours following death. There can be real benefit in saying the things you never quite got round to expressing. The grief ordeal is lessened and the chances of a full recovery increase. Even better if some of those words of forgiveness or appreciation can be expressed ahead of time!

May the Lord help you concerning this most vulnerable of issues. The death of His saints is precious in God's sight – and He will be with you as you honour their memory and embark on the next phase of your life.

Reflect and Pray

It is impossible that anything so natural, so necessary, and so universal as death should ever have been designed by Providence as an evil to mankind.

Jonathan Swift[8]

To conclude this section on how we can honour our loved ones, I am returning to another part of Robbie Davis Floyd's account of her daughter's sudden death.

> Usually, when birth is over, you drive home with a baby in the car seat or your arms. Death needs an escort too, and Peyton's godmother Sharon and I planned to be on the plane that would take Peyton's body home. She had flown in from New York. The next day Sharon, Richard, and I visited the site of the accident to try to figure out how this could possibly have happened. Ruts in the grass and four piles of shattered glass greeted us, showing how the car had swerved and the four times it had flipped. Among the tall weeds, I found the shards of a Japanese vase I had given my daughter at Christmas.

> Birth plans are generally made in clarity of thinking and well in advance; death plans have to happen in shock and

immediately. Peyton died on September 12 on her way home from New York to Austin to celebrate her twenty-first birthday with her family and friends. So it was utterly clear that we would not be having a funeral but rather a birthday party and that it had to happen on the actual day of her birth, September 16. Her dad and I had less than four days to pull it off.

To honour our daughter, we rose to the challenge. Even if we had had years to plan, the obituary Peyton's father Robert Floyd wrote could not have been more beautiful, nor could the Memorial Service/Birthday Party have been a more fitting celebration of Peyton's life. As in birth, so in death — ritual can carry you through!

Robbie Davis-Floyd[9]

And who said that Time should be an ordered man?
A man who breathes the morning air,
progressing steadily until
he slips into the night sleep.
Why, he slithers from nature's grasp
dashing back and forth through the years,
laughing at the turmoil he causes in my mind,
juggling my memories like an infant with its toy
until I don't know which are dreams
and which reality.

He can be a mean figure
who freezes time at the most unwelcome moments,
wanting me to savour an agony
Taking me through it frame by frame;
A slow-motion fully interactive picture of my pain.
On another day he may choose to drag me by the hand,
laughing, while I try to absorb every piece of this wonderful
life that's rushing by.
But constant even to this fickle creature of Time
is friendship.

He can speed with the winged feet of the wind,
or crawl with the first agonised attempts of a baby.
I need only to reach out through him

to feel the presence of those who share my life.
And though they may be faint ghosts of the past,
Time will carry them, as precious cargo,
and lay them down on the floor of my mind,
where we can laugh
and speak as if yesterday were tomorrow.

Alison Browne (aged 20)

References

1 In *A Severe Mercy,* Sheldon Vanauken relates the heart-moving
story of a couple whose love for each other led them to pursue
the very opposite of a modern fast-lane, two-career lifestyle.
Rather than neglecting each other in their quest for personal
fulfilment, Sheldon (Van) and his wife developed an all-
consuming love for each other, which, in turn, has had a
profound influence on the way many of his million-plus readers
have come to view love and marriage. Converted to Christianity
through the influence of C.S. Lewis and others, Van later came
to regard their love as somewhat selfish, but his book is more
than just a classic love story: it is a serious examination of
bereavement at its most intense.

2 1 Corinthians 15:26, Psalm 116:15

3 James Rutz's exciting chronicle of what God is doing around the
world highlights a small but increasing number of cases in
which believers are raised from the dead in response to fervent
believing prayer. Rutz J. (2005) *Megashift.* Empowerment
Press, Colorado.

4 *Allie's Song,* Allie Browne Copyright Tony and Brid Browne
1999 Herne Bay Kent. A collection of poems and writings by
Allie, who died at the age of 21 of cystic fibrosis.

5 Bright, R. *Grief and Powerlessness.* (1998) p.77. Jessica Kingsley.

6 Le Vaux, D. and S. *Dying Well.* (1996) p.105. Abingdon Press.

7 Grubb, N. *Rees Howells, Intercessor.* Lutterworth.

8 *Thoughts on Religion* 1765

9 Davis-Floyd, R. (*2003) Windows in Space and Time: A Personal
Perspective on Birth and Death. Birth: Issues in Perinatal Care.
Vol. 30 (4):22-277.* Robbie kindly gives permission for this arti-
cle to be reproduced.

Part Four

Minimising Grief's Desolation

N O ONE IS PRETENDING that there is a perfect way to grieve, but we will be looking here at a variety of strategies that will help to release our emotions and minimise the worst effects of grief's desolation.

Expressing Grief and Loss

As I stood there in silence—
not even speaking of good things—
the turmoil within me grew worse.
The more I thought about it, the hotter I got.
Psalm 39:2-3

What was it that had happened to cause the psalmist such distress? We are not told precisely, and in a sense, this makes it easier to apply his response to our own situation. When we too are feeling vexed with life, and intensely aware of our limitations, it is time to cast all our cares on the Lord.[1] After all, the only real alternative to doing this is to bottle up our emotions, and to allow guilt, oppression, failure and weariness to spill over into self-pity – that most deadly of all the soul's many enemies.

"There is no grief like the grief which does not speak," the poet Longfellow warned. A Turkish proverb repeats the same message: "He who conceals his grief finds no remedy for it."

Those who hold their grief inside themselves after a loss occurs usually do so because they want to remain strong for the sake of their children, or other loved ones. "Delayed" grief differs from "denial" in that it is not a deliberate attempt to avoid facing reality. Even so, keeping a tight rein on emotions that are bursting to find expression imposes immense strains. Sooner or later, repressed grief finds its way to the surface. When the initial anaesthetic has worn off, and overwhelming feelings flood back in, pray for the Lord and His people to be present to help them work their grief out stage by stage.

If family and professional commitments make it difficult for you to face the full onslaught of your grief, try setting aside specific times in which to let it out. Don't neglect to plan in some "out-of-the-house" events to distract from the intensity of it! As Catherine Marshall urges,

> One can at least take the cup with both hands and put it to one's lips at intervals, and then, for a while, turn to something else. Somehow, the cup becomes lighter, a little more bearable, its contents less bitter each time the cup is voluntarily grasped.[2]

Reflect and Pray

How are you handling your grief? Are you like a pent-up volcano, liable to erupt under the pressure of too many molten emotions? Or is the Maker of Mountains helping you to find ways to "regulate the flow" safely?

> *Father,*
> *provide me with people I can open up to safely –*
> *but may I not make the terms*
> *for letting others close so demanding*
> *that people lose the incentive to reach out to me.*
> *May I, in turn, be a source of strength and comfort*
> *for others in their grief and isolation.*
> *In Jesus' Name, Amen.*

When Impatience sets in

Do you not know? Have you not heard? The Lord is the everlasting God, the Creator of the ends of the earth. He will not grow tired or weary, and His understanding no one can fathom. He gives strength to the weary and increases the power of the weak.[3]

Isaiah 40:28-29

In the days before steam power, anyone crossing the oceans had to be prepared for times when lack of wind caused progress to be measured more by the centimetre than the kilometre. Prolonged periods of being becalmed did not, of course, usually prevent the ship from reaching its destination.

When something precious comes to an end, we may find ourselves tempted to slump into the slough of despond. Alternatively, we may want to throw ourselves into new projects or relationships, as if to reassure ourselves that we still have a role to play, or that we can still sustain an intimate relationship. All such feelings are entirely understandable - but it is as well to realise that impatience at this point can not only lead us into real danger, but can also cause us to miss out on other things the Lord has in mind for us.

At a subconscious level what may be happening is that we are trying to "get our own back" on the Lord for allowing such losses to come our way.

We are usually aware deep down, however, that our temptation to throw ourselves into some potentially short-term relationship may be nothing more than an attempt to compensate for the loss we have experienced. We must give God time to find His own unique way to fill the hole that has been left behind.

Some men plunge too quickly into new relationships in order to fulfil their own needs and sense of loneliness, but in the process leave their children feeling as though this new relationship "invalidates" the original marriage. At the very time when the children are still profoundly grieving the mother they have just seen taken from them, they feel now as though they are losing their father too.

It is important to remember that many psychologists consider adolescence to continue until the age of twenty five - in which case it would be a mistake to think that it is only young children who are affected by such decisions. In extreme cases lasting damage can be inflicted, causing the children to doubt all loving relationships, as well as the accuracy of their childhood recollections. There are no formulas here; only a great need to be led by the Spirit and careful in our communication.

Reflect and Pray

Lord, when nothing much is happening
give me grace to endure these slow and weary times.
Thank You that You already have in mind
what You are going to do beyond this recovery phase.
May I be in the right frame of heart and mind,
when You call me to some fresh adventure.
In Jesus' Name, Amen.

The Power of Resilience

Resilience: The power or ability to return to the original form, or position, etc., after being bent, compressed, or stretched; the ability to recover readily from illness, depression, adversity, or the like; buoyancy.

Dictionary.com

Researching the theme of resilience, Lyndall Bywater discovered that it enables us to "withstand shock without it causing permanent damage or rupture."[4] God has made us intrinsically resilient, and given us amazing protective mechanisms to absorb and recover from immense physical and emotional pain. Even though we may have suffered great loss, we must resist the temptation to sit back and settle for less: resilient faith helps us to bounce back again.

After the authorities had banned the apostles from mentioning the name of Jesus, there was a real danger that the fledgling church would lose its way. "It's no good, Jesus," they might have protested. "We've done our best, but it just isn't the same without You; we can't do any more!" Rather than giving up, or putting on a brave face and pretending that everything was okay, we read in Acts 4 that they turned to the Lord with still greater intensity, refusing to assume that they had failed just because they were meeting such strenuous opposition.

In times of shock, it helps to rehearse what God has said to us. Isn't it better to have our lives shaped more by God's promises than by how circumstances appear? "This is how things appear, Lord, and this is what other people are saying – but what do *You* have to say about it?"

No one enjoys these testing periods, but such was the disciples' strength of spirit that they were remarkably unperturbed by them. After all, Jesus had told them plainly that they would encounter many such difficulties.

Refusing to let the pressure make them retreat into themselves, the disciples rose to the challenge. Since the Divine Script Writer had allowed these scenarios to come about, He must have a way of bringing eternal good out of them.

May the Lord make us like the early Christians who "used" persecution to drive them to seek God more earnestly, and who refused to stop witnessing to what they knew to be true. When they asked the Lord to *"consider their threats"* it was their way of saying, "Lord, this is *Your* problem: *we* must get on with the mission You have sent us on."

How infinitely better this was than forming "A Committee to study Safe Responses in Times of Persecution." Calling on the Lord for boldness, the apostles cried, *"Stretch out Your hand to heal, Lord"* – and promptly went out and did the very thing the authorities had forbidden them to do: preaching the gospel everywhere they could.

There is nothing "safe" about being led by the Spirit! Those who are hostile to the work of the Spirit always cramp and oppose prophets and pioneers, and try to impose a more conventional course of action. We cannot afford to change the agenda God has given us just because the going is tough – or even because certain prayers appear to remain unanswered.

At a time when I was feeling overwhelmed by a number of daunting challenges, I picked up my much loved Living Bible and opened it at Hosea 6:1-2:

> *Come, let us return to the Lord.*
> *He has torn us to pieces;*
> *now He will heal us.*

He has injured us;
now He will bandage our wounds.
In just a short time –
two or three days at the most –
He will set us on our feet again,
so that we may live in His kindness.

This passage provided just the comfort that I needed, firstly because it spoke of the Lord working within precisely the time frame I needed Him to move in, and secondly because it raised my hopes that I would be able to enjoy "living in His kindness" beyond the immediate crisis.

The following day, while I was out walking the dog, I found myself caught up in an unexpected vision. I was eleven years old and running out to play for the school football team on a cold winter's morning. Unlike anyone else in the team I was wearing gloves to protect my fingers against the cold. "You took stick for standing out for what you know you needed to do," the Lord reminded me, "and you are doing the same thing now. Remember: the mockery didn't stop you rising to become joint captain."

I had long since forgotten all this, but now that the Lord highlighted it, I could remember being teased for wearing gloves. I also remember the wonderfully successful season we enjoyed the following year, during which two of us operated an unusual but highly successful arrangement as joint captains of the team.

This powerful reminder increased my trust that the Lord really was going to turn an immensely painful situation around. It was doubly special that He did so precisely three days later.

Reflect and Pray

Trust in the Lord with all your heart;
do not depend on your own understanding.
                              Proverbs 3:5

What areas of your life do you particularly need resilience in at the moment? Take time to identify and pray for the Lord to increase your resilience in the face of these threats and challenges.

Bringing Rest to troubled Souls

It is foolish to tear one's hair in grief, as though sorrow would be made less by baldness.

Cicero

During World War II, the Royal Air Force dropped enormous bundles of tin foil to confuse the Nazi anti-aircraft radar defences. They called these decoys "Window". Grief often leaves us feeling overwhelmed, however, by the amount of "noise" on the radar screens of our hearts.

Most of you will understand exactly what I mean when I speak of such intrusions. One minister I met, however, told me that he only ever needs a few seconds to bring his soul to rest, no matter how great the challenges he is facing. I have the feeling that he and I live on different planets! On the other hand – why waste time and energy "worrying" when the Lord wants us to have confidence in Him?

What we do not need are people brandishing platitudes at us. "Taking a stand in faith" does not mean living in unreality. What will help us are experienced saints who reassure us that the distress we are going through is normal, and who are prepared to stand beside us and love us back to full strength.

As we shall be seeing in the Appendix, "Tension – The Neurosis of Faith," some of us are more prone than others to experiencing anxiety in the aftermath of loss. For some this is a matter of temperament, for others it is the result of distressing episodes from our past. Speaking as one who arrived into the world on a hospital floor, with my mother unconscious and no midwife in sight, I understand entirely why people who have had difficult birth experiences are prone to feeling abandoned when too many pressures come their way.

Complications of attachment and separation in our earliest years can have a major significant impact on our emotional development, often causing insecurities to surface during times of loss – for grief is a time when strong emotions rage and old temptations abound. Let's also face this fact: that in our spiritual warfare, there are no vacations and no time-outs, and the enemy would be missing a trick if he failed to take advantage of our vulnerability.

In C. S. Lewis's masterpiece, *The Screwtape Letters*, a senior devil counsels his nephew, a junior tempter, in the ignoble art of luring the devout astray – whether into pastimes of no spiritual significance – or, alternatively, stoking their passions until they become ensnared in foolish affairs.[5] In either instance, serious spiritual warfare is going on behind the scenes.

Bearing this in mind, it is worthwhile checking from time to time to see whether grief is causing us to be consumed with some particular line of thought. Our waking thoughts are often an indication of where our dominant thoughts lie.

Each of us must bring our deepest longings to the Cross in the full assurance that we are loved and accepted at the deepest level of our being.

Reflect and Pray

As a mother comforts her child, so will I comfort you; and you will be comforted.   Isaiah 66:13

In his excellent books *The Freedom of Simplicity,* and *Prayer, Finding the Heart's true Home,*[6] Richard Foster shows how Christians through the centuries have proved the value of prayerful meditation in helping them to draw near to God. To take a particular theme or verse and meditate on it is hard to do when grief is tugging at our heart, but we will find great strength and comfort if we persevere.

Draw us deep into Your Word, Lord Jesus.
Let it fill our minds, and shape our thinking,
Until we instinctively choose the ways of Heaven.
Since Your Word tells us to guard our heart,
we resolve here and now
that we will allow no one and nothing

> *to take the place that is rightfully Yours.*
> *In Your name*
> *we rebuke the worries*
> *that blur our thoughts*
> *and consume our energies;*
> *for You are the source of our life,*
> *and we worship You.*
> *In Jesus' name, Amen.*

Too many Choices

Wer hat Wahl hat Qual – Choices bring pain.

German proverb

In all good dramas, much of the tension, like the action itself, centres around the choices that people make. Since most grief events in our own real-life dramas call for multiple decisions, may the Lord help us to choose wisely – especially when our emotions are already stretched and strained.

In the months after Ros's strange spasms began, we found it hard to know who to tell about what was going on. We finally shared the information with about sixty people, but soon found it exhausting trying to respond to their feedback.

Lovingly offered, most of the suggestions that came our way stemmed from experiences these people had gone through themselves, or which they had heard about from others. We found the sheer number of alternatives over-whelming, especially because they covered an impossibly large spectrum. It was rather like being told that Ros was suffering from mumps, measles, housemaid's knee and a broken leg all at the same time!

Since, by definition only one of these diagnoses could possibly be right, we found the whole experience profoundly disorientating. As a rule, we found that the more intensely people offered their suggestions, the less they witnessed to our spirits. The one "constant" that emerged was that this was first and foremost a spiritual assault – in other words, some-thing to resist rather than to adapt to. With this in mind I organised the day of prayer I described earlier which brought about the breakthrough.

Choices are easier to make when we know what it is we are trying to achieve. Taking a stand for our principles calls for considerable courage, however, when we know that they are likely to prove unpopular in certain quarters. There comes a time when, like Martin Luther, we can do no other. To hesitate at this point would be to concede ground to the enemy, and to risk missing our goal altogether.[7]

If I may take an example that meant a lot to us, even though it barely registers when compared to the more serious issues we are looking at elsewhere in this book, we wanted our last two children to be born at home. A consultant summoned Ros when she was forty weeks pregnant with our third child, and, without raising his eyes from his desk, told her that he wanted her to come into the hospital for an induction "because babies die if they are left in the womb."

He had chosen the wrong person to pontificate to! Aware that her gestation cycle regularly takes her well beyond her due date, Ros was able to stand her ground – but how many other women would have been able to withstand so much pressure at such a vulnerable time. If we had packed our bags and made our way to the labour ward, we would have missed a wonderful home water birth.

All too many stories do not have such a happy outcome, of course. Tragedy strikes unexpectedly, and we may be left grief-stricken and frustrated because we unable to secure the specialized help we needed. Or the medical staff lose interest because they consider the situation to be beyond hope, and they turn their attention to acute cases that may lead to a more "favourable" outcome.

More often than not, however, there are choices to make, and how we handle these "choosing moments" is all-important. Putting off making any decision at all is still a "choice" – though rarely a wise one. May the Lord inspire the choices we make in the short, medium and long term – and graciously sort out any foolish ones we have made!

Reflect and Pray

Faithful God,
be with us in the specific choices that we must make.
Align our hearts to Yours,
in true wisdom and humility,
and so help us to find
the paths that You have prepared for us.
In Jesus name, Amen.

When the Grass appears greener

I thought to Myself, "I would love to treat you as My own
children!" I wanted nothing more than to give you this
beautiful land – the finest possession in the world. I looked
forward to your calling Me "Father," and I wanted you
never to turn from Me. But you have been unfaithful to Me.
You've been like a faithless wife who leaves her husband.
                                              Jeremiah 3:19-20

The opening chapters of Jeremiah contain some of the most
poignant and tender laments in the Bible. The Lord has done
so much for His people, and it hurts Him when they proved
as unfaithful to Him as a wife who deserts her husband and
runs to take another. For Jeremiah, as for Hosea, there can be
no greater sin than turning our backs on our Heavenly Lover.
It grieves the Lord deeply.

The moment we lower the shield that Biblical truths provide us with, we are in danger of exchanging the truth about
God for plausible and sophisticated alternatives (Romans
1:25). Since this is as true for matters of the heart as for any
other area of our life, Paul tells Timothy to:

Keep a close watch on how you live and on your teaching.
Stay true to what is right for the sake of your own salvation
and the salvation of those who hear you.
                                              1 Timothy 4:16

When marital relationships are at a low ebb, it is easy to
fantasize that some new relationship will prove far more
fulfilling – especially if it appears to offer a way of escaping
heavy responsibilities.

For many years, Carlene[8] prayed for her husband to come to faith, but when this did not appear to happen, they moved to a remote part of the country, and the way was wide open for a marital disaster. In time, an "attraction" led to a full blown affair, which she managed to keep concealed. One year later, her husband was spectacularly converted, but because Carlene was so committed now to her new man, she was unable to rejoice at the answer to something she had once prayed night and day for.

Determined to pursue her affair, she rang to let me know that she was leaving her husband. Knowing how important the next few minutes would be, I prayed for the Lord to give me wisdom. Into my head popped an article I had read in the *National Geographic Magazine,* which describes in graphic scientific detail how such infatuations are like a mental illness – a psycho-physiological process that is highly likely to run out of steam after a certain period of time when a master valve in the brain suddenly switches off the "chemistry" that had, until then, been flowing so strongly.[9]

"In other words," I told Carlene, "the time will come when your feelings for your lover will switch off, and you will be left with no feelings for him, no family to turn back to, and, worst of all, no fire in your heart for the Lord." All too often I have shared such warnings to no effect, but on this occasion, a strong conviction came on her that things would work out exactly as I predicted. There and then she made the courageous decision to face the issue head on and to return to her husband – even though she very much doubted that he would be able to handle her infidelity.

"Why do you think the Lord has been strengthening him so much?" I replied. "Most husbands "know" in their spirits when something is wrong," I pointed out. "Surely one of the reasons the Lord has been blessing Mark so powerfully has been to prepare him for this?" Carlene agreed uncertainly, took a deep breath, and set off to restore the relationship. Her fears proved groundless. Mark forgave her immediately and the couple are now fully restored.

When a married person "falls in love," or runs away from a marriage, they are usually so caught up in their new passion that they mentally minimise the effect their affair will have on their children – some of whom may never fully trust them again. When they finally realise what they have lost, they are often devastated. They may also make the unwelcome discovery that the person they are attracted to has their own set of demands and dynamics – all of which impose their own requirements and responsibilities.

Many people's lifestyle these days is so intense that it almost encourages them to go in search of something to "compensate" for things they are finding too painful to bear, or which they perceive to be lacking in their lives. Where this searching inclines them to perceive another person as having more compassion or charisma than the person to whom they owe their chief loyalty, they may soon find themselves constructing elaborate hopes and fantasies around them.

As surely as there is a special anointing that causes people to open their hearts to each other in God-given friendship, it is as well to be aware that the powers of darkness are also highly skilled in kindling potentially fatal attractions. Counterfeit chemistry leads to emotional complications that can shipwreck marriages in exchange for nothing more substantial than a passing infatuation.

Just as David moved swiftly to secure an intimate audience with Bathsheba, such longings can develop rapidly from mental fantasies into dangerously co-dependent relationships. Only this week I heard about a vicar abandoning his wife for a curate half his age, leaving the parish in shock and grief. Such things affect far more than the people most directly involved.

When someone "suddenly" leaves, it is usually the end result of a process that has been going on for some time. For many, the process of infatuation begins (or accelerates) during times of grief, when a person is already emotionally vulnerable.

Just as the Lord uses shared interests – or hardships – as a starting point for promising new relationships, so the enemy seeks to do the same in order to bait the snare and spring his trap. Even seemingly well defended people – whether seventeen or seventy – can be induced to follow a path that will lead to exceedingly messy complications.

David's early faithfulness to the Lord was exemplary, but the effects of his affair with Bathsheba profoundly affected the lives of his children. No other sin leaves quite such a trail of misery as adultery. That is why Paul's warning remains as relevant today as it ever was: *If you think you are standing firm, be careful that you don't fall* (1 Corinthians 10:12).

If we find ourselves directing immense amounts of spiritual and emotional energy towards someone else, it is time to take stock. Is the Lord calling us to befriend this person and to lend them our strength? Or are we in danger of becoming infatuated with them? Check your timetable and your bank balance to see just how much you are doing to accommodate these new desires. As Catherine Marshall reminds us,

> *A man and a woman can live in the same house, in fact lie side by side in the same bed, and still be worlds apart. Don't make the mistake of thinking that the only lonely people are single people. Loneliness doesn't fly out of the window in the wake of the marriage ceremony.*[10]

As surely as we benefit from taking the Lord's promises and encouragements to heart, it is equally as important to heed His warnings. Since adultery almost never occurs where people are "heart accountable," have you got at least one person who knows what is really going on in your heart? Make sure it is not the person you are feeling attracted to!

Many hold back from seeking out the level of covering we are speaking of here, because they have seen pastors, leaders and family members over-reacting when someone has confessed to a growing attraction. I have come across leaders who have been summarily demoted, and even driven out of the ministry, not necessarily because "something has happened," but simply because the person concerned shared how they were feeling, and the leadership overreacted for fear of appearing to compromise.

In other words, the very course of action that should have prevented the problem from developing became the means of crushing souls who were battling not to give in to it. How tragic. Nine times out of ten, everything could have been defused by prayer and counsel.

Nothing is foolproof, but taking time to ponder the following safeguards will both enrich our relationships and make "accidental" attractions much less likely to occur.[11]

- Read and take to heart the message of Proverbs 2:16-19, 5:20-21, and 6:23-29.

- At any given point in your relationship with someone who is not your marriage partner, would you feel comfortable if either the Lord Jesus or your husband or wife were physically present?

- Take time to discover what qualities it is that your partner is seeking from the relationship (as opposed to what you think they want).[12] This will help you to direct your love and care where it is most appreciated.

- Lay down any unrealistic expectations you brought into the relationship. Much can be resolved if you will both appreciate what the other is contributing to the relationship, and acknowledge the pressures you are both under.

- Pray regular and specific prayers for each other. This can do wonders to focus and renew your love.[13]

Reflect and Pray

He who trusts in himself is a fool, but he who walks in wisdom is kept safe.   *Proverbs 28:26*

If you sense (or fear) that it would be unwise to share what is really going on in your heart with the "obvious" person, make sure that you do have *someone* to be accountable to. Don't sit tight and wait to see what happens. In a letter to someone who was experiencing a fantasy relationship with a woman in his office, Bel Mooney counselled:

> It goes without saying that you have to work at truly valuing and loving your wife anew. I tell you this. When you are old, and impending death is more than a troubadour's melancholic trope, the woman of your dreams (your wife, that is, not the fantasy woman) will, God willing, be at your side. She will be caring and loving, stroking your brow, wiping the soup from your lips – and still wearing, albeit with wrinkles, the face of the woman you loved deeply enough to marry.[14]

Wounds in the Household of Faith

Wounds from a friend can be trusted,
but an enemy multiplies kisses.   Proverbs 27:6

If you are anything like me, you will have known many occasions when you have received stinging rejections, and have greatly needed friends and counsellors to pull out the darts and arrows that have pierced your soul.

In one sense we are wise if we *prepare* people to experience such rejection. Even in Jesus' own day, when compelling evidence of His Lordship was mounting all around, more people followed their leaders' example in rejecting Him than embracing Him as their Lord.

We get glimpses in John's gospel of how much people's reluctance to follow through on their commitment affected Him. If that was hard enough to bear, Jesus then had to endure the greatest grief of all: being rejected by someone who was close to Him. Disillusioned because his Master refused to follow the path he had once hoped he would, Judas left the door of his heart wide open for Satan to enter in.[15]

Judas' rejection of Jesus was of an altogether different order from that of Peter, who also denied his Lord, not once but three times on the night He was arrested. Jesus knew that Peter's denial sprang from momentary weakness rather than from deliberate premeditated choice, which is why He made a point of seeking him out after the resurrection.

It was always Jesus' intention that Peter should serve as His overseer and spokesman, and in due time Peter showed himself to be a wise and trustworthy leader – despite, and perhaps even because of, his soul-searing failure. As Tozer brilliantly remarked:

> Repentance is, amongst other things, a sincere apology for having mistrusted our Lord so much – and faith is a throwing of oneself with complete confidence on Christ's mercy.

If you have been seriously betrayed or let down by someone close to you, you will know that there is no pain quite like it in life. If you have not, it is rather like me trying to describe an acute pain. You may do your best to put on an understanding smile, but a few minutes of the actual pain would be of far more use in helping you identify with it.

Job describes in graphic detail the effect his so-called "comforters" had on him.[16] Bombarded by unkind suggestions on the one hand from his fair-weather friends, and by immense external afflictions on the other, Job preserved his sanity by refusing to accept accusations he knew to be untrue.

When even his wife urged him to forget the God-thing altogether, Job replied in terms that most modern Christians would shrink from expressing quite so directly: *Shall we accept only good and not trouble from the hand of God (Job 2:10)?*

So far as God was concerned, it was this willingness to go through whatever He asks us to experience that proves the authenticity of His work in us. He is still in control even when everything looks and feels otherwise. As the Lord restored Job, so He can also find ways to bless those of us who have been bruised and battered almost to the point of wanting to quit the fray. That is why we too can declare:

> *When He has tried me, I shall come forth as gold . . .*
> *Even if He slays me, I will still trust Him.*
> *Job 23:10, 13:15[17]*

Reflect and Pray

At the end of the book of Job, when God breaks through and reveals Himself to His distressed servant, He makes no effort to give direct answers to Job's questions. Rather He speaks with passion about the most unlikely animals: wild donkeys, which cannot be tamed to work in the fields or to carry footsore human beings – and Leviathan, who is so strong and dangerous that he laughs at men's attempts to subdue him.

It is as though the Lord is saying, "You can't understand why I made these creatures, Job, but they have their role and place in My creation – and so too do these intense sufferings that You have been through. Don't be offended and don't hold back!"

Moving beyond the Reefs of Rejection

But as for me, my feet were nearly slipping.
Psalm 73:2

How do people who have experienced rejection react? Most commonly by withdrawing into their shell. Suppressing their natural emotions, they hold back from reaching out to others in case they end up getting hurt again. Does this sound familiar?

Not all withdrawal is unwise; it is certainly important to know when to protect yourself against further rejection. I understand entirely why a certain veteran prayer leader reached the point where he became fed up with people queuing up to "practise" their healing ministry on his wife, who suffers from severe multiple sclerosis.

Eager though both he and his wife are to welcome people with genuine anointing, they find it immensely wearying going over the same ground with people they have no heart connection with. Some who offer their help may feel pushed away – but perhaps they had not paused to think matters through from the couple's point of view.

C.S. Lewis posed a question which most of us ask ourselves at one time or another: "Does there have to be so much pain in loving?" Perhaps we would do well to look at this the other way round. Would refusing to love make things any better? Is this how God Himself works? What if He had weighed the odds halfway through Jesus' mission, decided that the Romans were looking fierce and the Pharisees were not for turning and pulled His Son off the job?

You are reading these words today precisely because the Father went right through with His mercy mission. No matter how empty your heart may feel, and how much in need of a refit, God honours those who persevere.

If you have been holed beneath the waterline by sharp rocks on rejection's reef, may the Lord direct you to people and places that will aid the healing process. You may find such repair work tedious and time-consuming, but, like a ship refitting in dry dock it is essential not to neglect the damage that has occurred. May He heal your hurts and rejections as you do this – including the *fear* of being rejected.

Reflect and Pray

Father, where scorn and rejection
have carved a furrow in my heart,
and throb as sharply as if blows and batons
were assailing my soul,
heal all traces of rejection in my heart,
and restore my trust in Your leading.
In Jesus' name, Amen.

Misunderstood

Then Jesus entered a house, and again a crowd gathered, so that He and His disciples were not even able to eat. When his family heard about this, they went to take charge of Him, for they said, "He is out of his mind." And the teachers of the law who came down from Jerusalem said, "He is possessed by Beelzebub! By the prince of demons He is driving out demons."

Mark 3:20-22

In *The Lion, The Witch and the Wardrobe,* Lucy, the youngest but most spiritually sensitive of the Pevensey children, suffers intensely when her brothers and sister refuse to believe what she has to tell them about the land of Narnia. Much the same thing happens in *Prince Caspian*, when she alone senses Aslan warning her that they are heading in the wrong direction. There is a cost to pay for seeing as the Lord sees, and grief at discerning His calling when others either cannot or will not follow where He is leading.

There is nothing new about this. There came a time when even Jesus's own family lost confidence in what He was doing – but our Lord refused to be disheartened by their lack of affirmation. If we too encounter hostility from those closest to us, we cannot afford to allow this opposition to put us off. Turning back would cause God and others grief, and jeopardize the work that He has given us to do – but we need courage to keep moving forward!

At the same time, there is no shame in acknowledging the pain we feel. When I began work on my first book, certain friends and reputable leaders tried hard to induce me to restrict myself to the teaching, and to edit out all trace of my own testimony. I felt strongly that real life stories would break up the blocks of teaching and provide access points to the truths I was seeking to convey. Because I was uncertain of my literary voice in those days, I compromised then more than I would today.

More recently, when the Lord called us to move to Shetland, He warned us that we would have to set our faces like flint to resist inevitable pressures not to move so far away. Having witnessed that there are no emptier people on earth than those who turn their back on a genuine call of God, we were determined not to allow anyone else's agenda to distract us from what the Lord was asking us to do. At the same time, we had our own grief to process at the prospect of leaving friends and family.

If you have come through a period of intense grief and sense that the time has come to embrace some new role or relationship, it can be immensely distressing when people oppose this. "You're way ahead of yourself," their attitudes if not their actual words imply. "Why, you're acting as if such and such had never even existed!"

There is a poignant reminder here to think before we speak! It is hard for us as outsiders to gauge where someone else is up to on their grief journey, and all too easy to make insensitive comments that reopen people's wounds at the very time when they are beginning to emerge into some new phase in their life. Why should we expect them to go on mourning if they have genuinely moved on beyond it?

Reflect and Pray

I am mocked and scorned for Your sake;
Humiliation is written all over my face.
Passion for Your house burns within me,
so that those who insult You are also insulting me.
                                        Psalm 69:7,9

Whether the opposition that we face comes primarily from people we are closely associated with – partners, parents, children, employers, co-workers and the suchlike – or because we have made things harder for ourselves by handling situations badly, the Lord can still bring us through.

When we find ourselves under intense pressure it is good to remind ourselves of how the Lord helped David. Shortly before Saul was slain, and he was summoned to become the new King of Judah, David experienced one of his most grievous trials. Providentially denied the opportunity to wage war against his own flesh and kin, David and his men returned home in time to find their village in flames, and their wives and families missing.[18] As if that was not shocking enough, his own men then turned on him, threatening to stone him. Just how bad could things get? As Matthew Henry reminds us,

> *When David was at his wit's end, he was not at his faith's*
> *end. The Lord can, and will, bring light out of darkness,*
> *peace out of trouble and good out of evil.*

Instead of giving in to despair, David *found strength in the Lord* (1 Samuel 30:6).[19] I love that expression. It speaks of immense resilience in the face of overwhelming loss. It would have been so easy to allow fear and tension to overwhelm him, but David plunged deep into the Lord's presence and gained precious reassurance: *"Pursue them – you will overtake them and succeed in rescuing them"* (1 Samuel 30:8).

Handling Dark Times: Tunnel Experiences

We think you ought to know, dear brothers and sisters, about the trouble we went through in the province of Asia. We were crushed and overwhelmed beyond our ability to endure, and we thought we would never live through it. In fact, we expected to die. But as a result, we stopped relying on ourselves and learned to rely only on God, who raises the dead. And He did rescue us from mortal danger, and He will rescue us again. We have placed our confidence in Him, and He will continue to rescue us. And you are helping us by praying for us. Then many people will give thanks because God has graciously answered so many prayers for our safety.   2 Corinthians 1:8-11

A few weeks before Rosalind's spasms began, a friend from church had a picture that we were about to enter a dark tunnel. Although she could see a bright light at the far end of it, she sensed that we were not going to reach that light immediately.

Other warnings followed hard on the heels of this picture. A few days later I had an intensely dramatic dream in which I was being pursued by a monster of a bull that was charging straight towards me. There seemed no conceivable way that I could avoid its lowered horns. I woke with the bull still racing across the field in pursuit of me.

A few days later I had another dream. On this occasion a thick cloud of midges was heading straight towards me. Again, there was no way I could avoid them. I could feel them crawling all over my face – and yet I had not been bitten.

I know enough about dreams to realise that if the same theme is repeated more than once, it is likely to be significant, and quite possibly urgent.[20] Often, the reason for such dreams and impressions is that the Lord is allowing us to glimpse the scenarios that Hell is seeking to bring about.

The Lord permits this so that we may rally our defences, spring to action stations and pray away the dangers we have foreseen – or, at the very least, reduce the effect they have.

At the same time – and here we see again the paradoxical nature of so much that we associate with grief experiences – we have also discovered that the Lord often uses these perilous and unpleasant situations to catapult us forward into some new phase of our lives.[21]

Within a few weeks of these dreams, we found ourselves beset by difficulties, culminating in the extraordinary spasms that convulsed Ros. The fact that we had experienced many such tests before helped us to endure those agonising months.[22]

We are also aware that attacks tend to come in proportion to the significance of the task we are engaged in. Not only is there often "backlash" after some major step forwards, there may also be intense "*pre*-lash." After all, the best time to attack an aircraft is while it is still on the runway.

When the powers of darkness are launching assault after assault against us, the more resolute we are in counter them with prayer and declarations of faith, the less power they have over us. It is better still if we can identify the source of the attack and come specifically against it. It is only when we heed our fears that we lose sight of the fact that God still has good things in store for us.

For the time being, however, His plans remained entirely hidden from view, because we were still in a "tunnel." Tunnels block out light, and cause any words that are spoken to bounce off the walls, echoing and distorting them to the point where we are not sure what it is that we are hearing.

From time to time, the path we are ascending is so rugged that we are required to advance by faith alone. When Jeremiah lamented how hard he was finding his calling, and the opposition that was coming even from his own family, the Lord's reply appears almost brusque.

"If racing against mere men makes you tired,
   how will you race against horses?
If you stumble and fall on open ground,
   what will you do in the thickets near the Jordan?"
                                        Jeremiah 12:5

Effectively, the Lord was telling him to use what he had learned during this present round of difficulties to help him cope with the tougher times that lay ahead.

Horatio Spafford must have understood this when he wrote this hymn, whose words have become well known all around the world.

When peace like a river attendeth my way,
When sorrows like sea billows roll,
Whatever my lot, Thou hast taught me to say,
It is well, it is well with my soul.

You might be forgiven for supposing these words to have been penned by an exquisitely happy man in a mid-summer rose garden, surrounded by his adoring family. In reality, they were written in the middle of the Atlantic, as Horatio made his way to rejoin his grieving wife.

Spafford had previously sent his wife and four daughters on ahead of him to Europe, but the ship had collided with another vessel, and all four of his daughters had drowned. Spafford had already experienced much suffering in his life, but this still greater test lent yet more authenticity to his words.

Though Satan should buffet,
Though trials should come,
Let this blessed assurance control,
That Christ hath regarded my helpless estate,
And hath shed His own blood for my soul.

Lord, haste the day when the faith shall be sight,
The clouds rolled back as a scroll;
The trump shall resound
and the Lord shall appear,
Even so, it is well with my soul.[23]

Sharing our emotional pain is important, but it would be naïve to expect griefs as great as these to disappear overnight simply because we have spoken them aloud. Like Job we may find ourselves lamenting:

> *If I speak, my pain is not relieved; and if I refrain, it does not go away. O God, You have ground me down and devastated my family.*
>
> *Job 16:6-7*

The best way to handle those agonizing times when we are unable to sense the Lord's presence is often just to act as if God is in control and knows exactly what He is doing – for the simple reason that He does.

It is not hypocrisy to act as if the Lord is close by – He is. This is why it is important not to hang on to truths and practices that have served us well in the past. Despite the dead weight of our feelings, we will benefit from attending to necessary practical matters. Apart from anything else, this will bring us the comfort of knowing that we are keeping on top of our workload, as well as sparing us from too much introspection.

Better times will return, and we will be grateful that we kept moving through the tunnel. The Lord is still on His throne, and even the most intense sadness will lift in time. The day finally dawned when Jacob declared, "You will no longer be called Son of my sorrow, but Benjamin, the Son of my right hand."

Neither do I imagine Rachel weeping to the end of her days.[24] Somewhere along her journey, the Lord will have found ways to call this grief-stricken woman back to life. Just as He found ways to restore Naomi after her great losses in the book of Ruth, so He will draw us out again into a more spacious place.

Reflect and Pray

I walked a mile with Sorrow, and ne'er a word said she. But oh, the things I learned from her, when Sorrow walked with me.   *Browning*

Think back to any "tunnel" experiences that you have been through. Did the the Lord give you a verse or a promise to hold on to before you were plunged into the darkness?

The Dark Night of the Soul

He has walled me in so I cannot escape; He has weighed me down with chains. Even when I call out or cry for help, He shuts out my prayer.

Lamentations 3:7-8

Grief falls into many categories – and none. You may be neither bereaved, nor divorced, nor even, God be praised, burnt out, yet you find yourself assailed by overwhelming sadness, perhaps even by all but compulsive urges to give up. Many of the greatest saints have experienced prolonged seasons in which they have felt all but completely bereft of any sense of God's presence.

Unlike the other griefs that we have considered in this book, the "dark night of the soul" can descend on us without any external loss or trigger. There are no words to describe the agony the soul passes through, when, for what may prove to be a prolonged season, we are more aware of His absence than His presence.

Although this is essentially a private grief, the Lord has caused the struggles of many who have experienced this seemingly inexplicable phenomenon to write it down as an encouragement to us to persevere.[25]

Do not all the best love stories include episodes of inexplicable separation? When we are in a "desert," we miss the comforting sense of God's presence – not to mention the excitement of seeing His Spirit moving in power. When it feels as though nothing is happening, and our hopes and dreams lie buried in the sand, there may be nothing that we can do to bring these desert experiences to an end. As Corrie Ten Boom reminds us, however, "When the train is in a tunnel, don't get out of your seat: sit tight and trust the driver!"

When we lose our "usual" sense of God's presence, what is in our heart becomes crystal clear. Strong temptations we thought we had long since conquered return to torment us, and self-will once again becomes a major issue. The question comes down to this: how hungry and thirsty are we to honour the Lord? Are we prepared to *use* the darkness as a goad for seeking to honour Him more?[26] Or will we give in to our doubts and disappointments and turn to other things to fill the vacuum? Truly, these times when the light of the Lord appears to burn low test our soul.

The Lord once gave me an insight into the scales that God uses to weigh and calibrate these desert times. He uses criteria that are so utterly different from our own that we would not even necessarily recognise them as scales at all. Be reassured: the Lord is still weighing our situation carefully. As Sebastien Valfrey puts it,

> *When it is all over, you will not regret having suffered; rather you will regret having suffered so little, and suffered that little so badly.*

Reflect and Pray

Reconcile yourself to wait in the darkness as long as is necessary, but still go on longing after Him whom you love.

The Cloud of Unknowing

Lord, where emptiness has scoured my soul
make my faith resilient and
my heart more full of trust.
For You created great swathes of desert
– steppe and glacier, veld and dune –
and You know how to sustain Your children
through desert doubts and droughts.
In the Name of Jesus, Who
neither sensed nor saw the Father's love
in Gethsemane's darkness, yet still obeyed –
and made the treasures of darkness
available to all. Amen.

References

1 See 1 Peter 5:7

2 Marshall, C. (2002) *To Live Again*. Chosen Books.

3 See also my an article on this subject: www.ruachministries.org/valeoftears/refs.htm

4 Lyndall is the National Prayer Coordinator for the Salvation Army.

5 C. S. Lewis. *Screwtape Letters*. Fount.

6 Hodder & Stoughton Religious (2005) and Harper Collins (1997).

7 You will find the teaching series I have written on the seven letters to the seven churches in Revelation helpful in this respect. See www.ruachministries.org/teaching/revelation.htm)

8 For reasons of confidentiality, this is not her real name.

9 National Geographic Magazine February 2006

10 Marshall, C. (2001) "They walk in wistfulness," in *To Live Again*. Chosen Books

11 I would commend in Nick Cuthbert's book *How to survive as a church leader,* Monarch (2006) and in particular the chapter "Run from the sexual snare."

12 See www.ruachministries.org/valeoftears/refs.htm

13 Try adapting the model found through www.ruachministries.org/valeoftears/refs.htm

14 Reproduced with her permission from her regular newspaper column in the Daily Mail.

15 See Luke 22:3, John 13:27

16 See Job 6:11-21

17 See also

18 1 Samuel 30:1f

19 The word *chazaq (strength)* occurs three hundred times in Scripture.

20 See Genesis 41:15-37

21 This is where it is worth recalling what I said earlier about the words for "tempt," "test" and "try" being one and the same in both Greek and Hebrew!

22 You may recall the "little whiles" that Jesus speaks of, during which His disciples would not be able to discern His presence. Cf John 12:35, 13:33; 14:19, 16:16-19

23 Cf Philippians. 4:11-13

24 Cf Genesis 35:18

25 The writings of St John of the Cross are particularly highly regarded in this regard. Mother Teresa's prolonged spiritual drought is a well publicised recent example. I have written in more detail about the dark night of the soul in my book *Intimacy and Eternity*, which you can access via our web site: www.ruachministries.org.

It would be a great mistake to assume that people who regularly receive inspirations and consolations enjoy a superior faith to those who experience prolonged seasons in which they all but lose sight altogether of the Lord they love so much. It might be nearer the truth of the matter that they are only able to stay the course at all because they receive such strengthening.

26 Cf 2 Chronicles 32:31, John 16:7

Part Five

Strategies for Resolving Grief

IF YOU WERE OBLIGED TO CARRY A BOMB, you would surely do so with the utmost care. Likening grief to a minefield, Sylvia Warner cautioned that "there is no knowing when one will touch the tripwire." Grief episodes themselves are unavoidable, but we shall explore precious and important strategies here that will help to minimise their impact, and even harness their apparently negative power.

The Sacrament of the Present Moment

You do not have to cope with everything –
only with this moment.
This moment is all the reality there is.
If everything seems to come on top of you at once –
give it to God.
Tell Him you can't cope on your own
so you are giving Him the whole mess to sort out.
Then forget the future and your worries.
They are no longer your worries.
                    Alison Browne (aged 19)[1]

There is nothing easy about grief! How right Shakespeare was when he declared, "Everyone can master a grief but he that has it."[2] In a dozen different ways, some people reveal their impatience that we *ought* to be recovering more quickly – which leaves us having to cope with yet one more layer of grief. If we make the effort to explain to these people how we are really feeling, it *may* lead to the depth of understanding we were hoping for, but equally it may serve only to reinforce their original opinion that we ought to be getting over it.

Unless we "cast our burdens on the Lord" in the way that Alison Browne suggests in the poem above, we are likely to become angry. Psychologists tell us that this is a normal response to loss and trauma. Judging by the number of times the psalmists direct their anger at the Lord we might certainly conclude this to be the case. It is not a phase to get stuck in, however, not least because it is usually those who are closest to us who have to bear the brunt of our outbursts.

Unless these people are exceptionally patient and understanding, (and how grateful we can be for those who are) our unhappiness is likely to reinforce their instinct to withdraw from us – which merely exacerbates our feelings of isolation. In other words, although anger may be a common response to loss, it is also something that we need to "own."

Once again we are coming face to face with the inescapable fact that the grief process involves considerable work, with no automatic guarantee of success. Some severed relationships may never be fully restored – in which case we must offer our profound regrets to the Lord, bless and pray for the people concerned, and trust Him to help us all rebuild our lives.

"In-between times", when nothing appears to be replacing the loss we have experienced have a way of exposing our lack of trust. We think of people who have let us down, and resentment sets in, like rain on a gloomy winter's evening. Or we look at those who appear to be doing far less than they could to alleviate our plight, and anger knocks on our door. Sin is crouching at our door, seeking to master us. Will we give in to it – or will we successfully resist it?[3]

God does not lead His children up blind alleys, but if the enemy can even begin to incline us towards entertaining such a notion, he is well on the way to blunting our cutting edge. Why settle for mediocrity and unbelief?

No matter how much we have lost, we are still richly blessed. We still have precious memories to sustain us, along with the certainty that the Lord will be with us as we set out to make new ones.

Even so, we must be careful how we process what is going on. Our minds are only too adept at adjusting inconvenient truths, and filtering out anything it finds too painful to confront.

If we insist on presenting matters from our perspective, while others would see things in a very different light, we may be like the Israelites looking back to their life as slaves in Egypt through rose-coloured spectacles[4] - or like Puddleglum, who viewed everything through a negative rated lens.

Forthright souls may challenge our lopsided impressions, but most prefer not to rock the boat, choosing for the time being to suspend the Scripture, *He who rebukes a man will afterward find more favour than he who flatters with his tongue* (Proverbs 28:23).

Inauthentic remembering cannot but distort reality, either by idealising the memory of some person, place or event, or by "demonising" it: that is, remembering only the hard times, and brushing all better memories aside.

Idealisation – whether good or bad – makes it more difficult for us to make the most of the opportunities that *this* day offers. That is why we do better to remember truthfully, "warts and all."

Reflect and Pray

"Behold, You desire truth in the inward parts, and in the hidden part You will make me to know wisdom."
                                              Psalm 51:6 NKJV

What *will* help us is to embrace "the sacrament of the present moment" as contemplatives call it. The more fully we seek to live each moment for the Lord, engaging Him in love and worship as well as petition, the less anxiety we will experience concerning all our tomorrows.

To embrace the present moment requires a delicate balance between remembering and trusting. As we call to mind ways and occasions when the Lord has helped us in the past, let these memories become a springboard for faith, from which to face our present challenges.

Harnessing Grief

When I am strong, I will fight,
and when I am weary of the fight
I will rest in You,
for Your love cannot be beaten.
When I am alone,
when I feel the icy touch of fear,
I will take it in my hand
and hold it out to You,
and in the heat of Your love
it will melt away.

When my heart feels isolated,
when no one can comfort me
and the crowd serves
only to remind me of how alone I am,
I will look within myself where You wait
and I will remember to allow You to love me.

Then when the joy is so strong
that I cannot take life in quickly enough,
I will remember to take a moment to sit with You
and appreciate the beauty You created.
And when the night comes,
I ask only that I be alive with peace and faith,
so that I may not fear
the new day that lies beyond.
                              Alison Browne (aged 21)

Some of us compensate for the losses we have sustained in life by "talking our grief out." Others of us prefer to immerse ourselves in physical endeavours; so much so that some might mistakenly assume that we were not grieving at all.

Others again express their grief emotions through writing, photography, painting or music, perhaps to "memorialise" the person or thing that we have lost. Journalling, too, provides a creative way to express grief emotions, without overloading our support networks. It can be helpful, too, to write with a particular person in mind, addressing updates to a loved one – or directly to the Lord Himself.

Books are such outstanding friends. They reduce our sense of isolation and involve us in each other's pilgrimages. God inspires those of us who have a call to write so that you can pick us up or put us down whenever you feel like it!

Given that by no means all the opinions we come across will prove helpful to our emotional or spiritual growth, we dare not allow grief to switch our discernment off. There are all too many who will tell us that God is no more than a distant power, who will do nothing to help or guide us. There are better ways to adjust to our new situation than to reduce our faith to fit such dismal assumptions – especially if they fly in the face of all we know about the God we love and serve.

Reflect and Pray

Lord, we cry to You,
don't let grief shrink our faith
or narrow our perspectives!
Help us to study and to read
beyond our normal reading habits,
and in so doing –
turn sadness into joy,
sight into insight
and make us more alert
to what You are saying and doing.
In Jesus' name, Amen.

Grief that Inspires Creativity

There is nothing more inventive than suffering.

Nazianzen

Many of the writings, compositions and paintings that speak most deeply to our spirits, have emerged from the shadow of dark times.[5] Just think of the impact that Joni Eriksson's books and talks have had, following the victory she won over depression in the aftermath of the diving accident that left her a quadriplegic.

Rather as countries with an abundance of water harness this natural resource to produce hydro-electricity, so we must find ways to *use* our strong grief emotions. Listen as the Abbess Hilda calls her community of nuns to move beyond any trace of self-absorption:

> *Trade with the gifts God has given you.*
> *Bend your minds to holy learning so that you may escape*
> *   the fretting moth of littleness of mind that would wear*
> *   out your souls.*
> *Brace your wills to action that they may not be the spoil of*
> *   weak desires.*
> *Train your hearts and lips to song, which gives courage to*
> *   the soul.*
> *Being rebuffed by trials, learn to laugh.*
> *Being reproved, give thanks.*
> *Having failed, determine to succeed.*
> *   Abbess Hilda of Whitby, 7th century*

Those of us whose work involves prolonged and intensive thinking often turn to pastimes such as painting or walking. Their repetitive rhythm requires little thought but soothes and releases our spirit, allowing ideas to develop in our subconscious.

People and situations often come vividly to mind when I am writing. I rarely feel so at one with my calling as when mind and spirit are working in tandem in such ways. Almost without pausing I lift them to the Lord. If I am too busy to pray in detail at the time, I make a note of the burden and return to it when I am less pressed.

If ideas for other projects come to mind, I welcome them. More "tidy" minds might be tempted to hold such thoughts at bay, lest they distract them from completing the project they were engaged on. Personally, I have not found this to be a problem. Inspiration comes as and when the Lord chooses, and I am keen to catch and store each precious drop. At any point, even many years later, the Lord can shape and refine the inspirational ideas that I have jotted down.

I do my best, therefore, to welcome whatever ministers to my spirit, or which makes me laugh. After all, where do we get our sense of humour from, if not from God? So long as we do not use humour to make fun of others, or to pretend that our grief is not there, what better antidote can there be to it than to laugh? It releases the flow of blood to the heart, and massages our vital organs!

Reflect and Pray

However intense your grief, the time will come when your creativity will surface again, provided you do not give up in the meantime. Take time to consider: which places and relationships have refreshed and revived your soul in the past? Make good use of them, for they will inspire you to carry on the daily task of living with renewed enthusiasm.[6]

The Power of Writing to heal

> *People who write about their traumas commonly experience fewest panic attacks and need least help recovering.*
> James Pennebaker

Writing provides us with a powerful tool to organise overwhelming events and make them manageable.[7] It was on Pentecost Sunday, 1985, shortly after the breakup of our ministry team, that someone brought me this word from the Lord: "I have a message, I have a pen. If you are willing, I will be with you." This is what I have been doing ever since, and in these next two sections we will be seeing just how therapeutic both writing and music can be.

James Pennebaker is the author of several pioneering publications that demonstrate how recording our traumas on paper can lead to genuine grief resolution. In a publication that pulls together the fruit of ten years of research,[8] Pennebaker shows that if we simply *describe* some traumatic event in our past – even giving full rein to our emotions as we do so – we will probably derive no lasting benefit from the exercise. His great discovery was that if we then proceed to record not only how we felt about it at the time, but also how we feel about it now, *that* is when something remarkable happens. By confronting the past, we as it were remove its horns and are free to move on again.

Can it really be so simple? Pennebaker discovered that people obtain the maximum benefit if they write four fifteen-minute bursts over a period of four days. Louise de Salvo, a creative writing specialist, confirms Pennebaker's findings,[9] and goes on to warn that anyone who does not put pen to paper will become increasingly irritated and even depressed until they do so!

Despite such encouragements, many people many of us find the thought of committing our deepest sorrows to paper daunting. We are bound to find reliving our most intense experiences emotionally challenging, but both Louise and James see this as *appropriate* pain: something that is *worth* enduring in order to reap the benefits.

In his subsequent studies, Pennebaker discovered that people who have been made redundant reported a much higher success rate of finding new jobs, and those who had lost their spouses made much faster recoveries as a result of following this pattern of writing.

The studies also showed that doing this on a regular basis reduced physical and mental stress and boosted the immune system. By contrast, those who neither spoke nor wrote about their traumas fared less well.

Those for whom writing currently holds no special place in your life may be tempted to skim over this section. If you know that there are hurts in your life that you have not yet recovered from, however, I would encourage you to try doing precisely what James and Louise recommend: four bursts of fifteen minutes of writing, spread over four days.

There is no need to edit and polish these passages. You are not writing with a view to anyone else seeing your work: all that matters is to tell the story, taking care to record how you felt about it at the time, and how you feel about it now.

A word of warning. When you first set out to describe some trauma, you may (intentionally or otherwise) find yourself omitting some vital part of the story.

It takes time and courage to reach such a place of inner honesty, but this is when you will begin to discern the hand of the Lord in issues which, until now, may have felt only like severe loss. Grief resolution proceeds apace as you come to see hidden blessings springing from even the hardest times!

Taking time out to write about specific traumas is therefore anything but self-indulgent. It has the power to stabilise our subconscious – which is, of course, the driving force behind how we really are. Just as the vast bulk of icebergs lie beneath the surface, so too do the greater part of our memories. Like a gigantic storehouse, the subconscious contains not only every experience we have ever been through, but also the imprint of how we felt and responded to those events. On a day-to-day basis we are largely unaware of these, but they are closer than we realise, awaiting only particular triggers to flush them into the open. As Mike Field commented,

> *I found it valuable specifically to invite Jesus to be Lord of my subconscious mind. Doing this put an abrupt end to very troubling recurring dreams I had been having since I was a child.*

Don't expect miraculous results every time you pick up a pen – but do expect attempting this exercise to have beneficial effects in terms of helping you to come to terms with things that have happened in the past.

If at some later stage you feel moved to share your insights with a wider audience, you will benefit from the practice you have gained in "writing to order," as opposed to writing only when you feel like it. This will help to school you for the serious discipline of shaping your original jottings,[10] for although writing may be the most portable of callings, that does not make it an easy option. Just as with anything that is of lasting value, it is less a question of *finding* the time to do the necessary work of editing so much as *making* the time.

Write to God, for God, and about God; write to loved ones and about loved ones, and pour out your hopes, dreams and memories. Turn thoughts and impressions into carefully crafted prayers for the people and situations you are concerned about. It can be incredibly powerful![11]

The Choice of the Day

Here is a great idea to help us look forward to each day. I learnt it from Kathleen Adams, who lectures widely on the therapeutic value of using journalling as a means of removing trauma. Kathleen urges us to write out the details of two or three topics or appointments every day on a small card. (I use a sheet of coloured paper). She rather delightfully calls this *"Le Choix du Jour" – The Choice of the Day*.

I find that making a feature out of these events does wonders in prompting me to pray for God to bless these events – even those which I might not instinctively have been looking forward to. This keeps me focused in prayer, as well as providing an easy way of looking back to ponder how these events worked out.

Kathleen also encourages us to write short "vignettes" about special times together that we have enjoyed. She writes that these "Captured Moments" become "like a written photo album, preserving precious memories for all time." This is a beautiful concept to explore. Why wait till a person has died, or a special season has passed, before recording it on paper?[12]

The Power of Music to heal

Music soothes our soul, sharpens our spirit, and draws us onto the Lord's wavelength. My friend Alex Robertson is a great believer that music is a wonderful tool for unblocking frozen grief and releasing creativity. It stimulates a different part of the brain than words, touching our worried hearts and freeing our blocked emotions.

As Martin Luther recognised, music soothes the soul and calms what he delightfully called "the agitations of the mind" as nothing else can do. All of us can remember times when songs or pieces of music transported us back to specific times and places, hooking us into certain moods or emotions.

Blessed though we are to have access to a wealth of recorded music, we may not always be able to locate a piece of music that expresses precisely what we are feeling. The great advantage of Spirit-inspired music is that we have no pre-existing associations to distract us. We are free to track wherever the Spirit leads.

Alex put his beliefs to the test recently by going into a tough prison to reach men for Christ, armed with nothing except his faith and his violin. Overcoming both his own fears and the curious stares, something extraordinary happened in the spirit realm as he began to play. The power of the Lord worked through the music, making it possible for him to gain first the prisoners' attention, and then their respect.

The fact that Alex was a classically trained musician and they were not did not matter because what was going on was essentially *spiritual* rather than cultural.

Unless you are one of those relatively rare people who do not respond to music, or are seriously depressed, there is every chance that the Lord can minister to you through this medium. If you sing or play an instrument yourself, may I encourage you to explore the endlessly creative world of improvisation?

Although I am not a skilled musician myself, I love to sit at the piano and play as the Spirit leads for people who come to visit. The Lord often uses the music to speak to their hearts, and to accelerate the resolution of their inner grief. Chords that are full of tension and slow to resolve often mirror unresolved issues in people's lives. Just as discordant sounds and rhythms symbolise extreme emotions, (confusion, fear, guilt and hopelessness), stronger chord sequences affirm trust and hope, and represent people's desire to take positive steps forwards.

Improvisation can lead to a release of prayer and prophecy, and short-circuit people's normal defensive mechanisms, whereas more direct questions about their feelings might lead only to embarrassed denials. At the same time, we must be careful not to manipulate emotions. Playing one note repeatedly against another, for example, might release such intense feelings as to be all but overwhelming.

There is no need, however, to limit ourselves to stereotypes. Minor keys are for much more than just expressing sad emotions. After all, many wonderful carols and dances have been composed in them.

Ruth Bright suggests that if we are feeling ambivalent towards someone we are no longer in contact with, we can express our feelings by beating a pair of Bongo drums, while someone else plays improvised music. (She suggests Bongos because they are less likely to remind us of musical classes at school than certain other percussion instruments.)

> *They give good tactile feedback to the skin and muscles, but none of the sense of using a weapon which a drumstick may give, and which is frightening for those who are only just learning to deal with their blocked anger.*[13]

It is hard for some of us to admit that we are still carrying layers of grief and anger. The way we play the drums may tell another story, and be a better indicator to our real state of mind.

Reflect and Pray

Write down the thoughts of the moment.
                                    Francis Bacon (1600)

Choose a favourite Bible verse and try singing the words. Or take a well known chorus or hymn and let new music flow. Or reach out into the deep and sing a new song from scratch.

Like beautiful wild flowers that bloom for a few short days, much of this music will be purely for the moment. We are singing and playing as an expression of where we are right now – and that is sure to be of both spiritual and therapeutic value.

There may be times, however, when we can return later to craft these songs and music into something of real merit.

The Blessing of Friendship

See, I have written your name on My hand . . . I no longer
call you slaves, because a master doesn't confide in his
slaves. Now you are my friends, since I have told you
everything the Father told me.

Isaiah 49:16; John 15:15

Do you remember speaking out the name of a loved one, or
writing it on the palm of your hand? Even so does the Lord
engrave our names in His heart. His companionship is the
best antidote of all to our grief – but as we have been hinting
throughout this book, few things inspire us like the support of
a friend. Many of us can identify with Paul's sense of relief
when his friend Titus turned up.

When we came into Macedonia, this body of ours had no
rest, but we were harassed at every turn; conflicts on the
outside, fears within. But God, who comforts the downcast,
comforted us by the coming of Titus, and not only by his
coming but also by the comfort you had given him.

2 Corinthians 1:3-4

How grateful Ros and I are for the friendships the Lord has
developed over many years. When we are in the company of
these "day and nighters," we sense the Lord's presence more
easily, and release timely and authoritative prayers for each
other, whilst helping each other to absorb the repeated
assaults of grief's battering ram.

Conventional wisdom has it that it becomes more difficult
to make close friendships once we have passed a certain age.
God's leading makes a nonsense of such artificial limitations!
He loves to join us to people we can bless and be blessed by,
regardless of age considerations.

If there is only a narrow window of opportunity during
which such friendships can fire up, then God will work fast.
One touch from Him can enable new connections to develop
farther and deeper in a few focused hours than many friendships ever progress to in a lifetime.

At any time the Lord can take existing friendships deeper, or launch entirely new ones. A widow in Tulsa called Shirley was serving breakfast to her children one day when the Lord told her to go to MacDonalds. She made all the protests that you or I would probably have made if faced with such a situation, but finally yielded to her leading.

She will be forever grateful that she did, for it was at that unlikely time of the morning that she met the man who became her husband. A widower minister called Terry Law just happened to be passing through the city at that precise moment, having prayed to meet his future wife. The rest, as they say, is history – and all because Shirley was willing to leave a cooked meal untouched on her breakfast table.

Reflect and Pray

Praise God for friends who allow us as much time and space as we need in which to share our pain. They, above all people, help us to discover our own voice, and to become our true selves in Christ.

Alison Browne, whose poems we have quoted extensively in this book, wrote that "a friend's love pushes aside the veil of tears." She also wrote,

> *Jesus – at times my love for You grows so urgent in my heart that I long to hug you physically. What can I do? Hug a friend, and in doing so you hug Jesus.*
> *Lord, I never want*
> *to take precious friendships for granted.*
> *Now, in the aftermath of loss and change,*
> *may old friendships continue to grow and mature,*
> *and new ones be forged,*
> *In the Name of our greatest Friend, Amen.*

Ceremonies that facilitate Grief

Coummunities and nations erect monuments to mark particularly important moments in thier history, and we too may find it helpful to celebrate our own landmarks – both the special ones and the more difficult moments. For example, there came a time when Rosalind felt that there was "one missing" in our family quiver. The Lord confirmed this, but tactfully did not mention the emotional roller-coaster that we would go through in the process. Before our youngest son was born we endured no fewer than five miscarriages!

We have no explanation for these losses. On each occasion, we had felt convinced that all was going well, and were taken completely by surprise when the loss occurred. The fifth miscarriage differed from the others in that when Rosalind passed the foetus, we were able to hold him, weep together, and hold a simple burial service. This made grief resolution easier than the more jagged experiences of the earlier losses.

Finally, we could bear the roller-coaster no longer, and set a "cut-off date." One month before the point of no return, Ros conceived again. She was so wary by now that she conducted seven pregnancy tests to make sure that everything was still alright!

Our grief over these miscarriages was "clean," in the sense that we had nothing to reproach ourselves with. Many losses, of course, are more emotionally ambivalent. In the case of an abortion, for example, it may well prove helpful to devise some suitable dedication to hand not only the foetus but also all the attendant guilt back to the Lord. It is the same when people feel they have no alternative but to walk away from relationships they had once assumed would be "forever."

Rather than staging one of those wildly euphoric "divorce parties" that are all the rage in some quarters, why not hand your original vows back to the Lord? This is surely as good a way as any to mark the end of one phase of your life and to re-commission the next.

Because symbolic ceremonies can be profoundly liberating, ask the Lord to show you whenever such a ceremony might be relevant. In the case of a dissolved marriage, for instance, it might be appropriate to remove your wedding ring and to declare before the Lord,

> I have been faithful before You Lord, and ask You now to set me free from my wedding vows.

Or, if matters have been less straightforward:

Lord, I confess that I have not been faithful to my vows.
As I come to You in repentance,
do whatever it takes to cleanse the depths of my heart,
and to heal all who have been hurt by my unfaithfulness.
In Jesus' name, Amen.

Breaking bread together is another means that God has ordained to remove our guilt and to affirm our determination to follow Him. In the words of the old prayer book:

Ye that do truly and earnestly repent . . .
and intend to live a new life . . .
and are heartily sorry for these misdoings . . .
draw near with faith.

Reflect and Pray

Lord, I come to You in need of closure about . . .
I repent where my actions or attitudes
have been part of the problem.
Forgive me, and cleanse me from the sense of guilt and
shame that I am carrying.
From this moment on, help me to live in the light.
In Jesus' name, Amen.
Elisabeth Harding

Gratitude that Sustains

Happiness doesn't depend on who you are or what you
have; it depends upon what you think . . . It is not a state
to arrive at, but a manner of travelling.
Dale Carnegie and Margaret Runbeck

Not everyone feels the need to express their grief as openly as we have encouraged in this book. My Granny, a widow for over half a century, took Alfred Lord Tennyson's words and made them her own: "'Tis better to have loved and lost than never to have loved." In her own case, she remained profoundly grateful for the life she had so briefly enjoyed with her husband – not to mention the son she bore him, and the son whom he then fathered – that's me, folks!

We saw earlier that the longer and louder we complain, the more we risk becoming inwardly bitter and externally isolated. I referred earlier to Joss Ackland's comment that not a day passes without providing him with opportunities to grieve. Let's put that the other way round: not a single day passes without providing many opportunities to express our gratitude.

Many of us only fully appreciate things (or people) after we have lost them. As this dawned on the French authoress, Colette, she exclaimed, "What a wonderful life I've had. I only wish I'd realised it sooner!"

During one prolonged period of grief, we went through many years ago, when pressures were piling in against us from all angles, we resolved to count our blessings, six by six. We kept a "Book of Gratitudes" jotting down at least half a dozen things each day to be grateful for. There was never any shortage.

I am not speaking here of life-changing experiences or world-shaking events, but simply of acknowledging the Lord's daily grace and goodness. A tasty meal, an inspiring film or television programme, a fresh insight, a startling sunset or a beautiful view. Thanking God helps us to realise just how much He *is* doing, even if the particular issue we are most concerned about still appears no closer to resolution.

Too often we leave the two-edged Sword of Praise hanging on the wall, more like an ornament than an integral part of our spiritual armour. It takes love as well as courage to take it out of its scabbard and to affirm that God knows precisely what He is doing. Thanksgiving is both joy to the soul and a weapon to be used against our doubts.

Reflect and Pray

Lord, forgive me that I default so quickly to grumbling.
Cultivate this spirit of praise and gratitude in me,
for it will keep me from despondency –
and others will catch the uplift that it brings.
In Jesus' name, Amen.

References

1 Allie's Song, Alison Browne. Copyright Tony and Brid Browne 1999 Herne Bay Kent. A collection of poems and writings by Allie, who died at the age of 21 of cystic fibrosis.

2 Shakespeare, W. *Much Ado About Nothing.*

3 Genesis 4:6-7

4 Numbers 11:4-6

5 Immediate examples that spring to mind in the literary world include Tennyson's *In Memoriam,* Hardy's letters to his late wife, Shelley's poem *Adonais* about the death of Keats, is an intense expression of feeling on the death of his fellow poet, Keats, just as Milton's *Lycidas* was. Henry King's *Exequy* is likewise a lament on his young wife's untimely death.

6 Parts of this book were written in beautiful surroundings in Shetland, Jersey and Dresden, with the final draft and proofreading being completed in Crete. Like Catherine Marshall, I hoped that writing in such inspiring places would give my book a special flavour, "like garlic rubbed on the salad bowl or a hint of rosemary in the soup!" The greater part of it was written, however, in early morning shifts between half past four and breakfast time, at a time when my mind and spirit were clear before the other demands of the day weighed in. See also my chapter Towards a Life of Reflection in *Intimacy and Eternity.* See http://www.ruachministries.org/valeoftears/refs.htm

7 Harvey, J. (2000) *Give Sorrow Words: Perspectives on Loss and Trauma.* p.11. Brunner/Mazel.

8 Pennebaker, J. (1990). *The Healing Power of Confiding in Others.* Morrow. New York.

9 De Salvo L. *Writing as a Way of Healing.* The Women's Press.

10 You may find my book *Craft of Writing* helpful in this respect. You can download it from: http://www.ruachministries.org/thecraftofwriting.htm

11 See my book *The Still Small Voice.* p.73. New Wine Press. On a more mundane level, there is also be much to be said for writing down lists of things we need to remember, since our memory and concentration are sure to be adversely affected by grief.

12 See link to Managing Grief through Journal Writing at http://www.ruachministries.org/valeoftears/refs.htm

13 Bright, R. (1988) *Grief and Powerlessness. Helping People regain Control of their Lives.* pp. 152-153. Jessica Kingsley.

Part Six

Fallout from Grief

Abraham went to mourn for Sarah and to weep over her.
Genesis 23:2

ONE MOMENT IT WAS AN ORDINARY DAY in the south of Russia, the next a nuclear disaster was under way that would ultimately impact regions thousands of miles away. Even now, many years after the event, lives are still being affected by the meltdown of the Chernobyl reactor. As we shall be seeing in this section, the fallout from grief sometimes feel almost "nuclear."

In the Immediate Aftermath

At the very time when grieving people find themselves obliged to shoulder many additional responsibilities, a new grief may come their way when certain friends appear conspicuous by their absence. In the case of a spouse dying, people who related to them as a couple often prove less welcoming now that they are single again. Unexpected awkwardness and even jealousies surface, with some people regarding them now as a potential threat to their own relation-ships. Needless to say, this merely increases their sense of no longer belonging.

Almost everybody these days pays lip-service to the idea that mourners should be encouraged to express their emotions, but the language they use to describe how they are "coping" often reveals that deep down they still admire a very different set of values. When they speak of the bereaved "breaking down" and "weeping uncontrollably," it may seem to imply that the person concerned would have done better to have held themselves together.

Let's not forget that something tremendously important has happened. A human life has reached its conclusion, and it is right that we should mark the occasion. Since death is the ultimate statistic (one out of one people die), funerals are a good time to remind those of us who still have time to run on our "lease on life" about the One who has the right to call in this "lease."

It is customary nowadays, either at the funeral or at a memorial service, to celebrate the life and achievements of the departed. The aim is to create an occasion which will be uplifting at the time and memorable in retrospect. This means having the courage to go beyond the sentimental to proclaim the eternal Gospel of Jesus in the face of death. Our concern is to pray divine comfort for those left behind, as well as to call all present – who may have but the haziest idea of what a relationship with the Lord Jesus is all about.

As well as surrounding the bereaved with a network of caring people who will continue to be there when the post-funeral sandwiches have been consumed, the aim is also to help everyone concerned to realise that the loss itself is final. To aid you in your preparations at what is likely to be a highly stressful time, we have included some links to provide suitable material for such events.[1]

A question that is likely to be uppermost in everybody's mind is "what about the children?" Since children are likely to exhibit feelings of unreality long after a parent or grandparent has died, attending the funeral service usually helps them to accept the fact that the loss is final. If denied this opportunity, children may develop the strangest imaginings about what has really happened.

Some children may be too young to cope with the intensity of the occasion, but most will benefit more from saying goodbye in this way to a loved one than to attend some alternative (usually some artificially arranged activity) while the funeral is taking place. Catherine Marshall would agree with this wholeheartedly:

Are we not handling the grossest insult imaginable to the young when we assume that they have not the spiritual or character resources to handle this test courageously and victoriously?[2]

An increasing number of people are choosing to have an initial service in a crematorium, attended by close friends and family, and then to hold a special memorial service later.[3]

Paying attention to the musical side of the funeral service can be as important as the prayers prayed and the words spoken, for, as we saw in the section "The Power of Music." Music is its own language, and God uses it to touch parts of our being that words alone cannot reach. Rosalind and I would certainly want our passing to glory to be marked in such a way.

Reflect and Pray

Both at funerals and on other occasions, many have found this poem inspirational.

You can shed tears that she is gone
Or you can smile because she has lived
You can close your eyes
    and pray that she will come back
Or you can open your eyes and see all that she has left
Your heart can be empty because you can't see her
Or you can be full of the love that you shared
You can turn your back on tomorrow and live yesterday
Or you can be happy for tomorrow
    because of yesterday
You can remember her and only that she is gone
Or you can cherish her memory and let it live on
You can cry and close your mind, and turn your back
Or you can do what she would want:
Smile, open your eyes, love and go on.

                                        David Harkins

Who Suffers most in the Aftermath of Loss?

Marriage is a long conversation that is never quite long enough.

Anon

If I were to ask you who suffers most in the aftermath of loss, you might be inclined to assume it would be people who were inseparable in life from their loved ones. After all, is it not those with whom we share our deepest experiences, and on whom we are most dependent, that we miss the most?

Immense beyond words though the loss of our closest confidant undoubtedly is, those who have endured a conflict ridden relationship often suffer still more. The fact that there is no time left to put things right, or to develop better memories makes the grief process still harder to bear.

It is important to understand the legacy that guilt-laden relationships leave behind them. When the person who has died, or separated themselves from us, only bestowed love and praise grudgingly, they may well have been misusing these intrinsically godly qualities to maintain power and control over other people.[4]

If challenged, they would doubtless have been quick to deny that they were doing anything wrong – or to claim that they were only doing it "for the other person's good."

The fact remains, however, that their entire way of relating was profoundly unloving and un-Christ like. The Lord *hates* it when we use power to belittle and depersonalise each other.

All of us need to be careful on this point, lest He has to go to extreme lengths to set His beloved children free from such unfair impositions.

Reflect and Pray

You, O God,
see trouble and grief;
You consider it
to take it in hand.
The victim commits himself to You.

Psalm 10:14

Lord, in Your name,
I resist and throw off all attempts
to straitjacket and control my life.
Forgive me, too,
whenever I make unfair demands on others,
or withhold love and care.
Grant me the insight and the opportunity
to put as many matters right as possible.
Refit and re-equip me for the next stage of life.
In the name of Jesus,
Who alone is perfect freedom, Amen.

Fallout from the Death of Children

On this mountain He will destroy
the shroud that enfolds all peoples,
the sheet that covers all nations;
He will swallow up death forever.
The Sovereign Lord will wipe away the tears from all faces;
He will remove the disgrace of His people
from all the earth.

Isaiah 25:7-8

Michael and Esther Ross Watson, a remarkable couple who spent many years ministering in Indonesia, experienced great tragedy when they attempted to adopt a child. While they were still in the process of going through the adoption process, she was taken from them and subsequently died. The next baby they were going to adopt also suddenly died – which completely devastated them. God had provided the room, the clothes and all the necessary equipment to welcome this child – yet suddenly the baby was no longer there – and the pain was overwhelming.

The next forty-eight hours were the darkest Michael and Esther had ever experienced. It was the one time in their life when they doubted the love of God. How could He have provided everything yet still have let them down?

It was while they were recovering at another missionary couple's house that a letter came from the orphanage, saying that they had another baby available for adoption. Did the missionaries think that the Ross-Watsons had sufficiently recovered to cope with such a thing? Amazed that this letter should arrive while they were staying there, Michael and Esther went straight round to the orphanage – and fell in love with the baby at first sight. Angela is now twenty-seven-years old, and God has blessed her greatly.

I was talking to Michael and Esther recently about this episode, and they recalled how, at the end of those dreadful forty-eight hours, a deep peace settled on them both. They are so glad God gave them this experience *before* they heard that the orphanage was trying to find a home to place the newborn baby.

Despite their earlier disappointment, God had been planning the very best for them – and all the baby things they had been given were soon put to good use!

In years gone by, virtually every family had children who failed to outlive childhood, and grief was considered a "normal" part of life in a way that we are no longer familiar with. Grieving together is an important way of acknowledging that hurtful things do happen on life's journey, and that we can survive the storms together. This is what David Woodhouse wrote concerning the death of infants.

> It was an occasional and sad ministry to offer comfort to parents whose child had died in a cot death, through miscarriage, abortion or still birth.[5] I found it important and comforting to hold a short service in which we commend the baby to the Lord at a separate time before the funeral, with just the parents, or mother present. I used the passage from Isaiah 40:11 where the Lord gathers the lambs in His arms, and carries them in his bosom while gently leading the mother sheep.
>
> Whether the baby is present or not, I talk through the option of the mother holding the baby in her arms and then symbolically lifting the baby to the Lord, handing him or her over to the Lord's safe-keeping until we meet again. I have found this to be a very powerful healing and releasing

pastoral event. We hand the child to Jesus for safe-keeping until we meet again in the Lord's presence.

The way we explain things to children when other children or a parent dies requires great care – not least because they interpret words and phrases very differently from adults. If we try to protect them from all exposure to grief, children may end up concluding that it is we, the grown-ups, who are unable to face what has happened.[6] This places them under an enormous strain, because they feel obliged to comfort us – and who is available then to help them talk about the loss that they have experienced?

Right from the outset, it is important to reassure the child that what has happened is not their fault. However obvious this may seem from an adult perspective, certain children (like some overly sensitive adults) easily project mountainous consequences onto molehill acts of misbehaviour. In other words, they somehow take it into their heads that *they* must somehow have been responsible for this terrible thing that has happened.

It is important for adults, too, to be prepared for an emotional backlash. Grief is unpredictable and volatile, and many couples pull apart emotionally in the aftermath of a child developing a major disability, let alone dying. Since this is the last thing any surviving children need, it is as well to be aware of the dangers, and to take extra care to protect and strengthen ties of friendship.

Grandparents suffer doubly. Not only do they have the loss of their own hopes and dreams for the loved one to cope with, but also the pain of seeing their own children enduring such terrible grief. This pain is all the more acute if it hooks into unresolved issues in their own lives.[7]

The truth is that almost anyone with a sensitive conscience is likely to feel some measure of guilt when someone either falls from grace or dies. It is perilously easy for us to feel responsible – especially when we remember all the times we have not been as thoughtful, kind or as prayerful as we should have been.

It will help if we are able to differentiate between "legitimate" guilt (when we really *have* done something wrong) as opposed to "neurotic" guilt (which has no basis in reality). As surely as God forgives us when we confess real sins to Him, it is far less helpful when we berate ourselves for things the Lord is not convicting us of.

Demonic tempters are quick to take advantage of such accusations. Their quest is simple: to turn our feelings of disappointment into a lingering resentment against God. C.S. Lewis exposes this strategy through his fictional mouthpiece, the master demon Screwtape:

> *Unexpected demands for a man who is already tired tends to produce good results. This means first feeding him with false hopes (presumption). Weaken their resolve to bear what they have to bear, make people doubt their happiness (it is too subjective after all) and live only in the "reality" – as if such happiness were not already reality.*[8]

Many years ago I was part of a church that prayed earnestly for a teenage boy who was suffering from Hodgkin's Disease. Despite much heartfelt prayer, the boy died. There was no need for anyone to consider the boy's home-going as a failure. Right to the end, the Lord's presence had shone through him, touching many by his vibrant peace and witness.[9] Yet the Church was so "set back" in their faith that several years passed before people felt free to pray again with any real conviction for the sick to be healed.

As always, we are responsible for the process, not the outcome. As surely as trying to live up to standards which the Lord is not asking of us is a recipe for disillusionment, at the same time we must be prepared to acknowledge when we really have failed, and be prepared to face the implications.

There is one other important thing to note in this context. When we do go to God in this way, we must be sure to *receive* His forgiveness by faith. What would be the point of confession if we did not actually believe that He is prepared to forgive us? It would be like pleading for a glass of water but then not drinking it. *As far as the east is from the west, so far has He removed our transgressions from us* (Psalm 103:12).

Reflect and Pray

Lord Jesus, as surely as You have guided countless millions through the swirling vortex of loss, guard and guide those who have lost loved ones through these churning eddies of grief.

Fallout for Children

What's done to children, they will do to society.
Karl Menninger

How can the fallout from the death of a parent be anything less than intensely distressing for a child?[10] Bereavement catapults children into taking on many of the roles and responsibilities of the missing parent long before they are really ready to do so.

"Parental inversion" robs children of much of the fun and freedom of childhood. As they make the more or less conscious decision to put their own grief on hold in favour of supporting the grieving adult, deep and disturbing seeds of anxiety can hardly fail to be sown in their soul. If left unattended, these can seriously hinder the child's ability to sustain mature friendships in later life, and to enjoy life's lighter side.[11]

> When a child senses tension, hears Mummy complain about Daddy, or lies in bed hearing arguments, she wants to do all in her power to keep them together. She hears comments that make her think that she must be the cause of the trouble . . . so it is not surprising that when the split comes she interprets it like this, "It's my fault. I have failed in my attempts to keep them together. That message goes deep." It is especially the oldest child who feels this and who "carries an augmented load of guilt."[12]

A young child who throws a tantrum, or bursts into tears when a loved one leaves the room, is protesting in the only way it knows how to do. If this fails to bring about the desired result, the child may become unnaturally quiet. This quietness often masks a profound resentment, which may continue even when the loved one returns – but now it has become a breeding ground for rage and anger, and can cause the child to become increasingly withdrawn or unpredictable when other forms of loss come their way.

Matters often come to a head during adolescence, which is a time of loss as well as of exploration. During these years when they are preparing to leave home, our children are already becoming markedly less family-oriented. More concerned now with what peers think and feel than with our family values, teenagers want to behave in an adult manner, yet continue at the same time to do the most unadult-like things.

Hypersensitive lest they be humiliated in front of their peers, and acutely unwilling to believe that anybody else has experienced the full extent of the emotions they are wrestling with, the stage is set for contradiction and conflict. "Why did the teenagers cross the road?" "Because their parents told them not to!"

No wonder teenagers react unpredictably when further loss occurs. It is like throwing oil onto a fire. Warning signs to indicate that trauma may be present include disturbing dreams, along with emotional detachment and age-inappropriate behaviour.

While it is right to do all we can to protect children from the side-effects of divorce, separation, and bereavement, we cannot afford to become over-protective. Young King Canute deliberately set himself in the path of the oncoming tide to remind the fawning flatterers who surrounded him that he was as much subject to the laws of nature as anyone else. Trying to shield children from all pain is equally as futile.

Adopting a "china doll" approach and over-controlling children's freedom ultimately stunts their development. More often than not it reflects the parent's inward-looking attitude. Better just to try and maintain open communications, and to pray that all that we have shared will stand our children in sufficiently good stead to help them cope when inevitable losses come their way in later life.

Perfectionists will throw up their hands in horror and try still harder to control their behaviour – but the prayerful will persevere in the hope that they are simply "building their testimony," en route to achieving great things for the Kingdom. May the Lord give us grace and wisdom to know when to intervene and when to remain watchful and prayerful – especially if they insist on making choices that we know can only lead to harm or disillusionment.

It does not take anything as radical as a literal bereavement to upset a child's sense of stability. It was obvious to us from an early age that our youngest son, Dominic, had learning needs that were making reading and writing immensely difficult for him. To our sadness, he passed through the hands of several teachers who were unable or unwilling to acknowledge the dyslexia that was so blindingly obvious to us.

The heartache has been all the greater because Dominic longs to read and write fluently, and feels intensely grieved at being unable to keep up with the rest of the class. It was a relief when a detailed report finally highlighted the issues we had long since identified. Of itself the report does not constitute a cure, but at least the matter has now been recognised. He is currently receiving a limited amount of outside tuition, but unless the Lord intervenes miraculously, he is likely to continue needing help as he gets older.

When children regale adults (and each other) with a string of problems in order to elicit sympathy, it is often because they are compensating for some internal sense of loss or inadequacy. Unaware of the real reasons behind these attitudes, teachers may dismiss these children as "attention seekers." "Attention-needy" would be a better description – a label that embraces an ever growing number of children in our increasingly dysfunctional society.

Some of the losses that children complain about appear relatively trivial to adult eyes. "The house isn't burning down," the parent protests, "so why make such a fuss?" Have we perhaps forgotten the heartache we felt when a favourite toy got broken – or when we were repeatedly overlooked or excluded as a child?

Likewise, those brought up in Christian homes, where the parents' hectic schedule kept them constantly busy attending to other people's needs, sometimes struggle to feel God's presence for themselves in times of crisis. Perhaps they have an inbuilt expectation that God, too, will always be too busy for them. This can undermine their sense of being unconditionally loved, and leave them insecure about their own identity.

At a still more serious level, how can children who grow up witnessing violence and abuse in their home, fail to carry the imprint of this into their adult life? Most commonly this manifests in a crippling lack of confidence. Sometimes, however, it can take a more sinister turn: an overarching desire to take revenge, for instance.

This is the dark backdrop against which so many are growing up today. May we help children to grieve constructively by helping them to understand at least some of the factors that make abusers as they are, without in any way minimising the seriousness of their actions.

Reflect and Pray

Lord, You see the hurts
that countless children sustain every day :
victims of famine, war and disease.
You know the hearts of those who have been scarred
by violence and abuse.

Where earlier attachments were cruelly severed,
or never allowed to develop,
we ask You to grant special resilience and protection
and to bathe each damaged soul
in Your special light and love.

May those of us who feel ourselves to be a failure
resist the temptation to push ourselves to the limit
in order to prove that we are acceptable.

May we learn instead the restfulness of love,
that yet enables much to be achieved.
Where we, as adults, have failed to provide our children
with the care and support they required,
we confess our failings to You.
Forgive us for the heavy price our children pay
when we fail to address our own shortcomings
and overcome our areas of woundedness.

Make up ground that has been lost in their lives,
especially in the lives of . . . and . . . we pray.
In Jesus' name, Amen.

Fallout from Divorce

You cry out, "Why doesn't the Lord accept my worship?"
I'll tell you why! Because the Lord witnessed the vows you
and your wife made when you were young. But you have
been unfaithful to her . . .

Didn't the Lord make you one with your wife? In body and
spirit you are His. And what does He want? Godly children
from your union. So guard your heart; remain loyal to the
wife of your youth. "For I hate divorce!" says the Lord, the
God of Israel.

Malachi 2:14-16; see also Matthew 19:8-9, 11

Scriptural teaching on divorce is crystal clear – but with the divorce rate cresting at fifty per cent of all marriages of less than twenty years' standing, almost all of us have more or less first hand experience of the grief that so often accompanies divorce. It is worth pointing out that the enemy tries very hard to make people feel that their marriage has reached the "irretrievable" stage, when, in reality, it might still be possible to turn it around.

To those who have made each other profoundly unhappy, separation may come as a considerable relief, but Sally Mowbray sounds an important warning on this point:

There come times in most marriages when you need to "set your face as flint" and hang in there. The Hollywood film idea of marriage lacks any semblance to reality. The path to a relationship breakdown is littered with small choices that lead relentlessly away from commitment and partnership and towards excitement, change and self-interest.

Like most schemes that Satan uses to pull Christians away (whether from God or other people), it is the accumulation of these seemingly insignificant choices that draw a person way off course until they suddenly wake up to what is going on, and wonder how they got to where they now find themselves.

Some, of course, rejoice at their new "freedom" – but that may be more a sign of their hearts hardening towards people they were once committed to than the Lord's explicit leading. Look at it from the other direction: even the small choices that we make through gritted teeth to honour and forgive do far more than we imagine at the time to hold relationships together.

Even though there is far less stigma attached to divorce these days than there used to be, how could there be such a thing as a painless separation? As a friend who was going through particularly unpleasant proceedings put it, "It really is the worst thing possible."

The high levels of domestic violence associated with broken relationships are a reminder of how volatile such issues can be. If one of the partners never wanted the separation to happen, divorce comes as an additional body blow, leaving them feeling that it has made a mockery of all that has gone before. Jennifer Rees Larcombe relates her desolation when her husband, who had supported her throughout her long years of confinement in a wheelchair, left her for a younger woman *after* she had been miraculously healed.

Jennifer charts the strong emotions she went through in the aftermath of this betrayal. In her case it was compounded by complete strangers making all manner of unkind suggestions as to what she must have done wrong to have caused the marriage to crash.

Jennifer's diary entries at that time are peppered with references to having no further desire to live. Like many who lose a loved one in such circumstances, or who feel that their reputation has been irreparably tainted, she experienced strong temptations to point her car at a tree. She records weeping with disappointment when the hospital rang to tell her that the latest batch of tests had revealed no farther sign of cancer. Writing on behalf of the many who have been blessed by her ministry, I am so grateful that God found ways to see her through that terrible time.[13]

For any who are reading these words who have allowed some other attraction to develop, may I refer you back to the earlier section on "When the grass appears greener?" It might just save someone from unnecessary and unpleasant consequences.

As always, grief that is suppressed and "swept under the carpet" is likely to resurface in other ways. Unresolved grief hinders all family relations but especially step-families. People are much more likely to separate and divorce again if they are still carrying "blocked" or "frozen" grief around with them from previous relationships. How can such things fail to have an effect on their ability to relate to the Lord?

In "Ceremonies that facilitate Grief," we recommended that newly divorced people find ways to "formalise" what has happened. It is a sign that they are allowing themselves to go through a similar process of grief and recovery to someone who has suffered a literal bereavement.

It is also worth remembering the effects that divorce has on others – not only on the children, but also many others who may have invested in the marriage, who will all have their own grief to work through as a result of it breaking down.

Most marriages are too complex to permit one party to be identified as being solely responsible, of course. Even when people find themselves suddenly and unceremoniously abandoned, the process that led up to the separation has usually been underway for some considerable time.

In *The American Way of Divorce,* Kessler charts seven emotional stages: disillusionment, erosion, detachment, physical separation, mourning, second adolescence (starting a new relationship), and finally exploration – the hard work of establishing a new identity and new close relationships.[14]

Most people do not experience all these reactions, of course, or at least not in this particular order, but what Kessler does show is that the person who initiates the break-up tends to be the one who suffers least. They have had more time to come to terms with the idea of being a free agent, and once they have open their hearts to this possibility, it may only be a short step before they begin exaggerating difficulties and taking provocative steps to make sure that nothing prevents them from achieving this separation – even to the point of spreading defamatory stories about their partner's behaviour.

Such a person is likely to come in for some degree of criticism for initiating divorce proceedings, but that is usually considerably less than the grief experienced by the person left behind. If the abandoned partner has had more than their share of grief in the past, this latest episode is likely to reinforce their expectation that life is sure to go on letting them down.

In their shock and anger they find themselves making things worse for themselves. At the very time when extreme diplomacy is called for, they lose their temper, and "waver between bravado and being pitiful."[15] The truth is that they feel as though their roots are being pulled out one by one – and, to their utter dismay, it is their own partner who is doing this to them.

To lose access to a person to whom they still feel profoundly attached causes agony beyond words. The risk is that if these underlying attitudes are not attended to, the abandoned person may become so desperate to find a love that will prove constant and consistent that they become increasingly incapable of sustaining any healthy emotional relationship.

Although some people are rejected without fully understanding the reason why it has happened, most recognise the areas they should have paid more attention to. Even if it is too late to save this particular relationship, it is still wise to take note of these things, and confess them to the Lord.

Reflect and Pray

Father, whatever has happened,
thank You that I am not an outsider to grace.
Forgive me for every way in which I have failed You –
especially in the matter of relationships.

Thank You for the blood of Jesus
that renews the depths of my heart
and the grace than enables me
to pick up the threads of my life.

Do whatever it takes
to bring me to the point of putting You first
and so being able to embark safely
on the new relationships
You have in store for me.
In Jesus' name, Amen.

Fallout from Relocation

The greatest use of a life is to spend it on something that will outlast it.

William James

Most of us derive a considerable percentage of our emotional security from our work or ministry. It provides us with much of our "identity" as well as our sense of purpose in life. No surprise, then, if we find adjusting to revised circumstances challenging.

Towards the end of 2001 a friend turned up at our house, wanting to know how I would feel if the Lord were to ask me to lay my ministry down. Very much hoping that He would do no such thing, I made the "proper" reply, that if He really were to ask me to do so, then of course I would do it.

As it turned out, her question was anything but rhetorical. Fast forward events a few weeks and Ros found herself making enquiries about a midwifery post that was being advertised on the Shetland Islands.

"Shetland?" I gasped, "but that would mean leaving every-thing behind."

Ros laid the telephone handset back in its cradle. She was looking thoughtful but intrigued. My mind was reeling. So far as I was concerned, God had led us to Shropshire, and so far as I was aware, we were here for the duration. Which only goes to show how little I know! Mind you, I doubt if I would have been prepared to contemplate such a radical change of direction had it not been for the question my friend had recently asked me – along with a prophetic word that a visiting couple had brought us.

They had asked to pray with us, and the lady shared a vivid picture that she had received. "Our life had been heading in one direction," she declared, "but the Lord is about to turn it a full ninety degrees." Well – how do you handle a word like that? It felt profoundly significant, but since there was nothing whatsoever we could do about it, we shared it with friends for the sake of accountability and then "pouched" it until the Lord did something to activate it. It looked as though that "something" might be starting to happen!

"Okay," I said, gulping hard, "but everything will be different up there. It would help if we had *one* point of continuity. How about giving Anna a ring and see if she would be prepared to come with us?" (Anna had been looking after our youngest, who was then two years old.) We rang her together, and popped what seemed to us a most improbable question: how she would feel about moving to Shetland?

Anna gasped when we asked her. Ten minutes later she e-mailed me her diary entry for the day I had first discussed the possibility of her working for us. "Robert and Ros have asked me to work for them. I would be delighted to do so, but I am afraid that it will get in the way of my calling to Shetland!"

Although we knew she had visited Shetland before, Anna had never shared this call with us. The first confirmation had come. Within days there would be several more, some of them equally as dramatic. To our great surprise, we found ourselves, a few months later, heading nearly a thousand miles north to live on the remote but beautiful Shetland Islands, where Ros had been appointed as the senior midwife.

Ros and Tim travelled up a few days ahead of me in the worst storm of the year. I will never forget setting out on a heavily overcast late February evening from Aberdeen harbour, trusting the guidance I had received, but weighed down with grief at leaving so much behind.

The storm had lessened to a Force Eight by then, but the swell was intense, leaving the ferry labouring as it smashed down into the huge waves. At some stage of the crossing, the Lord drew near and pointed out that He was doing the very best for us. The way He had provided a beautiful house called *Ruach* for us, overlooking some of the most spectacular scenery in the country,[16] had felt nothing short of miraculous, yet such was my sense of disorientation that it did little to lift my spirits.

Change is challenging, and some of us find it harder to cope with than others. The crucial thing is to try to adjust to the new realities as quickly as possible.[17] Although the Lord had given broad hints as to what I would be doing in terms of my writing ministry, we were effectively, starting again from scratch: not an easy thing to do at any stage of life, but harder perhaps in a remote location.

Our forty-two-month sojourn on Shetland brought many blessings, but also immense griefs. The move proved particularly traumatic for our thirteen-year-old son, who faced many challenges integrating into a school where he was the only English person.

When the Lord showed us that our time on the island was at an end, He warned us that we would be "shifting around" for some time to come. This was hardly the message we wanted to hear, but it prepared us for what was to come. We found ourselves obliged to move three times in a year – which meant being involved in four communities: something that stretched us to the limit. It took considerable energy to pack up each time, not to mention the emotional challenge of developing an entirely fresh set of relationships in each place.

Each season had its own blessings and rewards, but each by definition also *lacked* certain advantages that the others offered. We sensed that these were "transition" phases, but were taken by surprise each time by just how short-term they proved to be.

Now that we are living in an urban environment, we are no longer able to enjoy the spectacular views we once took almost for granted. The glories of the places we have lived in – Shetland, Shropshire and Devon – live on in our memories, and God has made up for it in other ways as we embark on our new callings: for Rosalind as a "midwife" to the midwifery students at Canterbury Christ Church University, and for myself in my role as Associate Minister of a thriving Anglican church.

Reflect and Pray

Lord, when You declare that time is up
on some particular phase of our life,
help us to collaborate with Your leading,
rather than fighting against it –
for You look at issues from every possible angle,
and have so much up Your sleeve!

Praying for Prodigals

At the age of forty, Esau married two Hittite wives . . . But Esau's wives made life miserable for Isaac and Rebekah.
Genesis 26:34-35

Many of us have experienced acute grief when loved ones turn their back on following the Lord. Leaders feel this pain particularly, fearing perhaps that the waywardness of their children (or partner) will "nullify" their own testimony. No wonder that God is calling so many to pray for "prodigals" (of whatever age) to experience Holy Spirit conviction and to come back home to the Lord.

Let no one pretend that this is anything less than immensely challenging! Billy Graham once commented that steering his son Franklin through his teen years was the hardest challenge he ever faced. The compassionate ministry his son has long been leading is testimony to the outstanding job he did.

Not all of us are so successful. When several of his sons showed alarming sexual tendencies, King David showed himself uncharacteristically indecisive in dealing with them. Quite possibly he held back from taking the firm steps that were needed because his conscience was busy accusing him of being a hypocrite.

The Lord had no intention of giving up on David because of His "mistakes," any more than He does when we fall from grace in some way. At the same time, we cannot fail to notice that David had opened the door for far-reaching troubles to afflict his dynasty.[18] Despite these, David was able to declare at the end of his days:

> *In my distress I cried out to the Lord;*
> *yes, I cried to my God for help.*
> *He heard me from His sanctuary;*
> *my cry reached His ears.*
> *2 Samuel 22:7*

Reflect and Pray

> *Despite all our mistakes, Lord,*
> *Bring our children back to You,*
> *and give them the resilience they will need*
> *to navigate through the losses*
> *that are sure to come their way.*
> *May they come to love You with all their hearts –*
> *and may their future homes*
> *be filled with that same love.*

The Hedge of Thorns

> *For this reason I will fence her in with thorn bushes. I will*
> *block her path with a wall to make her lose her way.*
> *Hosea 2:6*

In the second chapter of Hosea we find the remarkable story of how God called one of His prophets to marry a woman called Gomer, warning him in advance that she would be unfaithful to him.

Gomer is a symbol and reminder both of the nation's waywardness and of the Lord's determination to do something radical about it. By hedging her about with thorns, and building a wall to keep her from straying, He did not make it *impossible* for her to continue her self indulgence, but He certainly made it a great deal harder!

From this story we can deduce that it is perfectly permissible to pray for God to erect a "hedge of thorns" around people who are running away – whether from the Lord, their marriage, or from some other responsibility. There is no "formula" involved, but we can pray that God will block the path of those who are straying, and bring them back to Himself.

It is hard to think of a less attractive calling, but since Gomer's unfaithfulness is an allegory of Israel's spiritual infidelity, and we too live in a society that has turned its back on God and embraced many false "lovers," we can pray along similar lines for our nation to reconsider its wrong priorities.

A Prayer for a Prodigal

I spent time today with one
who used to walk with You,
whose love once spurred her on
to seek Your Kingdom first.

But now that faith has turned to ashes.
I see new passions stir among the embers,
awaiting only the spark
of some other master's fire.

Lord, spare this once-fiery soul
from a third-rate role;
rekindle her soul's desire,
to love and follow You.

Coping with Redundancy

Grief makes me so empty and hollow, Lord;
that I gasp for you to fill the void.
So many things are pressing in –

crowding and bewildering –
give me grace to focus my heart
and to make good use of my time and strength.

Does it get easier to make large steps of faith as we grow older? On the one hand it does, because we are fuelled by the memory of all the occasions when God has shown His faithfulness to us. On the other hand, it is only fair to acknowledge that most of us find change increasingly hard to cope with as we get older.

We should by no means underestimate the grief that accompanies experiences such as redundancy and retirement. Being made redundant is one of the sharpest shocks that most people will ever experience, removing at one stroke not only their professional role in life, but also many of the markers that identify who they are. Life moves on and people soon forget what they have done, and maybe even who they were.

The more closely linked people were as a work team, the more likely they are to feel a corresponding grief when the cut and thrust of that camaraderie is no longer there. For some people, the loss of momentum and status, to say nothing of income, may remain acute even many years after the event itself.[19]

There may be additional grief, too, in discovering that some whom they had looked on as friends turn out to have been no more than colleagues. Many will identify then with Sally Mowbray's experience:

> When my father died, my mother deeply mourned the lost connection with his working world. He was a vet with the Ministry of Agriculture, and so his relationships encompassed not only officials but also a wide range of farmers. This all came to an abrupt halt because her relationship with all but a very few had been exclusively through her husband.

> We also need special grace to cope when we know that we are being left behind as things develop and move on in the field in which we once worked, and which we are no longer a part of. It feels a bit like watching the departure of a train

we were travelling in. It moves on while we remain on the station platform – which now feels very empty. If specific rejection has also been part of this process (as opposed to natural retirement), the grief can run very deep, latching all too easily onto feelings of inadequacy: "There, I always said I wasn't good enough!"

In today's fast-moving "hire-and-fire" culture, most of us can expect to lose our job at least once along life's journey. We may try to act phlegmatically, and make light of this; but in reality most of us are more deeply upset that we like to admit. There is some basis for truth behind the caricature images of people setting out for work each morning because they lacked the courage to tell their loved ones that they had lost their job!

It is *normal* to experience moments of fear and anger in the aftermath of being made redundant. The fact that we possess skills that no one appears to want can be particularly hard to cope with. The thought of spending more time at home may sound attractive in the abstract, but it only takes a few comments along the lines of, "You shouldn't be here at this time of day!" to make us feel in the way and one too many.

People's instinct to chivvy us into looking for another job may be exactly what we need to get us moving forwards again – but it may also push us into steps we are not yet ready to take. Each of us responds to loss in very different ways. The most important thing is not to assume that we have no further contribution to make now that we have lost the role or position that was once so central in our life. It is utterly untrue that we are too old – or too anything else!

The Church has been slow to recognise the reality of the midlife crisis, that inclines so many to unwise actions. Neither does it always have much to say about the grief that redundancy and retirement can provoke. If reality fails to measure up to expectations that were never quite the Lord's, there is a real risk of people setting off in search of adventures of their own making, abandoning established relationships in the process, and condemning themselves to futile attempts to fulfil impossible dreams.

To any of you who find yourselves at such a place, let me remind you of the prophet's wisdom: *Stand at the crossroads and look; ask for the ancient paths* (Jeremiah 6:16).

The Lord will show you clearly what to do, even if it means hunkering down for the time being until the way ahead becomes clearer.

When it does, your problems may be anything but over! Certain career changes themselves prove difficult to handle. If you work intensively with people (as a nurse or social worker for instance) you may experience considerable strain when you are promoted to managerial positions, not least because your new role often takes you far away from the very people you originally entered the profession to serve.

To all intents and purposes you find yourself embarking on an entirely different career – and one that may be riddled with unexpected pressures and responsibilities. There are few more challenging things to cope with than having heavy responsibilities, unless you are also given the authority to make necessary changes.

Reflect and Pray

Gracious Father,
Guide and Restorer,
thank You for all the work and tasks I
have completed for You.

Where You have new ones in mind,
ease me into them –
and where these are not immediately forthcoming
keep my heart flexible and grateful
to make the most of what You have already given.

Be with all who are feeling the grief
of adjusting to major lifestyle changes
especially . . . . . .
In Jesus' Name, Amen.

Coping with Retirement

God is waiting for us here, at this very moment.
Michel Quoist

Grey Panther alert! Now that people are living longer, yes, even many beyond the hundred year mark, a new generation is emerging of people who are eager to make the most of their remaining time on Earth. Beyond the pummelling hours most people are expected to put in at work these days, retirement beckons. For many this proves to be a spiritually rich and rewarding time in which they are able to share with others the hard-earned wisdom they have acquired in the course of their pilgrimage, and to complete the goals and projects they have long been holding in their hearts.

In theory, embarking on retirement represents an unparalleled opportunity to develop our ability to "be" rather than just to "do." Because our lives tend to centre round the role that we play, and the position that we hold, however, it is hardly surprising if we feel disorientated when we lose or lay down some prized place in church or society. Apart from feeling the loss acutely, we may feel uncertain how to relate to others now that our role and status have changed.

This consideration alone makes a compelling reason for not allowing our "job description" to define us. Even though our working environment provides us with much of the meaning and context for our lives, we are who we are, rather than what we do. That is why we are called human *beings* rather than human *doings*!

The challenge is to rise above any sense of grief and disorientation we may be feeling in order to be able to make the most of it. By God's mercy, new opportunities *will* emerge – but the Lord may use the interim period to draw our attention to various things we have not had time to attend to before.

When financial constraints combine with loss of status, however, retirement takes on an altogether different hue. The full reality of this shock may not hit home initially. Death usually has a date, but that is not automatically the case with the onset of grief. In a subconscious reaction against the shadow of looming retirement, some remain at their posts too long, whether in church or in business. It takes grace to recognise the right moment to lay something down, and to release younger people into their calling.

Constant change is here to stay, and we need grace and flexibility to embrace it, especially as we grow older. At the same time, if change is *not* called for, we are most unwise to insist on it. As my father commented,

> In the nature of things, many of those experiencing grief will be elderly. Unless these are people who have made successful efforts to keep up with the times, change usually represents a menace. They simply cannot cope with new types of equipment, they do not understand the new ways in which they are supposed to be doing things, or why the old ways are no longer considered sufficient. This is not to glorify the status quo, it's just to recognise that they feel insecure and uncertain in a fast changing world.

Take the far from unusual example of one partner insisting on moving to a region where they have no friends or family. If their principal reason for relocating is because they are attracted by the scenery, or because they have happy memories of the place, it is wise to wait until they are more certain.

By no means everyone makes the change successfully from "visitor" to "resident." And if one partner dies, or the relationship breaks up, the "survivor" is often left in more or less complete isolation. For all manner of kingdom purposes (as opposed to just taking out an "insurance against loss") it makes sense to cultivate the friendships God has given us, rather than looking only to each other for friendship and support.

An Ode to Time

A witness to the passing of time;
You hold the answers,
to questions we have yet to ask.

So, tell me, what sorrows
all-enveloping at the time,
now lie still and at rest in your memory,
as once you never thought they could.

Tell me what worries
that once fed from your soul
have now passed and proved unfounded:
stormy clouds on a summer's day.

Tell me of the pain
that came and took possession of you,
and then left when you never thought it would.

Then tell me what you've learnt of time;
how waiting and wishing means moments lost
and empty days or even years,
When looking back.
And tell me what you've learnt of love . . .

Then you will have told me all that I have heard before,
but I'll continue to ask,
until my time passes,
only after this will I know,
because each man must learn the truth for himself.

Alison Brown (aged 14)

Reflect and Pray

*God of steep upheavals
and settled days,
You hold my life-span in Your hands;
ordain each step along the way.*

*God of the solid anchor,
and favourable breezes,
hoist my sails to catch
each wind Your Spirit blows.*

Fallout from controlling Church

Think of ways to encourage one another to outbursts of love and good deeds. And let us not neglect our meeting together, as some people do, but encourage and warn each other, especially now that the day of His coming back again is drawing near.

Hebrews 10:24-25

If the loss of a spouse is by far and away the sharpest grief most of us are likely to experience, loss of a job and moving house also rank high in the "Top Ten Stress Factors." Neither should we underestimate how much grief can be caused by difficulties in the local church. Of all the many sufferings Paul experienced, none taxed him more than his concern for the fledgling churches.

Besides all this, I have the daily burden of my concern for all the churches. Who is weak without my feeling that weakness? Who is led astray, and I do not burn with anger?

2 Corinthians 11:28-29

Every caring pastor finds himself assailed by such concerns, but I want in this section to consider the hurt and grief that so many in the Body of Christ experience when they are pushed, or pulled into a mould that does not fit them, and where they feel misunderstood and even intimidated by their leaders. If this comes on top of other griefs that they are carrying, then they may indeed find the church a hard place in which to bleed.

As surely as some churches exalt grace to the point where people effectively do what they want, others create a culture in which constant control and manipulation press down to keep people in line. Born of insecurity on the one hand, and pride of ownership on the other, such attitudes foster legalistic traits and an "empire-building spirit" that severely curtail the freedom of the Holy Spirit.

The process by which churches and organisations become taken up with their own vision and concerns, rather than with the best interests of their members, is a subtle but serious one.

When everyone and everything is sacrificed in order to fulfil the vision, the Lord often has to go to extreme lengths to rescue people from what may have become a hot house and a trap.

Such difficulties are equally as common "the other way round." All too many Godly leaders find themselves constantly thwarted by the demands of certain controlling people in their congregation. Whether the fault lies primarily in the leaders or the led, all such tendencies need renouncing.[20]

Some years ago we spent a most unhappy period in a church where the leader's domination of his flock caused us untold agony of heart. Week by week we would ask God to keep our hearts free from any judgmental attitude, but would emerge feeling far worse than when we had entered the building. We hated seeing people being whipped into line, and told in no uncertain terms where the door was if they didn't agree with all that was happening.

Attitudes such as this are abusive, and right on the verge of being cultish. How can effective ministry develop within the Body of Christ when everything revolves around the leader's whims and dictates?

The irony is that most of these leaders mean well. More often than not, their understanding of what Church ought to be sounds fine when talking to them on their own. It is when they are "up front" that a controlling spirit manifests itself, demanding such performance and compliance that it causes intense grief and distress to sensitive souls. It was certainly a relief to us when the Lord finally gave us the green light to move on!

Since when did "servant" leadership mean treating the congregation as slaves? God is looking for leaders who empower without controlling and who, like Jesus Himself, are full of both grace and truth (John 1;14,17).[21] Where such love and grace are lacking, and control is present, leaders are prone to rein in promising works of the Spirit, precisely because *too* much is happening away from their immediate control.

In John's second and third letters, the apostle passed on to specific friends some of the pearls of wisdom that God had given him.[22] In the second letter (the only one in Scripture that is specifically addressed to a woman) John reiterates his call that we should love one another.

Since this is something that comes more easily to women than to men, this might seem self-evident, but John is using the opportunity to warn her not to allow her loving heart to blind her to error. If false teachers come to the fellowship, she must not allow them into her home, or do anything to encourage them. It is the clearest of warnings couched in the mildest of rebukes. With supreme skill, John focuses on how a woman's greatest strength can become a potential weakness, allowing real error to creep in beneath the radar.

John's third letter, equally as brief, also touches on the subject of hospitality: a vital subject in those days before Travel Lodges, when Christians were the only people willing to accommodate visiting preachers. John commends Gaius, a generous-hearted elder who had been supporting godly teachers. At the same time he warns against Diotrephes, a dictatorial church leader, who rejected the teachers John had sent to him. Full of his own self-importance, Diotrephes was so hot on "truth" (as he perceived it) that he was actually expelling any Church members who remained willing to receive John's messengers.

If you have been on the receiving end of the sort of control and intimidation that occurs only too often when a man's strength becomes his weakness, the example of Diotrophes will resonate loudly. Such coercion often develops when a group of leaders are so intent on building a "successful" church or organisation that they hold the reins of authority too tightly, unable to trust others, or to release them into their giftings.

If you sense that your leaders are more interested in increasing the size of their church than in developing healthy relationships, you will almost certainly be carrying a heavy load of grief in your spirit May you have the grace to handle this creatively, rather than allowing it to crush your spirit. More than we perhaps appreciate at the time, God often trains us by putting us alongside less perfect leaders because we learn so much from their poor example and wrong attitudes. Apart from anything else, it makes us determined to live in a different spirit ourselves!

If you come to the conclusion that you need to move away from an environment that has become too controlling, be prepared for squalls! Controlling bodies do not easily give up their prey, even going so far as to imply that people who leave are dooming themselves to fruitlessness. If God is calling you to move on, however, you cannot afford to allow any threat or intimidation to hold you back.

All such tensions are doubly unwelcome in that they have no business to be anywhere near the Church. The fact remains, however, that a significant number of people opt out of Church altogether each year because they are unable to differentiate between following the Lord Jesus Himself (whom they instinctively warm to) and knowing how to cope with the dictates of "leaders with attitude".

Despite the many pressures and frustrations, the answer is not to stop meeting altogether. Church is still the place where God disciples His children, and from which He reaches out to the world. That is why it is so important to pray for God to raise up strong but sensitive leaders, and to work towards establishing structures that facilitate growth and godly experimentation. God wants us to enjoy being Church together!

Finally, I would like to conclude this section by returning to the different strengths that men and women bring to the Body of Christ. We are seriously incomplete without each other!

In all too many churches, however, the exclusively (or predominantly) male leadership has crushed the beauty and creativity the Lord has invested in women. If this is true for you, please don't harden your hearts against us. Can you find it in your heart to forgive what we have done to you? If so,

the Lord will hopefully find ways to develop all He has in
mind for you to be and to become.

Reflect and Pray

Father, where I have have been coerced and confined –
please lift the dead weight of oppression off me.
Where false prophecies and controlling words
have been spoken over me –
remove their effects right now, I pray.

But where I have been guilty of controlling others,
set people free from what I have said and done,
and help me to affirm people better,
and to relate to them in more Christ-like ways.
In Jesus' name, Amen.

References

1 Tony Cooke provides a concise overview on what to say, and
what to refrain from saying at funerals. For details, see
www.ruachministries.org/valeoftears/refs.htm as well as links to
web sites that provide practical advice for planning funerals.

2 Marshall, C. (2002) *To Live Again.* Chosen Books.

3 This gets round the problem some people occasionally experience
who attend fellowships that do not meet in a regular church
when they are unable to persuade the local vicar to include
items that sufficiently reflect their own heart and leading.

4 See especially Lake, T. *Living with Grief.* p. 60. Sheldon Press.

5 I would recommend Jack Hayford's *I'll Hold You in Heaven.*
Healing and Hope for the Parent who has lost a child through
miscarriage, stillbirth, abortion or early infant death. (1990)
Regal Books.

6 See Bright, R. (1998) *Grief and Powerlessness*, p.24. Jessica
Kingsley Publishers.

7 See www.ruachministries.org/valeoftears/refs.htm for a link to an
article that highlights the grief that grandparents experience.

8 Lewis, C.S. (1965) *Screwtape proposes a Toast.* Collins.

9 The whole issue of how we handle such disappointments is one
we may need to give considerable attention to. You may find
my article *"Dealing with Disappointment"* helpful.
www.ruachministries.org/valeoftears/refs.htm

10 There are a number of books on the market geared to helping explain death to children, e.g. *Water Bugs and Dragonflies,* by Doris Stickney, Continuum International Publishing Group Ltd. (2002), *Help Me Say Goodbye,* by Janice Silverman, Fairview Press, U.S. (1999), and *Sad Isn't Bad,* by Michaelene Mundy, (Elf-Help Books for Kids).

11 Repairing the damage caused by a fearful or repressed childhood is a skilled and important task. John and Paula Sandford have written powerfully on this subject in their splendid study, *Transformation of the Inner Man.* Victory House. We highly recommend their insightful writings.

12 Green, R. *God's Catalyst.* (1997) Christina Press.

13 Rees Larcombe, J. (2006) *Journey into God's Heart.* Hodder & Stoughton.

14 Kessler, S (1975) *The American Way of Divorce.* Nelson Hall. Chicago.

15 Harvey, J. (2000) *Give Sorrow Words: Perspectives on Loss and Trauma.* p.69. Brunner/Mazel.

16 See www.ruachministries.org/photogallery.htm

17 Research has shown that the prisoners who survived the inhuman deprivations in Japanese prison-of-war camps were those who "adapted," to their new conditions and refused to look back nostalgically to their previous way of life.

18 2 Samuel 12:9-12

19 To avoid giving too many examples, I have by and large stuck to generalities rather than exploring specific griefs – but you will know and grieve for wonderful business, industries and enterprises that are no more. Only this week I was reading Jackie Moffat's (2004)deeply moving account in *The Funny Farm* of the desolation that the foot and mouth epidemic brought to British farming. Bantam.

20 John Paul Jackson reveals important spiritual dynamics that may be at work in such situations in *Unmasking the Jezebel Spirit* (Kingsway). I have posted a detailed review of this book on our website. www.ruachministries.org/valeoftears/refs.htm

21 You can download my publication on leadership *Out Front,* from www.ruachministries.org/valeoftears/refs.htm

22 Following godly counsel can save us so much grief! You might find Dr James Richard's book *Stop the Pain* (2001, Whittaker House) helpful in this respect.

Part Seven

Lending our strength

Praise be to the God and Father of our Lord Jesus Christ,
the Father of compassion and the God of all comfort, who
comforts us in all our troubles, so that we can comfort
those in any trouble with the comfort we ourselves have
received from God.

2 Corinthians 7:5-7

I CAN REMEMBER THE SCENE VIVIDLY. It was just over a year after we had married, and Ros was in the utmost distress, having experienced her first miscarriage. Sheila had dashed over to be with her, and I can see her now, sitting on the edge of our bed, just holding Ros and loving her. Never underestimate the strength of such support and friendship!

There is nothing we need more during our times of grief than the help and presence of caring people. Many of us feel instinctively inclined, however, to steer well clear of the grieving. We rationalize to ourselves that they will be happier to be left on their own – or hope that because they received such a manifest dose of "divine anaesthetic" in the early stages they are doing just fine.

It is relatively easy to appease our conscience by making an occasional visit, or by sending a card. This is infinitely better than doing nothing, but there may be more that we can do for them.

In case this sounds as though we are committing ourselves to a long-term dependency, it is important to say first that grieving people often *need* a measure of short-term dependency in order to make a full recovery, and secondly that we are *not* speaking of a life-long commitment. Nine times out of ten their strength will return and our involvement will taper off.

In the past, such support was usually supplied "en famille," or left to the parish priest or church elders. By definition, these people can only care for so many. Since everyone fares best when they feel listened to and cared for, it is important for us to "lend" our strength to those whose reserves have been depleted, not only when a literal bereavement has occurred, but in the aftermath of any form of loss.

This section is aimed primarily, therefore, not only for those who are formally involved in grief and trauma counselling, but at helping all of us to come alongside those who are bowed down with grief.

As with every other aspect of life, blessing comes as we share what the Lord has given us, rather than "hoarding and holding on" to it.

Reflect and Pray

If you find yourself telephoning those weighed down with grief instead of visiting, or texting instead of ringing, or avoiding getting in touch at all – is it perhaps, because of unresolved issues in your own life?

Are you afraid that coming face to face with such raw emotions will expose your own insecurities?

Rather than remaining aloof or giving the appearance that we are expecting the grieving to "pull themselves together," let's overcome our fear of being emotionally drained and have the courage to come alongside.

> *Strong God, Saving God,*
> *as I don my lifeguard's vest*
> *and plunge into the deep at Your command*
> *help me to lend support to souls in distress,*
> *until those who are floundering*
> *are restored and re-empowered.*
> *In Jesus' Name, Amen.*

Coming Alongside the Grief-stricken

The heart of the wise is in the house of mourning,
but the heart of fools is in the house of pleasure.

Ecclesiastes 7:4

Continuing her moving account of the death of her daughter, Robbie Davis Floyd points out that just as a "doula" attends births in order to support the mother-to-be, so the presence of a supportive friend makes all the difference in our times of grief.

> It was a crazy thing to do, getting on the airplane alone. I thought I could handle it. Just before takeoff, I was still lucid enough to try one more time to reach my sweetheart, Richard Jennings, in a last-ditch effort to give him the terrible news in time for him to be able to meet me at the hospital in Roanoke. I had been calling all night, but he is a midwife and was not on call, so he had turned his phones off to get some sleep. I left a desperate message. Then, as the plane lifted into the air, I leaned my head back and closed my eyes, thinking that perhaps I could rest. That was when the universe imploded into a black hole, filled with specks of golden light. I was falling, choking, imploding into that black and gold no-space. I gasped for air – I couldn't breathe.

> Almost instantly, the doulas showed up. The woman in the seat in front of me moved back and held my hand. Her name was Kim. She asked me to talk about my daughter, the best thing anyone could have done at the time. A beautiful red-haired stewardess brought me water and oxygen and insisted I drink and breathe – again the best thing. During Jason's home birth, I had guzzled water and the midwives had given me oxygen in between pushing contractions – such an appropriate and empowering use of technology. This time it was just as important, and worked as well to keep me conscious and give me the strength to go on. Air and water – the elements of life.

> Just as doulas nurture you through the journey of birth, Kim and this red-haired stewardess nurtured me through my journey toward death. They never left me. In the airport in

Atlanta, I had to change planes but couldn't see more than two feet around me for the grayness everywhere. They walked on either side of me, holding my arms, to a room where Delta sheltered me. They brought me more water and food, and made me eat it, though I could barely swallow through the lump in my throat.

I was given a phone and told I could make all the calls I wanted – so many people still didn't know. Kim had a plane to catch but didn't want to leave me. I made her go. The red-haired stewardess told her not to worry because she would stay with me, and she did. She changed her plans and flew with me from Atlanta all the way to Roanoke, never letting go of my hand. Did I doubt the existence of angels?

At the airport in Roanoke she handed me off to a friend who had driven four hours from DC just to pick me up and escort me to the hospital so that I would not be alone. Sheer love from all of them, 100 percent support. May every doula do as well. You don't need to know a woman to support her in birth or in death. I was not alone.

Sharing Condolence

When we honestly ask ourselves which person in our lives means the most to us, we often find that it is those who, instead of giving advice, solutions, or cures, have chosen rather to share our pain and touch our wounds with a warm and tender hand.

The friend who can be silent with us in a moment of despair or confusion, who can stay with us in an hour of grief and bereavement, who can tolerate not knowing, not curing, not healing and face with us the reality of our powerlessness – that is a friend who cares.

                                              Henri Nouwen

Condolence, as Monica Lehner-Kahn aptly reminds us, is the art of giving courage. Deep down, the bereaved are acutely aware that they no longer fit in. Suddenly there is no one around with whom to share precious memories, and no one with whom to enjoy the dearly familiar rounds of life. The household's silence palls. With their past exposed and their future uncertain, fears of being excluded hook into other long-buried memories of being overlooked and passed over.

The more willing we are to enter their isolation, the more bearable we make life for them. Contrary to what we might suppose, most people do not expect us to come up with all the answers for their dilemmas: it is our presence that is most appreciated.

One of the many challenges about spending time with someone in grief is knowing when to sit back and let them "vent," and when to try to steer them beyond it. Our starting point is to remember that we are there to serve them, rather than to correct every distorted perspective. More often than not, it is best neither to collude with such perspectives, nor to rebuke them.

If the person becomes agitated and directs cutting remarks your way such as, "I feel dreadful – and you're not helping much!" count to ten and make allowances. It is likely to be a reflection of the enormous strain they are going through than anything personal. They may be feeling at odds with the doctor who diagnosed (or misdiagnosed) them, or with someone else entirely. Resist the temptation to snap back that they are not the easiest person in the world to help, and try saying something like, "What are you finding hardest to cope with?"

Bearing in mind that we are there primarily to serve and strengthen them, it can help to choose a seat at a lower level, so that the person is looking down at us, rather than up. Holding hands, an arm around the shoulder, a tender look – all such non verbal gestures can mean so much.

We may find going over and over the same ground tiring, but this is precisely what hurting people need to do. Telling and retelling the story of what happened is an important part in managing and reducing their trauma.

To be sure, there are those who consider grief a dangerous emotion – a luxury that deprives one not only of courage, but even of the will to recover. Others, like John Adams in a moving letter to Thomas Jefferson in 1816, recognise the *beneficial* effects that grief has had in terms of shaping and fashioning their soul.

> *Grief drives men into the habit of serious reflection, sharpens the understanding and softens the heart.*

As we shall be seeing in Part Nine, the griefs we experience often "qualify" us to share the Lord's own heart. To enable someone to express their sadness may therefore be the kindest thing we can do for them. They are embarking on a new quest to redefine themselves – a process that will involve many difficult decisions and, quite possibly, more than one false start.

Reflect and Pray

> *Think rather – call to thought, if now you grieve a little,*
> *The days when we had rest, O soul, for they were long.*
>
> *Men loved unkindness then, but lightless in the quarry*
> *I slept and saw not; tears fell down, I did not mourn;*
> *Sweat ran and blood sprang out and I was never sorry:*
> *Then it was well with me, in days ere I was born.*
>
> *Now, and I muse for why and never find the reason,*
> *I pace the earth, and drink the air, and feel the sun.*
> *Be still, be still, my soul; it is but for a season:*
> *Let us endure an hour and see injustice done.*
>
> A.E. Houseman

What if I put my Foot in it?

> *I have nothing to give to another, but I have a duty to open him to his own life, to allow him to be himself – infinitely richer than if he could ever be if I tried to enrich and to shape him only from the outside.*
>
> Michel Quoist

As a young parish worker, I remember my distress before making my first visit to someone whose husband had just died. What on earth was I going to say? I went in fear and trepidation – only to find that God had got there before me to make the ordeal a great deal easier than I had expected.

Make up your mind not to worry in advance what you will say, Jesus urged His disciples.[1] Not to worry, but rather to pray – that is the key. When Job's friends heard about the devastating troubles that had come his way, they set out together to sympathize with him.

> *They sat on the ground with him for seven days and seven nights. No one said a word to him, because they saw that his suffering was too great for words.*
>
> *Job 2:12-14*

Wildly inappropriate though their subsequent advice turned out to be, they began well, sitting quietly with their friend for an extended period of time. Only later did they hurl their misguided accusations and their pious platitudes at a man whom God was testing to an unprecedented extent.

Those of us whose lives have not been touched by tragedy need to be especially careful not to tell people in distress what to do. As Job observed, *People who are at ease mock those in trouble. They give a push to people who are stumbling (Job 12:5).* Whilst it may be helpful to share our own experiences, it is important not to make it sound as though we have known far greater losses ourselves. Grief is not competitive!

How people handle grief is a profoundly personal matter. Some can't wait to talk, in which case, we have only to follow where they lead. If they prefer to sit in silence, we need be in no hurry to fill the gaps. It is rarely helpful to look the sufferer straight in the eyes and demand to know how they are. Such an approach leaves them with no hiding place if they do not feel ready to provide an in-depth, "honest" answer.[2] A cup of coffee together can be more helpful than cheerful attempts to chivvy people's pain away, or even to reassure them that "things are bound to get better."

Insensitive and over eager visitors and evangelists can't resist taking advantage of the person's weakness, but this will prove profoundly counterproductive if it appears pushy or guilt-inducing. At the same time, we would be hiding our light under the bushel if we were not prepared to share the faith that means everything to us.

Michael Green shares the sobering story of a man who faithfully befriended a non Christian friend for many years. When this friend was later taken terminally ill, he tentatively tried to mention God. "Forget it, John," his friend told him. "If it had mattered that much to you, you would have mentioned it years ago."[3]

Nothing so helps people to sense that God is touching and holding them as the loving attention of people who really care. It offsets their fear that they are being "obsessive" about their loss. If we can cook for them, clean, tend the garden, care for the children or pets and run whatever errands are necessary, our presence and practical support will be worth its weight in gold.

A family person who is now on their own may really appreciate a phone call on a Saturday afternoon. It is remarkable how much blessing a loving letter can bring too.[4] People rarely think to write to children who have been affected by loss, yet they too have intense needs that will benefit from being thoughtfully addressed. As Francis Thompson reminds us:

> Grief is a matter of relativity . . . a gash is as painful to one as an amputation to another . . . Children's griefs may be little, but so is the child, so is its endurance, so is its field of vision, while its nervous impressionability is keener than ours.

As the Lord directs, the Holy Spirit may give us special authority to set people free from excessive grief and trauma. Nothing is better than to bring them into God's presence, provided that they are ready and willing, but this is not the time for assertive prayer or in-depth counselling. More often than not, we are there to help people prepare for the long haul, and to walk with them through what may well prove to be an exceedingly bleak and painful season.

With the best will in the world we are bound to put our foot in it from time to time, and to say (or do) things that hurt the person we are trying to help. I'm sure I must have often been too quick to say, "It must have been God's will," or "I know exactly how you are feeling!" At the right time, such words help people to feel loved and understood – but said at the wrong time or in the wrong way, there is a danger of it having the opposite effect. How can I claim to know how they are feeling if I haven't given them the chance to tell me?

It only takes a few such "foot in mouth" moments to make us wish that we had never got involved in the first place. Whatever has happened, do not let it hold you back from reaching out to those who are grief-stricken. Ask forgiveness for any insensitivity on your part – and pray to be more in tune next time round.

Reflect and Pray

If there is one phrase above all others I would single out as being helpful, it is this: "I'll be in touch shortly!" The reverse is also true of course. What can be worse than to say that you will come and visit, but then not make good on your promise? Is there anyone you "owe" a visit too?

> *Lord, I feel I have nothing to say –*
> *but I know how much a timely*
> *phone call, e-mail or letter means to me.*
> *Help me to overcome my reluctance*
> *and to reach out in Your strength.*
> *Thank you that You go ahead to prepare the way –*
> *and Your presence will accomplish the rest. Amen.*

Is this Grief contagious?

Courage is contagious. When a brave man takes a stand, the spines of others are often stiffened.   Billy Graham

Some of us worry deep down whether coming alongside people who are experiencing intense grief may not cause us to "catch" the grieving person's heaviness – or at least to feel end up feeling weighed down. Don't laugh, don't despise, and above all, don't be surprised. It is no idle myth that some husbands have been known to experience "sympathy" pangs when their wives are pregnant or in labour!

Neither is it unusual for a carer to start to take on the other person's peculiarities of speech or gestures, or even some of their physical symptoms. In the case of married couples we are, after all, one flesh. If we find ourselves experiencing *too* strong a degree of identification, we may need to be set free from the power of this physical or emotional transference, for if we leave such things unchecked, they may come to seriously affect our whole personality.

Transference represents the shift of emotions from one person or object to another. It is a common sign that we are beginning to relate to people not as they really are, but as if they were some other person altogether – or to take on their characteristics.

"Flesh gives birth to flesh, but the Spirit gives birth to spirit" (John 3:6). If we find ourselves adopting someone else's outlook on life uncritically, we may end up performing injudicious actions on their behalf. Such is the effect that both cults and dominant personalities can have on us. When we start looking to people to fulfil us in ways that in reality only God can do, we are asking too much of them, and may be heading into dangerous waters!

Reflect and Pray

Lord, set my soul and spirit free
from any transference that has drawn me
too closely into someone else's orbit.
Where I have pulled someone else into mine,
forgive me and release them.
In Jesus' name, Amen.

Weeping with those who weep

Others heard my groans,
but no one turned to comfort me.
Lamentations 1:22

The ultimate test of how much we care for someone is whether we can rejoice when they are rejoicing, and weep when they are weeping.[5] This is more profound than it may sound, for some of us really only come alive when others are weak, but feel redundant – resentful even – if they are doing well.

We cannot fail to be a blessing if we are prepared to weep when others are weeping – provided only that we are not doing this primarily in order to meet our own emotional needs. The last thing we should ever seek to do is to take advantage of their weakness to make us feel superior.

Those of us who are in ministry may need to take extra care in this regard. We may need to guard ourselves against getting so emotionally involved that it affects our judgement. Loving gestures, offered with no sexual intention, can likewise risk being misunderstood. As always, such relationships benefit from appropriate covering and accountability. It is wise to be especially careful when dealing with griefs that remind us of losses that we ourselves have experienced and which we may not have fully recovered from.

There is no shame or stigma in referring a person for more specialized help than we are able to provide. It is all part of the body of Christ functioning as it should. Someone else may have just the right mixture of skills and experience to reach them.

Unlike the volunteers who staff the Samaritans and other emergency help lines, I am fortunate in that I often get to hear the follow-up to people's stories, whereas they have the difficult and challenging task of drawing out people's hurts and woundings without discovering the outcome.[6]

Volunteers have an important part to play in providing emergency care, and are trained not to inspire false hopes. Phrases such as "I'm sure these tests will come back negative," or, "Your child is sure to come home soon," should never be used lightly.[7]

Wisdom often lies in mirroring back to the person the things that they have said, and leaving it to their own conscience, and the Holy Spirit, to do any work of convicting that is called for.

Because people often hold out against the Holy Spirit's prompting, however, knowing when to make more proactive suggestions can be a highly sensitive matter. Pray before speaking for them to be *willing* to face issues head-on.

When people respond with anger to your best efforts to reach out to them, pray for grace to know when to keep trying to come close, when to respect their need for distance, and when to encourage them to seek out the real reasons for their reactions. If people appear prickly, rejecting things that deep down we sense they would *want* to embrace, it is often because they are reacting to hurts which have lodged in the core of their being. For their long-term well-being it may well be wise to encourage them to seek appropriate help.

Reflect and Pray

Don't walk in front of me, I may not follow.
Don't walk behind, I may not lead.
Walk beside me, and just be my friend.
        Attributed to Albert Camus

Lord, guide and inspire each one of us
who find ourselves in any way "on the end of a line."
Direct the words we say the truths we impart
and the prayers we pray.
Accomplish much through every contact –
and use us to catch people in time.
        In Jesus' name, Amen.

Caring for the Carers

Then the Lord told him, "I have certainly seen the oppression of my people in Egypt. I have heard their cries of distress because of their harsh slave drivers. Yes, I am aware of their suffering. So I have come down to rescue them from the power of the Egyptians and lead them out of Egypt into their own fertile and spacious land. I have indeed seen."

        Exodus 3:7-8

The word "care" derives from an old Germanic word meaning "to grieve, experience sorrow, and to cry out with." Because people anticipate the grief-stricken being absorbed with their grief, they fear that this will leave them indifferent to anyone else's needs. Most of us are instinctively disinclined to embark on a "one-way" relationship, which is a major reason why so few are willing to spend time with people while they are in the intense throes of grief.

If the loss in question has had an impact on us, we will have our own grief to deal with too, in which case it may be doubly sacrificial to allow the primary mourner the space they need to pour out all their negative emotions. But is life not full of such sacrifices?

In the world of nature, the mother humpback whale goes eight long months without food in the warm tropical waters until it is ready to make the eight-week journey north to the feeding grounds while her calf draws a staggering one hundred pounds of milk a day from her.

Because the Lord set us apart for many years in the Body of Christ, Ros and I are used to receiving a high volume of requests for prayer from people who are going through extreme grief situations. We have been more than willing to do this – but we cannot deny that dealing with so many mega-intense issues takes its toll.

Since our emotional reservoir is far from bottomless, we, as friends and carers, must take care of our own mental and spiritual well-being. If we find ourselves becoming continually exhausted and irritable that someone is not recovering more quickly, it may be best to refer the grief-stricken person to someone else.

Caring deeply is one thing – but feeling indispensable is quite another. One particular snare to avoid is trying too hard to fulfil a primary role in someone's life, not least because we are likely to lose objectivity in the process. More often than not, the real reason for this lies in our need to earn approval and admiration. Since not even the best of us can be perfect friends or counsellors, John and Paula Sandford challenge us to give up trying to be, and to "resign from the post of General Manager of the Universe!"

If possible, take deliberate breaks from all forms of burden-bearing. We want to be around not just to help *this* person survive their emotional roller coaster ride, but to be there for many others in the future.

If we have been caring for someone long-term, we should not be in the least surprised if we feel guilty and insecure when our services are no longer required in that capacity. Only too clearly do we remember wishing to be free of the burden – but now that we are, it is completely understandable if we feel decidedly ambivalent about it.

Only the Lord can show us whether uttering strong sentiments against awkward colleagues or family members and lamenting our "lot" so loudly has played any real part in what has happened. Words certainly do have power, and we may quite possibly have some serious "house-keeping" to do at this point, both in terms of wiping the slate clean, and in resolving to be more careful in the future. Soul-searching that leads to genuine repentance is good, but it may only be a small step from there to berating ourselves with endless reproaches. May the Lord, who longs to be close to us, help us to fix our thoughts more on Him than on our many sins and shortcomings![8]

Reflect and Pray

Lord, in my pain and frustration
I said I wanted "this" to happen –
but now that it has,
I am not at all sure that it is what I really wanted.
Forgive me, Lord, my hasty words.
Set a guard over my mouth
and keep watch over the door of my lips,
so that my words more nearly reflect Your heart.
In Jesus' name, Amen.

God Honours Those who Honour Him

God honours those who set out in obedience to honour Him. Obedience, is the twin of faith, the language of love and the key to blessing.

Michael Ross-Watson

Finding our life's vocation requires overcoming the expectations we heap on ourselves – let alone those that other people demand of us. If David had listened to other people's ideas on the "Five Best Ways to fight Giants," and lumbered into action against Goliath the moment he donned Saul's suit of armour, he would not have lasted five minutes. It was only by consciously resisting the obvious way of doing things that he was free to use his God-given gifting.

Though there may well be kernels of truth in most of the comments and criticisms that come our way, which we do well to pay attention to, we dare not allow our life to be directed by other people's agendas. Just as many of the diagnoses people suggested concerning Rosalind's convulsions proved mercifully wide of the mark, there is nothing to be gained by trying to force ourselves to embrace perspectives that simply do not witness in our spirit. At the same time we must keep our hearts wide open for the Lord's genuine challenges and promptings.

Whilst ministering in Hong Kong recently, the Lord told Michael Ross-Watson to pay a visit to Jakarta. He had less than no idea what the reason for this journey might be, so he booked a ticket in obedience to stay for just one night. Whatever the Lord had in mind would have to happen rapidly! He still had no clear idea what he was meant to do when he landed in Indonesia, so he made his way to visit some old friends: a family of six sisters and their brother, who run a Christian bookshop.

When Michael reached the bookshop at three o'clock, there was nobody there. Learning that the brother, the patriarch of the family, had just died, Michael made his way to their house as fast as he could. "Is that really you, Michael?" the man's wife gasped. "We haven't seen you for years. Come and join the family for the evening – stay the night . . ." She ran into his arms and he spent time praying and ministering to the whole extended family – all seventy of them!

The family invited Michael to conduct the wake that evening, during which three people came to Christ. The following morning he was on his way again, having fulfilled what the Lord had sent him on this long journey to accomplish: to minister to precious saints who were grieving, and to bring others to faith. Just as Michael stepped out in faith and went the extra mile, may we be willing to do the same, if the Lord whispers His leading to us.

Reflect and Pray

Those of us who are used to "lending our strength" to others may also be the ones who are in most danger of suppressing our own needs. This is a plea to ministers and carers not to "neglect their own vineyards."[9]

> *Lord, it can be so difficult for us to say "no."*
> *We feel such a pressure to appear strong,*
> *and fail to attend to our own grief.*
> *Help us to do so, Lord,*
> *before exhaustion obliges us to.*
> *Just as we would feel no guilt*
> *about taking time off with a bout of 'flu,*
> *help us not to balk*
> *when it comes to working our own grief through.*
> *In Jesus' name, Amen.*

Returning to Society and moving on again

Were we not the first to speak of bringing back our king?
2 Samuel 19:43

After David's son had perished in his mutinous bid to wrest the throne from his father, David remained outside Jerusalem while intense discussions flew to and fro. "David has his flaws," many argued, "serious ones even. But think of all he did to rescue us from the hand of the Philistines. What are we hanging around for? Let's invite him back onto his throne!"

The process was far from straightforward, but David was finally restored to his throne in Jerusalem. On both occasions when David found himself on the run in the wilderness, he was strengthened by the presence of faithful friends.

From a carer's point of view, it is important to be aware of what support the grieving have, and to tailor our response accordingly. Are they, for example, from a tightly knit family who find it difficult to receive outside help? Or are its members so geographically spread out that they are, to all intents and purposes, simply not there for each other?

By and large, many employers still expect the bereaved to take a few days compassionate leave and then return to their place of work. Some people find the stimulation of company the best way to avoid too much self-absorption, whereas others are far from ready to re-emerge into a world whose parameters, so far as they are concerned, have changed forever.

Pressuring themselves to return too soon would be like trying to do fifty press-ups a day after a heart transplant. If they push themselves to do more than they are ready for, they compromise the healing process.

We have much to learn here from other cultures and religions. The classic Jewish model for expressing grief during times of bereavement, for example, encourages mourners to take more time than most westerners normally permit themselves for embarking on the road to recovery.

According to the Shiva,[10] three days are set to be aside for expressing intense grief, followed by four days for condolence calls. The visitor's aim is less to talk than to listen, and to attend to practical matters around the house. There then come thirty days of adjustment (Shaloshim) during which mourners gradually begin to pick up the threads of their lives again. Finally comes the Jahrzeit (the one year anniversary), which is often commemorated in the synagogue.

After this the mourner is expected to be incorporated back into the community, although yearly memorial prayers may continue indefinitely. This pattern makes it more likely that a mourner will reintegrate successfully than in our secular and highly fragmented society. A counsellor for Victim Support warns that,

> *The grieving process takes at least two years. The first year is all about the person saying, "This time last year we were . . ." whilst the second year marks the start of their recovery. There are likely to be peaks and troughs well beyond that; days when they imagine themselves to be completely "over it," and others that leave them feeling all but completely overwhelmed.*

Our all-giving Lord does not want anyone to be endlessly trapped within the narrow confines of their loss, or to linger too long in one stage of the recovery process. All bereaved people need special grace around Christmas, anniversaries and birthdays. These are times when people are inclined to tiptoe around, reluctant even to mention the person's name, in case it makes them upset. In reality, including them in the conversation usually helps them to mitigate the sense of feeling excluded.

Some find it helpful to draw a timeline chart, noting the dates of major incidents and displaying the highs and lows of their path through grief. Linking patterns of feelings and behaviour to specific events in this way helps them to be aware of the dates and times when they are likely to be particularly vulnerable. This is a sideways testimony to the power of the subconscious, that even when people are not consciously aware of these occasions themselves, their subconscious is.

In *A Severe Mercy,* Van experienced enormous pain every time he remembered shared objects or seasonal activity following the death of his young wife. He came to realise that when he found himself suddenly overwhelmed by tears (wet or dry), it was often a sign that he needed to process some past loss. Brutally ambushed the first time this occurred, the sting gradually lessened – but it is as well to be prepared.

Common sense indicates that anniversaries are not the best time for those whose grief is still raw to take on everyone else's griefs and burdens. However much other people may be in the habit of looking to them for emotional support, there is no shame in holding back somewhat.

Neither are these the times to blank out all feelings and memories, whether happy ones, or the inevitable thoughts of "what might have been." These too need expressing, for they may be quite different from the recriminatory "but what ifs" that do need guarding against. The time will come when they are ready to move beyond them, and to make the conscious decision to love again. At that point, they may well find themselves willing and wanting to "maximize" their loss by contributing to the care and well being of others.[11] As Abraham Lincoln declared,

> *Die when I may, I want it said of me that I plucked a weed and planted a flower wherever I thought a flower would grow.*

Reflect and Pray

But if You turn away from them, they panic.
When You take away their breath,
they die and turn again to dust.
Then You send Your Spirit and new life is created,
and You renew the face of the earth.
Psalm 105:29-30

Lord, it would be profoundly wrong for me
to wish and while these days away,
because You are turning this season of trouble
into a doorway for hope.
Since You make each moment interconnect with another,
help me to "harness" my grief and move on;
for each day is precious to You
and brings its own possibilities
to meet, to seek, to praise,
and to let faith triumph again
In Jesus Name, Amen.

References

1 Luke 21:14-15

2 See my article "What do you say when people ask you how you are?" www.ruachministries.org/valeoftears/refs.htm

3 Green, M. *How can I lead a friend to Christ?* Hodder and Stoughton 1995 p. 114

4 Leonard and Hilary Zunin provide us with templates to help us write to people who have experienced particular forms of loss. Zunin, L. and H. *The Art of Condolence.* (Harper Collins). The Zunin's also include a list of remarks to avoid – comments such as, "Be thankful that you have another child." "You must be so relieved really," and "Get on with your life!"

5 Romans 12:15

6 For an introduction to reflective listening, see the weblinks at www.ruachministries.org/valeoftears/refs.htm

7 Much of the work that volunteers do involves passing people on to others. It is sometimes a kindness not to hand out the referral information too quickly, as this can leave the person feeling as though they were not important enough to merit spending time with individually.

8 Richard Foster has written some excellent material on self examination in *Prayer.* (Harper Collins). You can also find helpful pointers in my article on avoiding hypocrisy, www.ruachministries.org/teaching/hypocrisy.htm

9 Song of Solomon 1:6

10 Shiva is the name for Judaism's week long period of grief and mourning for close relatives.

11 As I was putting the finishing touches to this book I came across a book called *A Grace Disguised* (2004) by Jerry Sittser, which testifies powerfully to the turbulent emotions experienced by a bereaved person as he dares to step out again. Zondervan.

Part Eight

If Grief takes convoluted Paths

THUS FAR WE HAVE CONSIDERED STRATEGIES that will help us progress through the grief tunnel. It sometimes happens, however, that nothing seems to be making any difference. We feel as stuck in our grief as ever – rather like Winnie the Pooh finding himself unable to squeeze through the door of Rabbit's warren. But how can we tell if the grief process really has become "stuck," or whether we are just making slower progress than we expected to?

Like warning lights on a car dashboard, the continued raging of unrelieved symptoms is perhaps the clearest pointer. In this section we shall explore some of the more serious paths that unresolved grief can take. Don't be afraid of the white-knuckle ride: it is much better to face these things and then find release from them!

Resisting Anxiety

> *Anxiety is the natural result when our thoughts are centred on anything short of God.*
>
> *Billy Graham*

Jesus often used the phrase *do not worry* because He knew how easy it would be for us to allow waves of anxiety to wash over us when serious losses come our way. We saw earlier how important it is to pray ourselves free from the deadweight of trauma in the aftermath of every major grief episode. We have also hinted, however, that as surely as ju-jitsu fighters use the force of their opponent's charge to throw them off balance, we must find ways to harness these strong emotions.

Often, it is the pressure that jolts us into seeking the Lord more earnestly. If we feel reluctant to embrace so decisive a break, it is worth reflecting that nothing may change until certain issues are faced head-on. Think how unwise it would be not to go to the dentist if toothache is raging![1]

Reflect and Pray

Though I am surrounded by troubles,
You will protect me from my enemies . . .
The Lord will work out His plan for my life,
For Your faithful love, O Lord, endures for ever.
                                        Psalm 138:7-8

For those who feel caught between a past they are unable to escape, and a future they are unable to face, there can be great power in affirming the truths the Psalmist is declaring here. Let the Spirit minister to specific areas you are struggling with.

Father, I give You the tensions that tussle in my soul.
and the fears that are knocking at my door.
Let anxiety not turn my heart to stone,
but rather let me catch these fears,
and turn them into prayer.
In the name of the One who puts fear to flight,
Amen.

Resisting Pain-prone Reactions

Sorrow is a fruit. God does not make it grow on limbs too weak to bear it.
                                        Victor Hugo

Whilst we have all watched people bearing hardship bravely, I am, for obvious reasons, more concerned here to help people who are faring less well. Dr Cecily Saunders once asked a patient in great pain what it was he was looking for from those who were caring for him. "For someone to look as if they are trying to understand me!" he replied.[2]

Not all of us are blessed with healthy genes and strong constitutions, and many of us find it difficult to adjust to new realities when our body begins to weaken and fail. Some project their frustration outwards at this point, and put the blame for their misfortunes on someone or something else: the treatment they are receiving, the ineptness of their doctor, or any one of a thousand other scapegoats. If those who are standing alongside are not alert to this ploy, they risk missing the real point, which may actually lie in the difficulty they are having in coming to terms with their mortality.

Those who are excessively goal-oriented, or who are suffering from mental or chronic illness, often have great difficulty trusting that there is a way forward in the face of the pain and disorganisation that loss brings in its wake. Longing to be in control of their circumstances, they may resort to using their pain as a deflection mechanism, and to make others feel guilty that they are not doing enough to help them. It is important to realise that all such manipulative behaviour backfires sooner or later.

When people start to use their pain in such ways, even comparatively minor ailments quickly assume major proportions. This is hardly surprising, since most forms of psychological pain revolve around feelings of guilt. Again, those who are trying to come alongside people caught in this cycle will miss the real point if they direct their efforts only towards their superficial complaints.[3]

Our litigation-conscious generation is becoming far too used to looking for someone to blame for any distress or difficulty that we go through. We will do better if we consciously choose to "bless and forgive" rather than proceed down this road.

Many newly-bereaved people likewise "blame" their partners for abandoning them. Deep down they wonder why they deserve to be treated like this. Superficially it may look as though such people are full of bitterness; it might be nearer the truth, however, to realise that they are simply "deflecting" something they are finding too painful to deal with.[4]

At the same time the Lord wants to remove the underlying humiliation we may be carrying around, either as the result of our own inadequacies, or from being unable to do anything about someone else's. May the Lord lift any guilt we have allowed to settle on us, for shame and guilt risk shrinking our zeal and limiting our freedom. This is not quite as straightforward as it may sound, for some of us are more prone than others to hold on to these things. Let me explain.

Those of us who have "pain-prone personalities" often suffer from deep-seated feelings of worthlessness, which fuel the sense of shame and humiliation that I have alluded to. Strangely, we often enjoy *better* health when we find ourselves up against particularly difficult circumstances. The reason for this is that we feel we are reaping what we deserve, and set ourselves to cope accordingly with whatever comes our way.

Deep down, we view punishment and pain as the proper outcome for our chronically ingrained guilt. By contrast, when things are going better outwardly for us (or for others) we may find ourselves less able to rejoice than we should be. That is because other people's success can make us feel no longer needed. The risk then is that people will tire of sharing "cheerful" things with us, because experience has shown that we are unable to enter into their joy.

Who is most likely to use pain in such ways as a form of comfort? It is surely those who have not been shown unconditional love, or who have been the victims of some kind of abuse. What are the tell-tale signs that it may be present in our lives? Not only inner anxiety but something as simple as the tendency to say, "Yes *but*" . . . every time someone proposes a path that would lead to a promising outcome. Because we consider ourselves unworthy of success, something deep inside baulks whenever we get within sight of achieving some worthwhile goal. Alternatively, we develop some untimely ailment, which causes us to miss out altogether.

If this pattern of using pain and grief rings bells in your experience, the following prayer is just for you. Ask the Lord to continue His work of sanctification in your soul – and refuse to let your pain-prone personality come up with human substitutes.

Reflect and Pray

Lord and Straightener of the heart,
I give You my many complexities.
Keep me from using pain as a substitute
for the authentic work of Your Spirit.
Free me from all distorted perspectives
that would knock my trust, or put others down.
Realign my heart with Yours
so that the fullness of Your love flows freely through me –
joy without measure
and comfort without manipulation,
In Jesus' name, Amen.

Resisting Grief going Underground

Let flimsy storm-tossed saplings become sturdy oaks!

Even though we cannot expect the recovery process to proceed at an even pace, there is no reason why the Lord cannot achieve a more or less complete work of healing in us. The crucial thing is to attend to any issues that look like becoming "sticking points" – for griefs that we avoid are sure to catch up with us. As this far from untypical story shows, they may even turn "pathological".

> A friend who lost her husband many years ago when her children were young never got over the loss. She constantly talked about him as though he were still there, or just away on a holiday. In every sense, she put her life on hold. Many years later, this woman had a conflict in her workplace, and was unable to cope and had a complete breakdown. It took several weeks of counselling before she was able to address the grief and lay her husband's memory to rest.

In *Great Expectations,* Dickens paints what must surely be the supreme example of someone who refuses to embrace the reality of her loss. From the moment she is spurned in marriage, Miss Havisham allows every part of her life to go into cold storage. The clock hands remained pointing to the minute the wedding was cancelled, symbolising the unhealed grief that locks her into the past. The only emotion she now permits herself is a consuming desire to use her beautiful ward, Estella, as an instrument for exacting revenge on the male species.

If we can risk a broad generalisation, "dry-eyed people" like Miss Havisham are more likely to suffer acute reactions than those who are willing to face their griefs as and when they come their way. Those who are unwilling to do so are highly likely to experience some sort of a "rerun" of these grief events – and quite possibly in a more serious form. As Jennifer Rees Larcombe warns:

> Some people seem to make their tragedy a way of life; it gains the attention, love and help of other people. If their problems were solved they would lose all that. Others stay miserable because they want the person who caused it all to feel sorry. This casts us in the role of victim or martyr – and if we do that too often we risk becoming permanently typecast.[5]

If we are tempted to indulge in what Jennifer calls the POM's and the POD's (the "Poor Old Me's" and the "Put Others Down" syndome), bear in mind the self-hatred that so often rides in on the back of rejection. If we learnt as children that people come running to meet our needs every time we fall over, we are quite capable of continuing this pattern in later life, albeit in rather more sophisticated ways, subtly exploiting our whims and moods to control our environment.

Overcoming loneliness and finding peace of mind means winning many a battle against self pity. If we spot ourselves resorting to "silent treatment," or some other form of emotional manipulation, be doubly careful: such things have no place in the Kingdom of God.

It is especially hard for people to face their grief when they feel obliged to disguise it for much of their life. Ministers, for example, are often concerned to give the appearance of coping at all times, not only for the sake of those they minister to, but also, perhaps, to "prove" that their faith is working.

I am thinking here particularly of the grief that people carry when they are involved in a secret or illicit relationship. Such people's need for pastoral care is often still greater than for those afflicted by the pangs of more "socially acceptable" grief – but it takes more courage for would-be helpers to offer their friendship and support.

The more ambivalent a person's position, the more likely it is that their grief will dip underground. This in turn makes them inclined to go a long way out of their way to avoid meeting certain people. No wonder James says, *Confess your sins to one another* (James 5:16): the Lord wants to spare His people the strain of living a double life! As our friends Paul and Gretel Haglin urge: "Have the courage to go in and rescue those whom Satan has taken captive."

Reflect and Pray

Have you noticed yourself holding back from mentioning certain people or episodes? Are you merely being wise – or actually suppressing grief? The risk is that you will build such sturdy walls to protect yourself (and your reputation) that you end up keeping other people – and even the Lord Himself – at a "safe" distance.

> *Lord, when You and I are both ready,*
> *bring my griefs to the surface,*
> *so that I can face them properly –*
> *for when I start pulling others down,*
> *I risk turning my back*
> *on all the good things You are doing in their lives.*
> *When I seek sympathy inappropriately,*
> *I risk choking everyone's joy.*
> *Where shame is gnawing at my soul*
> *let Your love light burn it away,*
> *for there is no shame in loving You;*
> *only the joy of finding Your arms open wide.*

Resisting the Stoic Approach

*You do surely bar the door upon your own liberty, if you
deny your griefs to your friend.*
                          Shakespeare: Hamlet III, ii, 352

Those brought up in the school of the stiff upper lip find it
hard to realise just how much they need at least one person in
whom they can truly confide for the sake of their emotional
well-being. If their very *vocabulary* for expressing grief and
loss is under-developed, there is still time to learn it!

Many years ago I spent a week with a man, whose son,
shortly after graduating as a policeman, had taken his own
life. Had he experienced intimidation in that particular Police
Force? Or too many pressures on the job? I will never know,
because his father, unable to come to terms with what had
happened, quite simply "petrified."

Night after night he would sit in front of the television
screen, immured in pain, permitting nobody to mention the
subject. On the face of it, the man's attitude appeared stoical.
In reality, it represented a complete refusal to face the reality
of a loss that had left him emotionally unable to receive either
human or divine comfort. It is the worst example I have ever
witnessed of the grief process becoming stuck fast.

Do you perhaps fear, subconsciously, that if you were to
allow yourselves to slow down, you would experience all
over again the original shock and trauma? Is it in order to
protect yourselves against this anticipated onslaught that you
keep your diary packed, and your grief, for the most part,
unattended to?

Or do you feel excessively elated much of the time, even if
others sense that something about your euphoria does not ring
true? More perhaps than you realize, you are in danger of
sinking into a severe "downer".

Unaware of how vulnerable you are, you rush into new
ventures, or exotic vacations. Because you take unreal expectations and unresolved emotions with you, however, the
consequences are unpredictable. Refreshing and restoring as
holidays so often are, there is no guarantee that they will

bring you any magic change of fortune, let alone of disposition.

I understand entirely why some feel it wiser to change their holiday patterns altogether in the aftermath of a bereavement in order to avoid being overwhelmed by past memories. It is important to create new memories, but, unless the Lord intervenes and removes our grief at one fell swoop, most of us will experience the truth Marcel Proust discovered when he observed, "We are healed of our suffering only by experiencing it to the full."

Sedatives and other medications may have a role to play in helping us to obtain sufficient sleep, and to keep depressive thoughts under control. At the same time, it is important to bear in mind that the overuse of any substance to numb feelings can perpetuate dependency and prolong the grief process. Subconsciously it can cause us to dread the emotional devastation we imagine we would be left to face without the "chemical safety net."

No wonder than that some of us adopt a stoical refuge and bury ourselves in our work, or in hobbies that involve accumulating vast amounts of information, or spending much time and money on technologies or possessions, but with no specific end or outlet in mind.

Although this assuages the soul in the short term, it is right to check such matters carefully with the Lord to make sure they are in line with His purposes – especially if they do nothing to help others or to advance His kingdom.

Many of us feel the pull to return to places where we have experienced some particular grief or pain. Excessive looking back makes grief hard to bear, but such visits can serve a useful purpose, especially if they are combined with some specific act of separation – writing a note and leaving it there, for example, or pouring out our hurt until grief turns to confidence that He has heard our cry and is "on our case."

Once again, it is as well to be aware that there may be many layers of guilt and trauma wrapped up in our grief. I heard one day of a man who visited the cemetery every week for five long years to visit the grave of a young child who, as I later found out, he had never enjoyed a good relationship with.

"The grief is one thing," he ruefully admitted, "but the guilt makes it ten times worse." It makes me wonder if perhaps the man I referred to earlier had unresolved issues with his own son that could never now be put right. How the Lord longs to set us free from labouring under such a burden. He sends His Spirit to free our spirits, and to break every yoke.

When grief inclines us to adopt stoic attitudes, we must take care not to become "resisters to change." As surely as it is appropriate for sailors to drop anchor in a storm,[6] there are times when we must resist our desire to preserve the status quo lest we put the brakes on all new ideas.

Unless what is being proposed is fundamentally wrong (as opposed to merely threatening) there is every chance that we will be delighted with the outcome of these changes – not least because what appears new and untested now many in time become part of the "comfort" fabric of our lives.

May the Lord likewise help us to respond with kindness when we find ourselves opposed by resistors, so that He may have the chance to bring about His very best.

Reflect and Pray

Lord, wherever stoicism has inclined me to denial
or false bravado,
enlarge my heart
to receive Your perspective.
I resolve here and now
to be open to all You have for me –
as individuals, families, fellowships and organisations.
In Jesus name, Amen.

Resisting the Impulse to flee

If a ruler's anger rises against you, do not leave your post.
Calmness can lay great errors to rest.

Ecclesiastes 10:4

Why have I begun so many of the titles in this section with the word "Resisting?" Because grief, like fear, distracts and weakens us, and makes us want to run away from our calling.

To take a common example, it often happens when an elderly spouse dies that the surviving member "flees" by selling their house and moving in with family members. Unsurprisingly, many cannot bear the thought of living with so many memories.

For others, however, the additional loss of their house, coming so hard on the heels of losing their partner, would merely add to their sense of no longer belonging anywhere. Paradoxically, the fact that they may be feeling buoyed up by the divine anaesthetic may incline them to plunge too hastily into something new.

Given that the newly bereaved are usually too distracted to make the wisest decisions, we must not only discern the best course of action, but also the *timescale* in which that best is to be achieved.

There is value in sleeping on major decisions – quite possibly for a considerable period of time. Impulsive and over eager people in particular may need reminding of the value of considering matters from a variety of perspectives before leaping to commit themselves.

Reflect and Pray

Lord, one step at a time Your wisdom comes.
We welcome it today and every day.
Just as You protected Mary and Joseph
when they were forced to flee,
so we ask You to do the same for us
when we face major issues at vulnerable times.
May the loss we have experienced
cause us neither to act in haste,
nor to lag behind Your schedule.
In Jesus' name, Amen.

Resisting making Contact with the Dead

You are in error because you do not know Scriptures or the power of God.   *Matthew 22:29*

Jesus knew exactly where He came from and where He was heading – but how do you think His disciples must have felt when He announced, *It is to your advantage that I am going away (John 16:7)?* They must have felt tempted to "know better" and to retort: "How can it possibly be better for You not to be here?"

Those who have experienced the sweetness of the Lord's presence stealing upon them might feel best qualified to answer that question, for these special times when the Lord's presence is close remind us more vividly than words alone could ever do of the nearness of His love for us. They, above all, are in a position to make sense of Dietrich Bonhoeffer's comment whilst in prison that, "Death is the supreme festival on the road to freedom."

Sometimes the most profound experiences happen in surprisingly matter of fact ways. At a time when he felt completely stuck in his work of preparing his translation of the New Testament, and utterly depressed in his life and faith, J. B. Phillips records how the recently deceased C. S. Lewis suddenly stood before him, having entered his bedroom through closed doors. In this vision experience, Lewis spoke just one short sentence to Phillips: "J. B., it's not as hard as you think!" This "appearance" was precisely what was needed to draw Phillips out of his depression, and to set him free again to continue his life's work.

Many of you will have your own stories of the "powers of the age to come" breaking through to bring you help and reassurance. Such experiences owe nothing to "spiritualism," but everything to the Lord deliberately withdrawing the veil somewhat between Heaven and Earth. Why does He do this? Usually to bring direction, or to reassure us that a loved one is safely with Him. Sometimes it is to help us let go of them.

A friend who was struggling greatly in the aftermath of losing her mother lamented that she had not felt the presence of her mother for some time. Without telling her husband what she was doing, she prayed that the Lord would show him that her mother really was with the Lord. That night, he had a powerful dream, in which he saw his wife's mother with the Lord, specifically giving her blessing to them as a couple in a way that she had never managed to do on Earth.

Shortly after her husband died, Catherine Marshall went into the hospital room where his body lay and suddenly realised:

> I was not alone. For a while there was a transcendent glory. Although I did not understand it then and can't explain it now, I knew that Peter was near me. And beside him, another presence, the Lord he had served through long years stretching back to boyhood experiences on the moors of Scotland.[7]

In time this experience faded, and Catherine Marshall was left longing for further reassurance that Peter really was still "alive." What the Lord said to her then will be of help to us now.

> Once again you have been trying to put feeling before faith. Because you haven't been able to feel Peter's presence, you have assumed that he is lost to you forever. Simply have faith that he is with you whenever you need him. Assume it – and the feeling and the proof will come later. Accept this on faith.[8]

Given that not all of us may be privileged to receive such "audible" confirmation, we do well to bear Jesus' words in mind.

> *Because you have seen Me, you have believed; blessed are those who have not seen and yet have believed.*
>
> *John 20:29*

Experiences such as these remind us that the dead in Christ are by no means gone forever. Who knows what role they may still be playing on our behalf? We may one day discover to our delight that our loved ones continue to be involved in our pilgrimage, but now from the infinitely richer vantage point of sharing God's presence and perspective.

Understanding nothing of this interaction between Heaven and Earth, the Sadducees tried to catch Jesus out, but He cut right through their chicanery:

> *Marriage is for people here on Earth. But that is not how it will be in the age to come. For those worthy of being raised from the dead won't be married then. And they will never die again. In these respects, they are like the angels. They are children of God raised up to new life. But now, as to whether the dead will be raised – even Moses proved this when He wrote about the burning bush. Long after Abraham, Isaac and Jacob had died He referred to the Lord as the 'God of Abraham, the God of Isaac and the God of Jacob.' So He is the God of the living, not the dead. They are all alive to Him.*
>
> Luke 20:34-38

Jesus was pointing here to the wonderful continuity that exists between those of us who are part of His Church on Earth, and those who have died in Christ. Clothed now in their spiritual bodies, we can be very sure that they are able to think and praise on a much higher level than ever they could on Earth. What joy there will be when our time comes to meet with them in glory!

Contrary to certain popular superstitions, Scripture does not say that we will *become* angels – it tells us that we will be *like* the angels.[9] Since this is to be our destiny, let's get into training. What to angels do? They stand before the throne of God in worship, and are sent out from there on specific missions. Are we not called to do the same – first to draw close to the Lord, and then to go out to do His work, full of a Heavenly love that is free from all trace of lust and selfish exclusivity?

We are to steer well clear, however, of the many deceivers who are waiting in the wings to exploit our yearning to contact loved ones who have passed beyond. Although God in His mercy may occasionally grant some comforting sense of a loved one's presence, we dare not make this a general expectation, let alone go looking for opportunities to make contact with them after they have died.

The Scriptures categorically forbid all types of divination – whether by palmistry, pendulums, horoscopes or the like. We are specifically instructed not to get in contact with the dead through mediums. The Hebrew word for spiritist is a "knowing one," but much of the information that fortune-tellers provide is completely false, and comes from so deceptive a source that no wise person should have anything to do with it.

The spirit powers that are at work through mediums are perfectly prepared to trade platitudes about the afterlife, and even to accord insights into future events and physical healings – but if this permits an entry point into someone's heart it is by no means the good deal it may at first appear.

Given how wonderful Heaven is, it was perhaps inevitable that the enemy would find suitable propagandists to publish so-called tales from beyond the grave in order to lull people into believing that the afterlife is certain to be sweet.

Interviewing people who had clinically died, but subsequently returned to life, Dr. Richard Kent found a strikingly similar pattern. Each person described how significant moments of their life passed before their eyes – but in the clearer light of eternity, most of these were *not* the events that had appeared the most important at the time on Earth. The real issue is whether they had loved God and the people God had placed around them.

Dr Kent's findings are a powerful incentive not to leave getting right with God to our deathbed.[10] In stark contrast to the so-called wisdom of the therapy TV chat shows, Jesus does not give a blanket reassurance that everyone will automatically fare well in the next world. Rather, as a matter of urgency He warns us to fear and honour God.[11] The Scriptural teaching is clear: *It is appointed for men to die once and then to face judgement* (Hebrews 9:27).

I shared in "Angelic Assistance" how the Lord delights to send ministering spirits to our aid. He wants us to be aware of the ministry of angels, and confident of their ability to help. At the same time, we must be wise, for there are many deceiving spirits around. New Age and neo-pagan publications are full of stories of encounters with angels, and highly dubious out-of-body testimonies.

If you have had any involvement in such things, you will know a far greater freedom in your spirit if you repent of all such things in the name of Jesus, and ask people experienced in these matters to pray you free.

Reflect and Pray

Someone may say to you, "Let's ask the mediums and those who consult the spirits of the dead. With their whisperings and mutterings, they will tell us what to do." But shouldn't people ask God for guidance? Should the living seek guidance from the dead? Look to God's instructions and teachings! People who contradict His word are completely in the dark.

Isaiah 8:19-20

Lord Jesus, You said that You were going
to go and prepare a place for us,
so that we could be where You are.
Help us not to try to pierce the veil
in ways You cannot own.
Keep us from falling prey
to the temptation to consult occult powers.
Our past is safe in Your hands,
the future is Your concern,
and You will show us what we need to know
as and when we need to know it.
May we experience more and more of
Your leading from day to day.
In Jesus' Name, Amen.

Resisting the Temptation to Suicide

My particular grief is of so flood-gate and o'erbearing
nature, that it engluts and swallows other sorrows.
                    Brabantio, in William Shakespeare's Othello

A striking feature in the autobiographies of many fine
Christian ministers is how they have been through times
when they have felt so far down that they have wondered if
they will ever come up again as they wrestle with the devil,
who has been a murderer from the beginning.[12]

Amongst all the many strong grief surges, the temptation
to take one's own life is particularly insidious when it strikes
unexpectedly, often just when we think we are on the point of
recovering.

It may also coincide with the initial numbness beginning to
lift. Deprived of that special protection, feelings of anger,
guilt, futility and uselessness hurl themselves at us like storm
waves, threatening to overwhelm our vulnerable defences.
Like Job, we may find ourselves protesting at the intensity of
the struggle:

Why is light given to those in misery, and life to the bitter
of soul, to those who long for death that does not come?
Why is life given to a man whose way is hidden, whom God
has hedged in?

                                        Job 3:20-23

If someone or something we greatly cherish is taken from us,
we may feel little desire to outlive the loss. Likewise, if our
self-esteem is at a low ebb, we may no longer regard ourselves as a "proper" or "acceptable" person. We may even
feel as though we do not deserve to go on living at all.

Since the end cannot justify the means, it can never be right
to do something that is itself fundamentally wrong and take
our own life. The forces of darkness may whisper that we are
only doing so in order to bring about some supposedly greater
good – that we will get to Heaven quicker, and set the world
free of the burden of having us around. But these are the
words of a murderer, not a friend.

How can we be the judge of where we are up to in God's plan for us? Taking our own life would merely remove us at one fell swoop from being able to fulfil God's many purposes for us. More than ever we need to raise the shield of faith, and pay less heed to our emotions. Although the grief process may feel agonisingly long drawn out, it sometimes only takes some relatively small acts of kindness or encouragement to lift our spirits from the depths of despair.

As to the entirely understandable temptation many of us experience when extreme pain sets in, we can do no better than to repeat what the Archbishop of Canterbury recently declared:

None of us has the liberty to determine the day of our death. Almost all forms of legislation for assisted dying open the door to unjust and destructive pressures on people.[13]

The suicide rate is high amongst troubled teenagers and dejected young men, just as it is amongst those who are going through the pressures of a mid-life crisis, and over-wrought eighty-year-olds. In the aftermath of an elderly person taking their own life, loved ones often put around the story that they died of natural causes. By relating this often enough, they may all but come to believe their own version of events. In the long run, telling one story in public whilst knowing that the reality lies elsewhere invariably complicates the grief process.

It is not so easy to fool the subconscious, let alone discerning onlookers. Our dream life often picks up on what is going on in our inmost being. Since this is the most discreet way the Lord has of showing us where we are really up to, it can be helpful to keep a dream log, and to note any recurring patterns. The Lord may be using them to highlight matters we should be attending to.

Some people's attempts to take their own life are driven by the desire to punish others for their supposed lack of love and attention. From their perspective, the prospect of people being remorseful at their death feels almost like an achievement.

If people are unselfish enough to recognise how much their suicide would devastate friends and family, they might be far less inclined to do anything irreversible. It is worth being aware, however, that people who have given up on life are much more likely to succeed in their attempt to commit suicide than those who are merely angry.

When it comes to approaching people who may be at risk, there is no evidence to suggest that asking an overwhelmed person whether they are contemplating doing anything drastic actually inclines them to fatal action. The reverse is usually the case. The chances are that they will be grateful for the opportunity to discuss it – and quite possibly be willing to be talked down from the proverbial "ledge."

Just as meteorologists broadcast storm warnings ahead of time, so those who suspect they may be "at risk" are wise if they prepare strategies to help them during those times when compulsive feelings return in force.

- Know who and what to keep away from.
- Make a list of people to contact
- Have specific Bible verses to hand such as I have displayed in Appendix 4. Use them as a vital part of your rescue pack.
- Use the "Jesus prayer:" *Lord Jesus Christ, have mercy on me.*

People who are prone to "hearing voices" must be still more careful not to yield to compulsive commands to self-destruct. Even when we feel at our most overwhelmed, we are still accountable for our actions. The powers of darkness may be the ultimate authors and whisperers of these dangerous delusions that push people over the edge, but they make full use of any previous involvement we have had with occult practices, as well as generational sins and weaknesses.

Other people's dismissive attitudes and unhelpful words may also have affected our spirits far more deeply than we realised at the time. The freedom that comes when these things are lifted through prayer is enormous.

For our spiritual well being it is essential that we check what we think we have heard with others – and to examine our spiritual track record carefully. We may come to realise that we genuinely do hear from the Lord in certain areas of our life, but are regularly (spectacularly even!) wide of the mark when it comes to certain personal or emotional issues.

Even if we are feeling intense shame as a result of mistakes we have made, and the losses we have sustained, nothing will be solved by committing the western equivalent of hara-kiri. There is no better way to survive this often prolonged phase than to resist whatever it is that our plaguing thoughts are telling us – and even to dare to affirm the opposite. So long as we are still around, God can send His renewing power at any moment, and turn even apparently hopeless situations around for good. By His mercy, He will often do so much sooner than expected.

Reflect and Pray

God knew exactly what He was taking on when He called you to His service. When you hurt, He hurts, too, and He is concerned to get you back on our feet again. *In all your distress, He too is distressed* (Isaiah 63:9). When dark powers hurl themselves at you, and whisper self-destructive thoughts, give God time to work.

Turn this phrase into a banner and unfurl it when particularly strong temptations are assailing you: "Give God time!" By refusing to destroy yourself, and all that God has invested in you, you are not only resisting the worst the devil can throw against you, but are giving the Lord the opportunity to bring about something entirely fresh and beautiful. He will. You'll see. The best is yet to come!

Resisting the Desire to take Revenge

Everyone says forgiveness is a lovely idea, until they have something to forgive, as we had during the war. And then, to mention the subject at all is to be greeted with howls of anger. It is not that people think this too high and difficult

a virtue: it is that they think it hateful and contemptible.
"That sort of talk makes me sick," they say. And half of you
already want to ask me, "I wonder how you'd feel about
forgiving the Gestapo if you were a Pole or a Jew?"

C.S. Lewis

For long hours Jesus hung on the Cross, the agony of the nails adding to the excruciating pain from the stripes on His back. As the sun beat down on on His exposed head, thirst and hunger combined to take their toll on His body until He finally weakened and died.

At one level, we know that what happened on the Cross was the foreordained means by which God intended to save the world. At another level, it came about because one jaded disciple succumbed to greed and betrayed his master. We may be inclined to dismiss the thirty pieces of silver Judas received as if they were of no account, but the amount represented several months wages for a skilled worker: six or seven thousand pounds perhaps in today's terms. Is there any limit to the depths people are prepared to stoop to for love of money?

The distance between trusted friend and turncoat betrayer is not always as great as one would like to imagine. Many years ago, a godly man, who has long served as one of my mentors suddenly declared, "You're going to be betrayed one day!" Several years later this did indeed occur – and the pain was overwhelming. Shortly after it happened, I had an intense vision of the scene in the Garden of Gethsemane. I could *feel* the grief involved as Judas did what he did to betray his master. It ushered in the most painful episode in my life: one that took several years to even begin to recover from.

These things are rarely as clear cut as they were in Jesus' case. Most of us have our own part in the proceedings to repent of when relationships break down. I know that I did in this instance. Forgiveness has an important role to play then in ensuring that such experiences do not disempower us entirely. Be warned, however: this is not always an easy or a once-off event. It is easy to *assume* that we have forgiven someone who has hurt us deeply, but we may only discover whether this really is the case if the person continues to cause us problems . Or if they fall into trouble and we find that there is nothing in us that rejoices over their plight.

Once again, David is an excellent model for us to follow. Saul had caused him the most acute distress imaginable, yet the lament he composed for him is exquisitely generous.[14] Is our heart equally generous towards those who have made life hard for us?

This is not to underestimate the effects such betrayal can have on us. If you have ever been seriously "targetted" and abused, You will know how much it can damage your self-esteem and confidence – not to mention playing havoc with your trust in the stability of life.

It is by no means always obvious how we should respond to such things. Sometimes it may be perfectly legitimate to have recourse to normal legal or pastoral procedures, but whenever we find ourselves longing for vindication, it is usually wisest to leave such matters firmly in the Lord's hands. He alone knows the full reason why people behave as they do.

In terms of reaching out to those from whom we are estranged, Scripture urges us to make haste and be reconciled as quickly as possible.[15] Sometimes, however, there may be wisdom in staying away from someone while they are still in the first flush of their anger, lest we come under the influence of that spirit ourselves.

Venting our feelings directly with the person who has hurt us can actually make relationships worse, especially if the other person takes our outburst badly, or is unwilling to consider the matter from any other point of view.

There is also the danger of us overreacting. I have found that when I lose my temper, I usually lose a great deal more besides. I discover afresh the hard way that the *anger of man does not bring about the righteous life that God desires* (James 1:20). The Scriptures point us in an altogether different direction. *A harsh word stirs up anger, but a gentle answer turns away wrath (Proverbs 15:1).*

If we manage to share our perspective gently, and are both willing to make adjustments in order to strengthen the relationship, then everything is still possible. The Scriptures celebrate that God *devises ways so that a banished person may not remain estranged from Him (2 Samuel 14:14).*

Jesus calls us to love our enemies, for He not only comforts us in our grief but delights, too, to forgive the perpetrators of it. Heaven will be full of those who once sinned grievously. Look how quick God was to respond when even seriously evil kings such as Ahab and Manasseh sought his face – to say nothing of Saul the Pharisee.[16] Heaven will be full of such trophies of grace, as well as those redeemed from less dramatic sinfulness.

Sadly, there is nothing automatic about sinners turning to God. Jesus loved Judas and called him "friend,"[17] but He did not reach out to him after his act of betrayal. I am reminded of Augustine's penetrating insight: "One of the thieves was damned, do not presume; one of the thieves was saved, do not despair."

Reflect and Pray

Do not say, "I'll pay you back for this wrong!" Wait for the Lord, and He will deliver you.

Proverbs 20:22

If we get to the root of most relationship breakdowns, what do we usually find? Seeds of envy that have turned into strong-holds. As the Scriptures warn, *envy rots the bones (Proverbs 14:30, 27:4).* The Lord Jesus lived amongst people filled with strife and envy, yet He took on none of their traits. We could say the same about King David. Deep down, David felt no need to prove himself. But how about us? Does envy have any foothold in our life? If it does, it will be a certain cause of grief.

Lord, check my heart for any trace of this deadly poison. Keep me blessing, not resenting,

trusting, not dismissing,
and honouring, not denouncing.
Set me free from from this base emotion –
for if I am envious of others,
I am disapproving of the way
that You have ordained things.

Resisting the but-what-ifs

Child, I am telling you your own story, not hers.
I tell no one any story but his own.
Did I not explain to you once before
that no one is ever told what would have happened

C.S. Lewis[18]

On a perilous voyage to find the seven friends of King Caspian's father, the *Dawn Treader* anchors in the remote Island of the Duffers. Entering a magician's house, Lucy finds herself unable to resist the temptation to perform the spells she reads about in a book. One of these enables her to overhear a conversation back home in England. This turns out to be anything but a blessing, for she overhears a so-called friend siding with another girl in speaking against her. Aslan tells Lucy in no uncertain terms that she has no business to be prying in this way, but urges her not to think too harshly of the girl: she was acting under peer pressure and did not really mean what she had said.[19]

We need such reminders to respect proper boundaries. Why waste time asking questions that we can, for the moment, find no answer for? Once we allow house room to the "but what ifs" and the "if onlys," we soon risk their faith-deadening refrains drearifying our hearts.

It is so easy in the aftermath of loss to go over and over events, wondering if things would have worked out differently if only certain events had not happened, and we had not acted as we did. To be sure, we may not always have acted wisely, but the beauty of the Lord's dealings with us is that He takes us as we are, and leads us on from there.

A change of environment can do wonders to keep us from too much brooding. So too can worship. We have seen that under the anointing of the Holy Spirit, music can touch parts of our inmost being that words alone cannot reach. Put on a CD and lift your heart in praise – it is a wonderful antidote for fear and doubt.

As surely as we must often make the effort to "switch channels" when our minds become stuck, I hope you will forgive me for mentioning the "electronic companions" that we pass so many hours in front of. We are blessed to have access to such an impressive range of dramas, sports, music, news and documentaries, but we are wise to keep this far from insignificant portion of our lives under the Lord's guidance.

Idle channel flipping, like endless hours playing computer games, or shopping and surfing on the Net has the potential to isolate as well as to "connect" us, and to distract us from getting on with the hard work that alone can accomplish our real hopes and dreams.

In our "reduced-through-grief" state, most of us are happy to use television as a "pacifier" at times. The danger comes if we fall into the way of thinking that its tightly crafted dramas are where the *real* action is taking place. That is when people start living out their hopes and dreams vicariously through the fictitious dilemmas that the soaps portray.

At the very least, it is wise to check whether the Lord is happy for us to watch particular programmes. The more we reduce our dependency on television, and from spending unnecessary hours at the computer terminal, the more time and energy we will have for Kingdom business – which itself is a wonderful antidote for dispersing the pangs of grief.

"God has given us two hands," Billy Graham reminds us, "one to receive with and the other to give with." Ring a friend and arrange to do something together. Reach out and perform some kindness for someone. The Kingdom consists of many small acts, which Love expands and multiplies.

Since grief is not a time to absorb negativity, if it is at all possible, make sure that you spend quality time with people whose words and attitudes build you up and encourage you. Life is not just for television stars, or for people in the public eye – it is for all of us to live to the full.

As a deliberate act of the will, catch yourself whenever you find yourself rehearsing imaginary conversations with people who have caused you grief, or with whom you particularly want to make a good impression. You know from only too much experience where these inner dialogues are likely to lead – to endless turmoil and gloomy dead ends!

Reflect and Pray

Lord Jesus,
give us the determination to rise above the but-what-ifs.
and to find creative ways to live
that will refresh and inspire others.
So far as it is possible, keep us from people
who drain and intimidate us –
but when we do have to be in contact with them,
may we not allow their influence
to crush our seeking of You,
for You never permitted anyone else's agenda
to direct Your days or to rob You
of Your peace and purpose.

Resisting excessive self-consciousness

To be no part of a body is as to be nothing.
John Bunyan

Long before the days of polished mirrors, when proud knights admired their reflections in wayside pools, and sought to catch the eye of favoured maidens, the seeds of today's image-conscious society were already in flower. Most of us today are so concerned with our self image that it is bound to affect the way we handle that most self-absorbing of emotions: grief.

All of us have our own ways of projecting the image of ourselves that we are eager to convey. Those of us who have an inflated sense of our own importance, however, or who crave position and admiration, are likely to find the impact grief has on us particularly hard to bear. Considering how lacking in empathy some people can be towards the grieving, it is easy to see why we may be tempted to adopt subterfuges that enable us to "manage" our image. To some extent we all do this, but there is a considerable risk of this process becoming self-deceptive as we begin to hide – even from ourselves – just how much we are hurting.

If we find ourselves continually acting a part, it may be because we are trying too hard to impress. This can continue after we are no longer in contact with these people, or even after they have died. It is important for our future freedom that we do not allow their wishes to influence our lives unduly.

Juggling all that needs doing from day to day is hard enough, without having to worry about how we are coming across to others. We might fare better if we paused to ask why it is that we are so concerned about our image. Is it because we are lacking any clear sense of our own identity? Are our efforts to keep things under control causing us to avoid relationships that actually could and should have been mutually beneficial?

It is only a small step from here to falling prey to something that is particularly displeasing to the Lord: hypocrisy.[20] Those who suppress their pain, rather than lean into it, all too frequently end up turning to artificial stimulants or sedatives. We can only sound already well publicised warnings. Alcohol may induce relief in the short-term, but its long-term legacy leaves people almost invariably wracked with guilt.

If our ultimate aim is to avoid situations that "tarnish" our beloved image by exposing our anger, anxiety or anguish, we may well find ourselves making light in public of our loss. In reality, almost any loss represents an enormous body blow.

Reflect and Pray

A friend once compared our minds to a hard disc that uses up so much of its memory servicing its own operational needs that there is little room left for any new data to be added. We spend so much of our time and energy thinking about how we look, and how we are coming across, but if we could just get our focus more off ourselves – how much more time and energy we would have to give to God and to others!

> *Lord, hearts that are fully focused on You,*
> *neither foment regrets*
> *nor foster the envy that honours greed and pride.*
> *Why fence in scorn and freeze out love*
> *when You call us to lay such things aside?*
> *O Lord of Heaven's Armies,*
> *Eternal Comforter, draw near;*
> *restore the threads that hold our hearts to Yours,*
> *and lead us to Your throne.*

Resisting Aftershocks

> *The tsunami-lashed Andaman and Nicobar Islands have suffered 9,500 aftershocks since the undersea earthquake on Boxing Day that sent giant waves crashing into the emerald green archipelago.*   News24.com22

Deadly aftershocks often follow hard on the heels of earthquakes and tsunamis – and it can feel like this in grief, too. As the waves continue to buffet, all our instincts are to cry out, "Lord change our circumstances!" But since the Lord could have prevented whatever it was from happening, there may be better prayers to pray.

When loneliness and loss beat upon our shore, it is good to remember the many times when waves of love and blessing have swept our soul. By God's mercy these good times will return, and sweep aside our present sadness.

If it feels for the time being as though we are being dragged along in the undertow of these waves – like someone opening their mouth at the wrong time and finding the ocean filling their lungs – we must somehow learn to ride them, just as a surfer catches the waves and uses their power to take them surging towards their destination. This is but another way of expressing my earlier image of throwing a jujitsu fighter by the force of his own charge.

If anyone is thirsty, let him come to Me and drink, Jesus invites (John 7:37). From the depths we cry out, "Lord I am battered and all but drowning – but Your word says *Come to Me* – and Your water is fresh and sweet to my soul. That is why I will pray, "Lord, come to my heart and change me," rather than just "change the circumstances, please!"

This heartfelt prayer draws us into the silence of God – which is less loneliness than presence: an adventure waiting to be explored. How much better is this than storing up resentments, which at any moment can lead to make comments that are far better left unsaid?

Isn't this what our souls have always been longing for? In this silent seeking, we join our hearts to millions around the world, and hear the echo of His surprising yet profoundly reassuring promises:

> *He who loses His life for My sake will find it . . . Everyone who has left houses or brothers or sisters or father or mother or children or fields for My sake will receive a hundred times as much and will inherit eternal life. But many who are first will be last, and many who are last will be first.*
>
> Matthew 16:25; 19:19-20

Or as Jean Pierre de Caussade put it, "One often has more delight in finding refreshment anew than one ever had grief in its loss."[21]

References

1 We have seen that "normal" grief embraces a host of unpleasant symptoms. The question of when grief becomes "abnormal" is by no means straightforward. In extreme cases, when people are exhibiting extreme self-absorption, aggression, and a potentially dangerous disconnection from reality that inclines them to refuse all offers of help, there may come a point at which civil consciousness obliges us to inform appropriate people – pastors, police, doctors, social workers and so on, of their condition. We may have to wrestle with a variety of issues here, associated not only with personal loyalty but also the potential consequences, especially if we know and love the person deeply. Integrity and wisdom, however, may occasionally require us to be an instrument of referral.

2 Lishman, W. (1971) The Psychology of Pain, p.17 in *From Fear to Faith, Studies of Suffering and Wholeness.* SPCK. London.

3 See www.ruachministries.org/valeoftears/refs.htm for a link to an article on pain-prone personalities.

4 This is a common depressive reaction.

5 Larcombe, J. (2007) *Beauty from Ashes, Readings for Times of Loss.* Bible Reading Fellowship.

6 Cf Acts 27:29

7 This experience occurred when she entered the hospital room to see her husband's body.

8 Marshall, C. *To Live Again.* (2002) Chosen Books

9 Mark 12:25

10 Although we should not attribute undue authority to stories of death bed experiences, a number of impressive testimonies can be found at http://bibleprobe.com/nde.htm. Those recorded by Dr Maurice Rawlings concern people who tell their stories immediately after recovering from cardiac arrest. It was found that these people tend to forget all memory of negative experiences within a few days. See links at www.ruachministries.org/valeoftears/refs.htm for more details.

11 Luke 12:5

12 John 8:44

13 See www.ruachministries.org/valeoftears/refs.htm for link to news article.

14 2 Samuel 1:19 f

15 Matthew 5:23-25, Matthew 18:15

16 1 Kings 21:25-29; 2 Chronicles 33:12-13; Acts 9:3-4;

17 Matthew 26:50

18 Lewis, C.S. (2001) *The Horse and His Boy.* p. 139. Collins.

19 Lewis, C.S. (2000) *The Voyage of the Dawn Treader.* pp.123-4. Collins.

20 See www.ruachministries.org/teaching/hypocrisy.htm

21 Jean-Pierre de Caussade. *Self-Abandonment to Divine Providence.* (2008) Baronius Press.

212

Part Nine

The Wider Picture

I T IS OFTEN when we are prepared to look beyond our own grief that the Lord ministers more powerfully through us. In a world where most people are looking out only for themselves, it blesses the Lord when He finds people who are eager to share the things that are on His heart. That is why we will move far beyond personal recovery in this section, to begin exploring things that are grieving His heart.

Escaping the gravitational Pull of Grief

For sorrow, long-indulged and slow is to humanity a foe.
Langhorne

If everything in life has a starting point, then, by definition, most should also have a finishing point. The mere thought of a prolonged grief drawing to a close is a lovely one to contemplate – not least because the "end" often marks the start of many new beginnings.

Sometimes this happens of itself, as spring silently emerges out of winter. At other times, it is up to us to make the effort to fully hand over our hurts and losses to the Lord and so pull away from the gravitational instinct to grieve, lest it become permanently entrenched. As Lord Byron put it,

Selfish sorrow ponders on the past,
and clings to thoughts now better far removed.
Childe Harold's Pilgrimage

In one form or another, many of us sense when the time to move on has come. After months of mourning the death of Israel's double-minded king, the Lord challenged Samuel,

"How long will you mourn for Saul, since I have rejected him as king over Israel? Fill your horn with oil and be on your way."

1 Samuel 16:1

Effectively, God was urging Samuel to invest his energies elsewhere. Later, when David allowed his grief for the son he had been forced to banish to unbalance his judgement, he became more concerned for Absalom's safety than for the welfare of his troops.

This so incensed his chief of staff that he warned him that he would have no army left unless he roused himself from his stupour and went out to encourage his troops.[1] Joab's challenge recalled the king to his duty. It was misplaced love on David's part to trade the lives of his men out of loyalty to someone in whom the fuse of hatred flamed so relentlessly.

Some of us may find ourselves holding back from embarking on new projects and relationships because, like David, we may subconsciously be trying to "make up" for not having been as faithful or as kind as we would have liked to have been in the past. Such "compensating" can cause us to miss out on worthwhile opportunities, and to deprive the people the Lord is leading us to of precious truths that we have learnt about His love and faithfulness.

One of the clearest signs that we are on the path to recovery is when we find ourselves no longer constantly trying to "find" the person (or role) that we have lost. We may even have reached the point of realising that the Lord has been *using* some of the events that we initially considered to be an unmitigated disaster. Best of all, we are willing now to embrace the *new* things that are coming our way.

We know that we are well on the way towards healing when our mind turns to subjects that have caused us great distress in the past, and are able to think about them without our emotions spiralling downwards in grief or guilt. Precisely because life can never be as it was, there is no point in trying to perpetuate the way things were before. That does not mean that we will never again know happiness. There is every likelihood that we will – especially if we can thank the Lord for what He is doing, rather than hankering for how things were.

Reflect and Pray

It is such a joy when all but forgotten feelings of contentment begin to return. Like snowdrops and daffodils pushing their way through the frost-bound earth, it takes us by surprise to glimpse such happiness again. Even a hint of "spring" rejuvenates our heart, and inspires us to aim for higher goals. Our grief may not yet have gone for good, but even now fresh blessings and deliverances are on the way. That is why the Lord says,

> *I will return her vineyards to her*
> *and transform the Valley of Trouble*
> *into a gateway of hope.*
> *She will give herself to Me there,*
> *as she did long ago when she was young,*
> *when I freed her from her captivity in Egypt.*
> Hosea 2:15

> *Lord, I greatly desire to reach*
> *Your highest calling for my life.*
> *Wherever grief*
> *is threatening to spiral out of control,*
> *rein it in and rule in my heart.*
> *Even as I have mourned the passing of one season,*
> *help me take whatever steps I need to take*
> *to allow this new one to unfold –*
> *even if You are not ready yet to act on the things*
> *that I am most immediately concerned about.*
> *In Jesus' name, Amen.*

Never underestimate the Power of Prayer

In the same way that one can observe the effects of counsel-ling, painkillers or antidepressants . . . prayer is measura-ble. No one knows them as well, as deeply, as closely, as personally as their God. This is a time to capitalise on that

*relationship; to draw help, strength, courage, wholeness
and health from it . . . The act of seeking makes the
relationship closer.*

Dr Robert Buckman

We who love the Lord know that prayer is the life-blood of
our relationship with the Lord. Dr Robert Buckman, who
wrote this fascinating testimony to the power of prayer,
specialises in caring for the dying, but is not a man of prayer
himself. He is by no means the only "secular" source to
affirm its efficacy.[2]

When griefs and pressures piled in on every side, Paul
never missed an opportunity to ask others to pray for him.[3]
May the Lord help us to get into the habit of doing so too.

When ultrasound scans showed that baby Yelena had a
seriously enlarged heart, the Church in Shetland started praying. By the time the family reached Aberdeen for an emergency operation, to the mystification of the medical staff, the
baby's heart had returned to normal.

The fact that God intervenes in such ways to heal some
people, however, can itself be a cause of grief for those who
remain unhealed despite enormous faith. There is a fine line
between pressing in by faith, and knowing when to pray for
the grace to accept matters taking their natural course. There
are no simple answers here, let alone any "formulae". God
does some things supernaturally, either as a token of His love,
or because of the specific plans He has for us.

Take hold of appropriate Scripture verses and pray for the
Lord's healing touch to come on all that is out of line with His
will. There will always be blessing as we do so, provided we
do not tell God what to do, or roll the blame for any lack of
physical improvement back onto the person concerned –
especially if promising early signs do not progress into the
complete healing we were longing for.[4]

Reflect and Pray

Prayer is not only a spontaneous response to difficulty but
also as a *strategy* that requires both thought and planning.

Every time we meet together with brothers and sisters in the Lord, we share matters that are worthy of prayer. It is so often when we turn from "coffee and chat" to "coffee and prayer" that God releases His insight and His power. May the Lord give us the vision and the courage to move beyond sharing information and say "Let's pray together." Try it!

Spirit of Prayer,
harness us to bear real fruit before Your throne,
and to bring You great joy in the process.
In Jesus' name, Amen.

Burden bearing in the Spirit

The world scoffs at a man weeping for his neighbour's sins
as if for his own, or even more than for his own, for it seems
contrary to nature. But the love which brings this about is
not of this world.

Angela of Foligno

Many of the Biblical writers used the Hebrew language to play on words – and I was tempted to spell the title of this book "Veil" of Tears. We are familiar with the concept of walking through "the valley of the shadow of death" – but is grief not like a veil that separates us from so much that we love and prize?

Thus far we have considered God's compassion for those who are experiencing personal loss. As we turn to ponder the corporate griefs that engulf societies and even nations, I have often been tempted to wonder, if I may put this reverently, how God avoids having a nervous breakdown.

After all, while the rest of us dip our hands into the woes of the world and then relax in a shower and take the evening off, God never removes His gaze from the sufferings His children are called to endure.

What is needed, therefore, is a *spiritual* response to intensely distressing situations. Jesus does not despair over them, for that would be to deny the Hope that flows within the Godhead, but He most certainly does mourn over them – and He is eager to find others who will do so too.

Just as certain women dedicate themselves to sharing more of God's heart by "taking the veil," so the Lord invites us to share the grief that is in His heart. As He brings us face-to-face with situations that are dishonouring Him, we will often find ourselves expressing our feelings in sighs "too deep for words".[5]

It is at this point that we find ourselves glimpsing a surprising fact: this "veil" of tears actually becomes a means by which we come to share more of the Father's heart. This can be as true for the social injustices under whose weight the world groans, as for the impositions that both false religion and political correctness are increasingly placing on God's people – to say nothing of the flood of immorality that saturates our land.

Perhaps the sharpest pain of all comes from seeing just how far so many parts of the Church, as well as our society, have strayed from the Lord's heart. I have taken to calling this pain "Lot's Syndrome."

> God rescued Lot out of Sodom because he was a righteous man who was sick of the shameful immorality of the wicked people around him. Yes, Lot was a righteous man who was tormented in his soul by the wickedness he saw and heard day after day.
>
> 2 Peter 2:7-8

Many of us are prepared to share our joys with many people, but we reserve our deepest griefs for a few tried and trusted friends. Sharing God's heart in this way sets us free from the self-absorption of grief, and leads to such heartfelt intercession that it draws us onto His wavelength.[6]

If we get things out of perspective at this point, however, we can end up confusing our own prejudices and emotions for genuine spiritual discernment, in which case we will soon feel weary and weighed down – and risk becoming a bore to others!

To avoid taking on burdens the Lord is not asking us to assume and overloading ourselves, it is good from time to time to check and reposition our burdens. Imagine a log

making its way downstream. Is it in the middle of the current,
or is it becoming snared and snagged on its journey?

Reflect and Pray
Fine-tune our spirits, Lord,
to pick up the burdens
You are drawing our attention to.
Place the filter of Your Cross
between our own desires and longings
and the pain we come across,
so that burdens flow freely through us
to the mercy of the Cross
without getting stuck in the realm of our soul.
In the name of the One who ever lives
to make intercession for us, Amen.

Sharing the Father's Grief
Can I see another's woe and not be in sorrow too?
Can I see another's grief and not seek for kind relief?
William Blake

Every experienced counsellor faces the challenge that if they
give themselves wholeheartedly to someone, they risk being
sucked into an emotional vortex that will leave them as
weighed down as the people they are trying to help. If they
remain too aloof, however, they may find themselves unable
to reach the person's heart.

It causes the Lord much heartache when His perfect Love
is rejected by the people on whom He has set His heart. How
can we draw closer to Him this way? By allowing our sufferings to develop in us a deeper compassion. Just as we have
been at pains throughout this book to emphasise the importance of giving full expression to our grief, so we are in true
biblical tradition when we cry out to the Lord from the bottom
of our heart and at the top of our voice for the things we are
most concerned about.

In his powerful chapter "Wrestling Match," Philip Yancey
outlines the urgent and indeed abrupt nature of the prayers of

many of the saints as they struggle with perplexing griefs and sufferings. If this at times this makes them sound decidedly discourteous rather than meek and reverent, Yancey argues that God infinitely prefers people to deal with Him directly than to remain indifferent.[6]

May I encourage you to spend quality time in the company of the prophets? The writings of the prophets steep us in the Lord's presence and perspective in a way we will undoubtedly need in the uncertain times that lie ahead. It is in these all too often undiscovered parts of the Bible that we hear God sharing His longings and griefs, may I urge you to find modern translations and insightful commentaries that bring these Scriptures to life, which will draw you more fully into their world?[7]

Reflect and Pray

Lord Jesus, just as You mourned over the multitudes
because You saw them as sheep without a shepherd:
let me share more of what You are feeling –
even when You are mourning;
I aspire to join in spirit with that
pantheon of heroes and heroines,
who in every time and clime,
have trod the path to glory:
from the saints of ancient Rome;
through a thousand prison cells,
where precious souls are bruised
beneath a hail of deadly accusation.
Draw me closer to Your heart
so that I can take a prophetic stance
as I pray and interact
with nations (. . .)
communities (. . .)
and professions (. . .)
May I share the same love and passion for them
that I feel for my own friends and family.
In Jesus' name, Amen.

When Grief and Deception Engulf Nations

Our capacity for self-delusion is boundless.
                                        John Steinbeck

Although King Henry VIII considered himself a Christian, he passed edicts that ran entirely counter to God's law, spreading great grief and even terror in the process. By dissolving the monasteries and confiscating their assets, he left the poor with nowhere to go. Advisers who did not agree with him likewise risked being put to death. This was the fate of John Fisher, who had once been close to the king. When the time came for Fisher's sentence to be carried out, he made his way to the scaffold in his best clothes.

> "This is my wedding day," he explained, "and I ought to dress as if for a holiday." Carrying his New Testament, he was led to the execution platform. There he prayed, "Lord, grant that I may find some word of comfort so that I may glorify You in my last hour." The first words he saw as He opened the Scriptures were these: "Now this is eternal life; that they may know You, the only true God, and Jesus Christ, whom You have sent" (John 17:3). "That will do," he said. "Here's learning enough to last me to my life's end." Within minutes, he was dead.

We live in a day when we, like John Fisher, must take a stand, because God's laws are being systematically set aside. May the Lord strengthen us for this task, not because we believe that we can ever set up an earthly Utopia before the Lord returns but because it is important to let people know Who the Lord really is.

As a society we are excessively at the mercy of our passions. That is why, on a purely emotional level, the shock of Princess Diana's tragic death unleashed an unparalleled wave of mourning throughout the United Kingdom. In the early stages, at least, this flood tide of grief served as an unwitting focus for many people's own unresolved hurts and losses.

More ambiguously, hordes of people flocked to visit the small town of Soham in Suffolk, where Holly Wells and

Jessica Chapman were so brutally murdered. What was it that motivated these "grief tourists?" Was it just morbid curiosity – or were they in some way attempting to find resolution for some unresolved grief in their own heart?

Most of these visitors did nothing to help the community to pull together in the aftermath – unlike in Hungerford, which has recovered well, despite the intense media attention, from the dreadful day twenty years ago when Michael Ryan shot sixteen people dead with an automatic rifle. Many American institutions have had to face similar challenges following the spate of shooting incidents on college campuses.

If we are prepared to work towards forgiving even such intense wickedness, there is less likelihood of offences being prolonged, and the temptation to resort to seeking revenge is sharply reduced. But whilst special grace is often given to those most immediately affected, it is often from the ranks of colleagues and bystanders that the slow-burning flames of resentment are fanned. In worst case scenarios this leads to the onset of full-blown vendettas. In rather less dramatic ways, this is a risk we all face when we hear negative comments about others. This is how one friend summarised Jesus' important teaching on the subject:

> *Forgive your enemies and pray for those who persecute you – and that includes those of you who are looking on. Be careful to let go of the offences and not allow them to lodge deep down in your heart!*[18]

The question of how nations recover from the grip that grief and deception impose on them in is a crucial one to grapple with. Consider, for example, the devastated German people, who found themselves obliged to embark on a grief process at a national level for the second time in thirty years in the aftermath of their defeat at the end of the Second World War. The myth of Aryan supremacy had been exposed, but what was to take its place? Not another Hitler, as happened after their humiliating defeat in 1918, but, in the case of East Germany, another totalitarian regime, this time in communist uniform.

Many Germans preferred to sidestep entirely the issue of who had started the war and to perpetuate the blame game. They argued angrily that the damage done to German cities through Allied air attacks was morally as indefensible as anything their nation had done to the Jews.

The weight of historical opinion remains divided about the value, let alone the legitimacy of the Allied attacks that killed so many civilians, but there is no such ambiguity about the concentration camps. Gradually, as people woke up to the shocking realisation of just how far their beloved Führer had misled them, it was like the heart wrenching shock that cult members experience when they finally recognize the enormity of the deception that they are caught up in.

Psychologically, it is profoundly disturbing to see how quickly a nation can come to accept fundamental injustices and pathological depravity. Robert Jay Lifton studied the actions of the Nazi doctors during World War II, and concluded that many of these perpetrators of evil conditioned themselves with surprising ease to living a double life – each part acting "independently" from the other. One moment a cultured man is playing classical music; the next he is sadistically torturing a prisoner.[9]

Does this not parallel those cases we hear about from time to time, when an apparently ordinary (and sometimes overtly religious person) perpetrates some immense evil? Ever since Robert Louis Stevenson's pioneering descriptions in *Dr Jekyll and Mr Hyde* of the complicated processes by which apparently mutually contradictory tendencies can exist side by side within one person, such people have tended to plead various forms of mental instability when finally cornered or brought to court.

At this point, most perpetrators play up the extent to which they themselves have suffered. Their emphasis is almost always along the lines that "this would not have happened had I not been treated the way I was," rather than, "I have done something seriously wrong." Keen though they may be to absolve themselves, the fact remains that most people with multiple personalities make a more or less conscious decision at some point to "switch over" to their "dark side," even if, in extreme cases, they lose track somewhat of their actions once they have made this switch.

Such egocentricity lies at the heart of the "shadow arche-type" which Jung considered to be resident in us all. This corresponds perhaps to the sinful nature that Paul inveighs against in Romans chapter seven, but whose existence most of us are surprisingly loathe to admit to, where rage and envy, covetousness and greed lurk. Those who are willing to change often need setting free from the "power source" of distorted ideas or doctrines that the cult or ideal has superimposed on them.

Returning to the German example, many in the nation were by no means heart-convinced Nazis. All, however, needed both grace and deprogramming to recover from the ordeal of the Nationalist Socialist years.

It is a tribute to how seriously Germany has sought to face shameful episodes from its past that it now has the fastest growing Jewish community in Europe.[10] The work of *Trauer-arbeit* ("Grief-work") in post war Germany has been compli-cated, however, by the continued activities of various pro-Nazi sympathisers, but overall, Germany must surely rank with South Africa as the most comprehensive example in history of a nation doing its best to face its past.

If the best way forward is for nations to confront their wrong actions and to extend forgiveness, then the South African "Truth and Reconciliation Commission" is a splendid model. Using Desmond Tutu's book, *No Future Without Forgiveness* as a model, it set out as a serious attempt to face the immense grief that the apartheid system unleashed.

More than 21,000 testimonies of abuse and cruelty were heard, often in the presence of their perpetrators. Over 1,300 people received a full amnesty in return for their frank and full confession of the ordeals that they subjected their victims to. May the Commission's motto, "The truth shall set us free"[11] prove prophetic at this critical time in South Africa's history, when crime rates are so alarmingly high.

Unlike South Africa, Serbia has shown considerable reluctance to face up to atrocities committed against Kosovar Albanians. Serbia's default mechanism has been to peddle the line that they are victims rather than perpetrators. This not only holds them back from acknowledging their guilt, but has proved a serious obstacle to it regaining its proper place among the nations.

There are many complex issues to consider here, not least whether it is right or even possible to repent of sins that previous generations committed. I believe that God does hear prayers along such lines, and that leads some of us along the path of such "identificational repentance." We can readily discern the need for it.[12]

None of us can be sure that we are untainted by the prevailing attitudes in our society, unless we specifically seek God for Him to set us free of them. Many converts in China, for instance, have absorbed a guilt-filled ethos which doubtless has its origins way back in history, but which has witnessed many unpleasant recent manifestations.

During the intense suffering of the Maoist revolutionary years, for example, village meetings were characterized by the "naming and shaming" of individuals for their faults and failings. These new Christians are prone to feel ashamed at their lack of spiritual fruit – though, by western standards, many of them are leading people to Christ in truly staggering numbers.

As an infinitely more self-confident generation emerges in China, it is vital to pray that the Lord raises up His children to exercise influence in high places, lest the new-found infatuation with Mammon leads the soul of the nation still further astray than communist propaganda had done.

To avoid possible misunderstanding, let me make it clear that this is in no way to imply that our own nation is in any way "better". Those who understand spiritual cultures and atmospheres would probably say the reverse. Quite apart from the legacy of national pride and economic exploitation that continue to take such a toll, do not our media moguls have their own equally destructive ways of shaming people and ruining their reputations? Our sinfulness may lie deeper beneath the surface hidden than in some societies but that does not make it any the less serious in God's sight.[13]

These are entirely relevant issues to pray and ponder as great swathes of humanity swallow the lies that the forces of Antichrist are sowing.[14] May more and more see through these false values, and reject the false standards that are being proposed to them.

I have recently completed a teaching series on the seven letters to the seven churches in Revelation. These, like the rest of the book of Revelation, are powerful messages from God's heart to remain true to Him at times when the temptation to compromise is particularly strong.[15]

At the same time, I find myself asking difficult questions about western values. Can it ever be right to oppose terror with torture? How will future generations of Americans, let alone non-Americans, regard the "water boarding" torture techniques recently practised on Middle Eastern suspects?

All this has major implications for us as we confess the many ways in which we fail to honour Christ from day to day, as individuals and as a Church, as well as in the life of the nation. Many have come to recognise our need to offer specific prayers and acts of forgiveness for the many ways in which we (the British people) mismanaged and abused so many in the far-flung Empire that the Lord trusted to us rule. Those who are not British will doubtless be able to call to mind comparable examples from their own nation's history.

Reflect and Pray

The Lord's verdict against Sodom was that it was *"arrogant, overfed and unconcerned"* (Ezekiel 16:49). Does this not epitomise our guilt in the West today? Having so long disregarded the Lord Jesus Himself, it was inevitable that we should espouse self-centred philosophies that every year become more brazenly anti-Christian.

The message of both Biblical and subsequent history remains as clear as ever: God hears the heart cry of those who care enough to mourn – and who are prepared to work towards facing these issues head-on.[16] There are many promising signs, not least the increasing coming together of intercessors, evangelists and those involved in social action to work towards making the Lord again known in our land.

> *Lord, we long for Your name to be honoured in our land!*
> *Forgive us that we have pushed You to one side,*
> *as if you were an inconvenience in Your own world.*
> *Forgive us our pride and self-satisfaction,*
> *and lead us into richer better expressions of our faith*
> *as individuals, families, communities and nations,*
> *seeking more to serve and honour others*
> *than to impose our own conformities.*

Lest We Forget

> *The response to Schindler's List is proof that the most offensive word in any language is "forget."*
> *Richard Corliss[17]*

What grief leaders cause when they manipulate circumstances in order to further their own purposes, whilst doing all they can to conceal their actions and intentions. How can we not grieve when the western world shows itself willing to rouse itself whenever there is a serious threat to its standard of living, but is prepared to turn a blind eye to almost anything else?

Jewish survivors of the Holocaust deliberately did all they could to keep the memories of family members and role models alive.[18] This determination not to hide from the stark realities of atrocities that had been committed contrasts with the Japanese, who have been far less forthcoming when it comes to acknowledging the magnitude of their war crimes.

Linked as this is to the crucial need not to lose face, this long tradition of playing matters down culminated in the

Emperor of Japan making perhaps the greatest understate-
ments of all time when he announced his nation's surrender
at the end of the Second World War, declaring that the war
had developed along lines "not necessarily to Japan's
advantage."[19]

Echoes of such attitudes continue to this day to be an
impediment to people coming through to maturity in Christ.
Much concerted prayer is still required for the spiritual soil in
Japan to be conducive – first for people to receive the Gospel,
and then to develop as wholehearted disciples.

Throughout recorded history, governments have responded
to dwindling popularity and prosperity by offloading the
blame for their failings on convenient scapegoats.[20] Just as
Nazi Germany followed Russia in launching devastating
pogroms against the Jewish people, so the powers of darkness
excel at stirring up at hatred between nation states, and between different tribes and sectors within nations.

Forgetting that nothing we do passes unseen in Heaven,
governing powers that heed neither internal morality nor
external checks all too frequently end up oppressing the
innocent. "*A single death is a tragedy*" Joseph Stalin once
cynically declared, "*but a million deaths is just a statistic.*"

Three nations that come immediately to mind in this context are Myanmar (Burma), where the military continue the
horrendous ethnic cleansing of the Karen and other minority
tribes, North Korea, where believers are suffering more
acutely than in any other country in the world, and the Congo,
where more than four million people have lost their lives as a
result of the civil war[21].

In the whole realm of intercession there can be no substitute to being led by the Spirit when it comes to knowing how
to respond to events of such immense cruelty and magnitude.
In *Healing America's Wounds,* John Dawson provides powerful Biblical insights, and testimonies from around the world
of how God's people are addressing the root causes of hatred
between estranged peoples and groups, and bringing about
healing and reconciliation.[22]

Reflect and Pray

Arise, Lord! Lift up your hand, O God. Do not forget the
helpless.   Psalm 10:12

Survivors of genocidal episodes have to cope not only with
the immensely complicted fallout from these atrocities, but
also with the psychological challenge of adjusting to a world
bereft of familiar friends and landmarks. As one survivor put
it, "our most urgent need is to find ways to survive survival."

Why not take this thought and turn it into prayer for all who
suddenly find themselves on their own, or in radically altered
circumstances?

As we direct our gaze wider, and cry out to God to intervene on behalf of the grieving, remember the tribes in Myanmar (Burma), the child victims of the Lord's Resistance
Army in Uganda, and the millions of African children who
find themselves obliged to raise young siblings as the result
of their parents dying of AIDS.

Prophetic Laments and the Power of Music

My spirit is poured out in agony
*   as I see the desperate plight of my people.*
My tears flow endlessly;
*   they will not stop*
until the Lord looks down
*   from heaven and sees.*
My heart is breaking over the fate
*   of all the women of Jerusalem.*
*   Lamentations 2:11, 3:49-51*

Many of us spend much of our time bemoaning our lot.
Although this may give us a feeling of momentary relief,
more often than not the spirit of complaining draws us a long
way away from affirming in faith that *I have a delightful*
inheritance because the bound-ary lines have fallen for me in
pleasant places (Psalm 16:6). Indeed, it sits so heavily at
odds with our calling that it may actually endanger it.[23]

The many spiritual laments we come across in the Bible
may at first sight sound like people getting their complaints

off their chests, but the Lord detects where real faith and longing are present. [24] Jesus declared in the Sermon on the Mount, *Blessed are they who mourn,* and He demonstrated this quality Himself when He wept over the fate that He could see awaited Jerusalem.[25]

When the King of the Kingdom returns, there will no longer be any need to cry out, *"how long, Lord?"* For the time being, however, we must continue to mourn the evils that humankind is doing both to Creation and to each other.

We have seen that one of the finest features of King David was his willingness to grieve for those who had opposed him. It was not only on hearing the news of his friend Jonathan's fate that he was profoundly moved, but also when he learned of the death of those who had caused him great distress: Saul and Abner. Concerned that Israel should realise that it lost the services of mighty leaders, he composed powerful and moving laments in their memory.[26]

Jeremiah wept when the well intentioned King Josiah died, and he wanted others to do so too, for he rightly foresaw that the new king would not pursue the excellent reforms the young king had initiated.[27] In powerfully persuasive poetic oracles, Jeremiah prophesied year after year how dire it would be when God's judgement devastated the land.

When it finally occurred, the scenes he records in the book of Lamentations are so terrible they almost defy description. It is no coincidence that he chose to recount these in poetic form, for poetry is a most effective medium for relating such horrors – especially when it is accompanied by music that graphically depicts this dimension of mourning and lament.[28]

Such inspired music is a perfect vehicle for going deeper in intercession. It enables us to identify with the raw passion of the situations we are concerned about, and to feel God's heartbeat. This is so precious and powerful a concept that I have long sought to combine music, mourning, prayer and prophecy in the way we lead our prayer conferences. Reflecting on his own long experience of pioneering in this field, Richard Williamson recently wrote this challenge:

In our music making, there has been a danger that we have been moving away from the creative "prophetic" stream that flowed through us in earlier days in favour of a "safer" stream where everything is nicely sewn up and "acceptable" – and as musically perfect as possible. Of course we need to do things well – but have we lost our willingness to step out and express God's heart through musical languages taught to us by God Himself by the inspiration of His Spirit?

One musical language I believe that God wants to undergird our worship with is the language of holiness. God is calling us to offer our lives to him afresh – lives that are holy and abandoned to Him. In doing so, He can use our music to bring a new vision of who He really is to a world and to a Church that is in desperate need of hearing God's voice and seeing His face. Not a "cosy" over-familiar vision of God, but an awe-inspiring encounter with Almighty God who is holy – the Creator of the Universe and the Lord of History: a God who is rightly to be feared.

A second language I believe God wants us to develop further is the language of lament, exile and identification. We have "sung our songs of victory" and worshipped God as our healer and our friend – but the Lord is also looking for those who can express the grief in His heart, and also the pain that is in so many people's lives today.

Such music may not necessarily need words (spoken or sung) – but it will identify closely with the cry of our hearts and call forth the Song of the Lord, both in worship and in heartfelt intercession.

A third language we need to nurture is the language of hope. Hope in a world falling apart, hope in the Church and hope for the glorious fulfilment of the Kingdom, leading up to the return of the King. This is the language of glory – displaying the glory of His splendour and encouraging us to look forward again with expectancy.

Reflect and Pray

It is important to develop the habit of praying wider. With at least one in ten of the world's Christians living under severe persecution, we have no excuse for remaining in ignorance about their plight, or for not supporting the work of movements that reach out to the Suffering Church.[29]

The Courage to keep going

For your sake we are in danger of death at all times; we are treated like sheep that are going to be slaughtered . . . For I swear, dear brothers and sisters, that I face death daily . . . As a result, we have stopped relying on ourselves and have learned to rely only on God, who raises the dead. He rescued us from mortal danger, and He will rescue us again.

Romans 8:23 TEV

Any one of the repeated beatings or prolonged confinements that Paul experienced in oppressive Roman prisons might have deterred a lesser man from pursuing his God-given assignment. It would certainly have been easy for him to hunker down into "survival mode," but Paul had learned not to be at the mercy of circumstances, but to press on into the heart of God.

In this he seems to me to be in the direct spiritual lineage of Jacob, who wrestled with the angel and refused to let him go until he blessed him.[30] With supreme courage, we like Paul must resist "the thief, the murderer and the destroyer" and pursue our mission, refusing to bow the knee to the subliminal invitations the powers of darkness send our way: "I'll stop bothering you, if only you'll stop being such a thorn in my side!"

How infinitely poorer the Church would be without the letters Paul took the trouble to pen from prison! May the Lord likewise strengthen our resolve to be *active in sharing our faith, in season and out of season, so that we will have a full understanding of every good thing we have in Christ (Philemon 6, 2 Timothy 4:2).*[31]

In *Life in the Overlap* Jean Darnell describes how she once sat down by mistake in a first-class railway carriage. Another woman entered her compartment, clearly depressed and in no mood to talk. This suited Jean fine. She was exhausted from her speaking schedule and had no desire whatsoever to indulge in small talk. The Lord had other ideas, however, and insisted that she reach out to the woman. It turned out that she was on her way to a solicitor's office to finalise a divorce.

By God's grace, Jean was able to lead this woman to the Lord. When they reached the terminus, she rang her husband to tell him what she had done. He was a long time answering. "I'm sitting on the edge of my bed with a gun in my hand," he replied. "I just can't go on living without you."

The amazing outcome to this story is that this family is now serving the Lord – and all because Jean stepped out of her comfort zone to share the gospel.

Reflect and Pray

Holy God,
steep my soul in the truths of Your Word
until they fill my mind.
Shine the clarity of Your light
into all that is out of focus,
and breathe faith where unbelief reigns.
Where powers of darkness are scheming and resisting,
I take my stand in Jesus' name against them,
and declare myself willing
to step outside my comfort zone
whenever You call.

Cultivating an Eternal Perspective

Then as I looked, I saw a door standing open in heaven, and the same voice I had heard before spoke to me like a trumpet blast. The voice said, "Come up here, and I will show you what must happen after this." And instantly I was in the Spirit, and I saw a throne in heaven and someone sitting on it.   Revelation 4:1-2

We have come a long way on our journey, from the first waves of shock and trauma until we can now speak freely of moving on beyond our grief. Towards the end of his life, the

Lord reminded the evangelist David Watson of *His* priorities and perspective.

> All your writing and all your preaching are as nothing in comparison with your relationship with Me.[32]

In both *Extraordinary Miracles in the Lives of Ordinary People,* and *Intimacy and Eternity,*[33] I shared a wonderful experience of the nearness of Heaven that I was privileged to be accorded many years ago. This both launched my ministry, and has continued to influence my whole outlook on life and eternity ever since. From time to time the Lord's presence draws close, and I catch the echo of Paul's encouragement to *let Heaven fill my thoughts,* (Colossians 3:2 LB).

Too much striving after earthly aspirations diminishes our spiritual hunger. If something sharp is required to refocus our priorities, why be surprised if the Lord allows razor-edged trials to come our way? Anything is better than settling for complacency!

Reflect and Pray

Take courage. No matter how much you have suffered, or may yet have to go through, God is preparing you for a lifetime in His presence. When God is ready, He will usher you into the greater fullness of His Heavenly Kingdom.

> All the things that have deeply possessed your soul have been but hints of it – tantalising glimpses, promises never quite fulfilled, echoes that died away just as they caught your ear. But if it should really become manifest – if there ever came an echo that did not die away but swelled into the sound itself – you would know it. Beyond all possibility of doubt you would say, "Here at last is the thing I was made for."
>
> Your place in Heaven will seem to be made for you and you alone, because you were made for it – made for it stitch by stitch as a glove is made for a hand.   C.S. Lewis

> *Lord, You know, You see, You hear –*
> *every cry, every sadness, every sigh.*

You know exactly what I am going through
and where You are taking me.

I give to You each grief that I have borne:
each dented dream,
each failure of faith or friendship.

Take these shards and slivers, Lord,
so that none turns septic
and taints my heart.
Make of these fragments
a full and pleasing mosaic.
I bless and forgive each person, young or old,
who has caused me grief or hindered my path.
I receive Your forgiveness too
for all the wrong that I have done ,
when I have caused others to stumble.
I bring You all who are in need
of Your profound refreshment:
and make myself available to You and to them,
In the name of the One Who strengthens me
from day to day,
and enables me to share in Your eternal life.

References

1 See 2 Samuel 19:5-7

2 The British Medical Journal also published findings that show remote, retroactive, intercessory prayer leading to shorter stays in hospital and briefer duration of fever for patients with bloodstream infections. Encouragingly, it concludes that prayer should be considered for use in clinical practice. With the experience we mentioned earlier of Ros, who was prayed free from her spasms, we echo these findings wholeheartedly! "The Effects of remote, retroactive, intercessory prayer on outcomes in patients with bloodstream infection: randomised controlled trial." You can find the link at www.ruachministries.org/valeoftears.refs.htm

3 E.g. 2 Thessalonians 3:1-2, cf Colossians 4:3-4, Hebrews 13:18-19, cf 1 Thessalonians 1:11

4 Tens of thousands prayed all over the world for David Watson, the beloved and greatly used evangelist, when he was diagnosed with liver cancer. David enjoyed a period of grace when strength returned, a time he used to write *Fear No Evil*, the moving account of what turned out to be his final year. Ultimately, however, this proved to be "time given back" rather than the full healing so many were hoping for. Sadly, some "blamed" him for his apparent lack of faith.

5 Romans 8:26

6 Yancey, P. (2006) *Prayer. Does it make any difference?* Hodder and Stoughton.

7 For an introductory overview, see the section on the Prophets in David Pawson's *Unlocking the Bible*. Collins 2003.

8 The quote is used by permission but the author prefers to maintain his anonymity.

9 Lifton, R. (1986) *The Nazi Doctors*. Basic Books. New York

10 The numbers increased substantially during the 1990's as a result of large numbers fleeing the crumbling Soviet Union.

11 See www.ruachministries.org/valeoftears/refs.htm

12 I was struck recently by a less than obvious example of the need for this. Many Poles, in despair and indignation at the appalling suffering inflicted on them by both Russians and Germans, themselves carried out many atrocities. Is that legacy now being reflected in the high levels of violence that are currently affecting certain Polish cities? Or is it just an unrelated coincidence that fascist skinheads gangs are on the rise? As we pray for this vicious cycle of sowing and reaping that has dominated Poland's past to come to an end, may more and more of the Lord's redemptive gift be released through this broadly God-fearing nation.

13 Of particular concern at the moment is our immigration system. We have allowed in many who have no love for our nation, but we are also guilty of having sent many away who desperately needed a safe haven, and who now face an uncertain and even perilous fate.

14 2 Thessalonians 2:5-12

15 You can access this teaching series via our website, www.ruachministries.org/valeoftears/refs/htm

16 Shortly after 9/11, a unique civil event in America's history was held in the Yankee Stadium. Lutheran Pastor David Benke was suspended from his post for praying in the presence of other religions). Nevertheless his prayer, "Tower of Strength," brought a measure of healing not only to those immediately traumatized by loss but to many others in the nation who were

grieving. See www.ruachministries.org/valeoftears/refs.htm

17 Time Magazine. 14/3/94

18 By contrast, Dan Bar-on has noted an almost desperate eagerness among many second and third generation descendants of Nazi concentration camp guards to "move on from the past, by deliberately not referring to it." Bar-on, D. (1995) *Fear and Hope*. Harvard University Press. Cambridge. By contrast, a considerable amount of nostalgia can be found these days in the former East Germany for the highly repressive D.D.R. – perhaps because the regime appeared to offer people a "simpler" structure for their lives than today's more complex free for all.

19 Max Hastings has written extensively on this subject. See www.ruachministries.org/valeoftears/refs.htm In Okanaura, for example, civilians were told to take their own lives rather than fall into the hands of the American invaders. As recently as in 2007, all references to the thousands of suicides that followed the giving of this instruction were removed from text books.

20 See Staub, E. (1989) *The Roots of Evil: the Origins of Genocide and other Group Violence*. Cambridge University Press.

21 www.ruachministries.org/valeoftears/refs.htm

22 Dawson, J. *Healing America's Wounds*. (1995) Regal Books.

23 See 2 Corinthians 10:9-11

24 There are 43 personal laments in the Psalms, and 14 communal ones: in other words, 57 out of 150 psalms in all, compared to 17 Psalms of Thanksgiving and 32 Psalms of praise.

25 Luke 19:41

26 See 2 Samuel 1:11f, 3:31f.

27 See pp. 590 and 593 of David Pawson's excellent *Unlocking the Bible*. Collins.

28 Ruth Fazell has written a moving oratorio out of the poems left by child survivors of the concentration camp at Terezín (Theresienstadt). In 1941, the Nazis converted this small town, to the northwest of Prague, into a transit concentration camp. To the outside world, Terezín was presented as a "model Jewish settlement" – a resort-like atmosphere with stores, café, bank, kindergarten, school and flower gardens. In reality, Terezín was an overcrowded way-station for the death camps, to which the transports would come to take adults and children alike to the gas chambers of Auschwitz. Many died in Terezin itself, as a result of the horrendous overcrowding. Many of the prisoners were musicians, writers, poets, artists and intellectuals. In the midst of such depravity, they and their children turned to art to transcend their pain. While regular schooling was prohibited, classes were held clandestinely and many of the 15,000 Jewish children who passed through the camp were encouraged to paint and write. Of those 15,000, only about 100 survived. You can hear excerpts of Ruth Fazell's oratorio by following the links at www.ruachministries.org/valeoftears/refs.htm

29 www.opendoorsuk.org, www.csw.org.uk, www.barnabasfund.org

30 See Genesis 32:24-30

31 See *Witnessing for Jesus* www.ruachministries.org/articlepub.htm

32 Watson, D. *Fear no Evil.* (1998) Hodder & Stoughton.

33 Marszalek, T. (Ed. (2007) *Extraordinary Miracles in the Lives of Ordinary People.* Harrison House. For a link to access Intimacy and Eternity, see www.ruachministries.org/valeoftears/refs.htm

Appendix One

Exequy: A Funeral Celebration

I GAVE THE FOLLOWING TALK at a funeral reception recently after a friend's mother died. It pulls together many of the themes I have touched on in more depth elsewhere in this book and I include it in the hope that it will be of interest as well a spiritual resource. For obvious reasons, I have removed specific names.

"We have just heard truly wonderful tributes about your mother. May they go some way to compensate against the profoundly shocking time you have been through. After fighting such a long and intense battle for your mother's life, when her prospects for recovery hung in the balance and lurched between promise and decline, you are bound to have many emotional ups and downs.

You have found it hard not knowing until very near the end if she was going to make a full recovery, or whether she was about to go and be with the Lord. You were torn between the shadow of an oncoming death that you were determined to withstand at all costs, and recognising that death is also the "gateway to everlasting life."

For many long weeks you rode the tempestuous waves of two oceans surging against each other – and now that the raging storm has passed, you have to adjust to the different demands of a flatter sea in the aftermath of your loss.

Now is the time to give expression to your accumulated grief. There is absolutely nothing wrong with this: grief is every bit as valid an emotion as love and joy. This is what C.S. Lewis wrote in *A Grief Observed* following the loss of his own beloved wife, after only a few short years together.

Bereavement is a universal and integral part of our experience of our love. It follows marriage as normally as marriage follows a courtship, or as autumn follows sum-

mer. It is not a truncation of the process, but one of its phases.

Lazarus' house was the nearest thing to a regular family home that Jesus knew. When Mary and Martha sent news that their brother was desperately ill and at the point of death, I wonder what they would have thought if had they overhead Jesus say *Lazarus is dead, and for your sake I am glad I was not there, so that you might believe.* (John 11:14)

Mary and Martha reproached Him for the delay, pointing out that he would not have died had He been present. Jesus knew perfectly well what He was about to do, but when He saw the sisters' grief, it affected Him deeply. The shortest verse in the Bible is simply this: *Jesus wept (John 11:35).* They are words full of depth and power and meaning.

Whenever we hear in the gospels of Jesus feeling compassion, we mentally prepare ourselves for something special to happen. When He saw a funeral procession at Nain, He raised the widow's only son from the dead. When He saw the crowds as sheep without a shepherd, He took pity on them and multiplied the loaves and the fishes in order that they should not faint from hunger on the way.

Compassion, like grief itself, is an intense emotion. The Greek word could almost be translated as a "gut ache." *In all our distress, He too is distressed (Isaiah 63:9).* It is right for us to feel things deeply, and then to go a step further and to turn those feelings into prayer, for God is only ever a prayer away.

There was so much wisdom in Jesus' decision to wait – but then comes that wonderful moment when the Father shows Him that the time has come to act. Are there any greater moments in life than when Heaven breaks through and Jesus comes to our rescue after some particularly long and searing trial?

To the joy and amazement of many, Jesus called Lazarus back to life, even though he had been four days in the grave. The Pharisees, who were too set in their ways, and too proud in their hearts to follow the Way that Jesus was showing them, became still more determined to do away with Him.

When the two of you were about to get engaged, you made the effort to travel a thousand miles north to come and visit us in Shetland. Even though you had never been to these remarkable islands before, you sensed how special they were, and immediately felt a profound spiritual connection with them. Every homecoming is precious – especially in a place where, until the coming of powerful modern fishing vessels, it must always have been a great relief to see loved ones returning safely home after long and dangerous trips on the wild northern waters.

"Hamefarin" is the delightful Shetland word for homecoming. The word is used particularly to describe people returning to their homeland after being off the island for many years. For many there is a profoundly spiritual quality about this "hamefarin" – the sense of returning home to roots and families.

Over the years, many Shetland folk left their beloved island home and went to settle in places such as New Zealand and Nova Scotia. Typically, these people imbued the next generation with a deep sense of love for their homeland. They taught their children the dialect, the culture and the music. At the slightest opportunity they would take their fiddle down from its peg and play – first to their children and then in the wider community. They told their children such vivid stories about the islands that when they themselves visited the islands, they often experienced a profound sense of coming home.

What can be more precious than such a "hamefarin"? It is not only the homeless who pine for a secure and stable home. Now that this grief has come your way, you are finding yourself longing to return to the way things were, and to people and places that bring you comfort and joy.

As surely as your mother's roots went deep in her faith, and you are exploring yours, there is a spiritual belonging that anchors the soul and that makes sense of everything else –

even though the ups and downs are bound to continue as grief carves its path through your life.

Sometimes this river will be in full spate but sometimes it will be much quieter. You have needed to strengthen your "riverbanks" during these past few difficult weeks in order to protect yourself. These walls will remain up for some time to come – rather like the London flood barrier. They are part of God's divine anaesthetic, enabling you to bear the unbearable and to tide you through these darkest hours. Later, they will not be needed, or, at least not to the same extent, and then it will be right to let the barriers down. To continue sheltering behind them would keep others whom you need to be close to at a distance – and maybe even the Lord Himself.

The truth is that we need each other in order to recover. The concepts Simon and Garfunkel lauded in their song "I am a rock, I am an island" were profoundly mistaken. They celebrated that they had no need of love or friendship, for friendship causes pain.

I love the music, but I cannot agree with the sentiments. Life is too rich to shut ourselves off from our life source. We are not a rock or an island; we are human beings made in the image of God with a deep longing for love, laughter and acceptance.

May I take this opportunity, therefore, to spell this message out: your grief will take as long as it takes to recover from. Don't be dismayed if other people become impatient, and assume you ought to have got over it by now. Since when did God ever deal with "oughteries?" Each of us has our own set of memories to celebrate and to negotiate our way around. You are bound to experience backwashes and eddies as the river of grief surges along, but you will benefit greatly by making the effort to stay close to those who are willing to accompany you on this journey. As Gregory the Great put it,

When we are linked by the power of prayer, we, as it were, hold each other's hand as we walk side by side along a slippery path, and thus it comes about that the harder each

one leans on the other, the more firmly we are riveted together in brotherly love.

Lean together into the pain. It is rather like a birth, where positioning and breathing are so important. With every difficulty, lean together into the pain. There will always be a way forward. The closer you are linked together, the better you can hold each other along life's way. There comes a point, however, beyond which each one of us must journey on alone, like Reepicheep in the Voyage of the Dawn Treader, courageously sailing on alone to Aslan's country.

The more we look to Jesus, and seek to lead lives worthy of our calling, the more we will look forward to that final journey. After all the careers and achievements we laboured so hard to develop have reached their conclusion, we will discover that they are not the things that matter most when we make the final transition and stand before the Lord Jesus, either as our Saviour or our judge. He is not that interested in what sort of car we drove, or where we reached on the career ladder – but He is interested in whether we received His love deep in our hearts, and shared it with others.

Those who are in Christ and have preceded us to Heaven will be there to greet us. A few weeks before your mother made the final journey home, she had a dream in which she saw Jesus coming for her, flanked by Mary and Joseph. I had a strong sense then that her earthly pilgrimage was nearly complete. I knew then that I needed to help you to let her go. Years ago I came to understand a remarkable truth: that what we sow does not come to life until it dies. So often it is only as we let go that God moves to accomplish His most precious work.

Let me read some of Paul's teaching in the fifteenth chapter of his first letter to the Corinthians. I'm taking it from Eugene Petersen's inspiring paraphrase, The Message.

> Friends, let me go over the Message with you one final time – this Message that I proclaimed and that you made your own; this Message on which you took your stand and by which your life has been saved. (I'm assuming, now, that

your belief was the real thing and not a passing fancy, that you're in this for good and holding fast.)

The first thing I did was place before you what was placed so emphatically before me: that the Jesus, the Messiah, died for our sins, exactly as Scripture tells it; that He was buried; that He was raised from death on the third day, again exactly as Scripture says; that He presented himself alive to Peter, then to his closest followers, and later to more than five hundred of his followers all at the same time, most of them still around (although a few have since died); that He then spent time with James and the rest of those he commissioned to represent Him; and that He finally presented Himself alive to me.

It was fitting that I bring up the rear. I don't deserve to be included in that inner circle, as you well know, having spent all those early years trying my best to stamp God's church right out of existence.

But because God was so gracious, so very generous, here I am. And I'm not about to let his grace go to waste . . .

Let's face it – if there's no resurrection for Christ, everything we've told you is smoke and mirrors, and everything you've staked your life on is smoke and mirrors. Not only that, but we would be guilty of telling a string of barefaced lies about God, all these affidavits we passed on to you verifying that God raised up Christ – sheer fabrications, if there's no resurrection. . . . If all we get out of Christ is a little inspiration for a few short years, we're a pretty sorry lot. But the truth is that Christ has been raised up, the first in a long legacy of those who are going to leave the cemeteries . . .

Some sceptic is sure to ask, "Show me how resurrection works. Give me a diagram; draw me a picture. What does this "resurrection body" look like?" If you look at this question closely, you realize how absurd it is. There are no diagrams for this kind of thing.

We do have a parallel experience – in gardening. You plant a "dead" seed; soon there is a flourishing plant. There is no visual likeness between seed and plant. You could never guess what a tomato would look like by looking at a tomato seed. What we plant in the soil and what grows out of it don't look anything alike. The dead body that we bury in the ground and the resurrection body that comes from it will be dramatically different . . .

This image of planting a dead seed and raising a live plant is a mere sketch at best, but perhaps it will help in approaching the mystery of the resurrection body – but only if you keep in mind that when we're raised, we're raised for good, alive forever! . . . The seed sown is natural; the seed grown is supernatural – same seed, same body, but what a difference from when it goes down in physical mortality to when it is raised up in spiritual immortality! . . .

In the same way that we've worked from our earthy origins, let's embrace our heavenly ends . . . With all this going for us, my dear, dear friends, stand your ground. And don't hold back. Throw yourselves into the work of the Master, confident that nothing you do for Him is a waste of time or effort.

When the Sadducees, who understood nothing about the realities of eternal life, came to Jesus and asked Him a potentially tricky question about whose wife a woman would be if she lost her husband and married his brother, Jesus cut right through their argument.

> *You are making a serious mistake because you know neither the power of God nor the Scriptures. God is the God of Abraham, Isaac and Jacob – He is the God of the living.*
> Matthew 22:29

In the aftermath of loss, many long to make contact with their loved ones, perhaps to reassure themselves that they are in a safe place. I am sure that your mother is living now with Jesus, where there is crystal clear clarity and perfect continuity, and this is therefore not a temptation for you, but it may be for some who are here today. As a result, many end up visiting spiritists and mediums, not so much because they want to know the future, but because they want to revisit the past. To say the least this is most unwise because it brings us into contact with spirit powers that God specifically tells us to steer well clear of.

God does not want you to be endlessly looking backward, because people who persist in looking over their shoulder usually bump into things! Although it may seem far away and remote, there will come a moment when you realise that you really have begun to move on. Let's pray together.

> *Jesus, Author and the Finisher of our lives:*
> *You aren't impressed with celebrities and*
> *You don't despise the grieving,*
> *but You do draw close*
> *to those who set their hearts*
> *on seeking You.*
> *Comfort all here today who are mourning.*
> *Open our hearts to a deeper sense*
> *of coming home to You,*
> *for seeds once planted in our hearts*
> *have the power*
> *to grow*
> *in the most surprising ways –*
> *and Your love is only ever a prayer away.*
> *Thank You!*

Appendix Two

Praise Carts and Protective Mechanisms

FOR THE BENEFIT of those who wish to come alongside people who are manifesting more severe psychological side effects, this section is going to explore some of the ways by which people develop "protective" mechanisms to help them cope with their grief.

Although these lightning sketches will inevitably veer us more towards a "text book" approach (and contain rather stronger meat than the average person might wish to deal with in the immediate throes of grief) you are sure to find material here that will prove helpful in every phase of life.

I hit on the idea of using the letters PRAISE to illustrate these essentially psychological concepts for the simple reason that it was the first word I thought of that incorporated the starting initials of the themes I wanted to explore. Given that praise "carts off" so much of our emotional baggage, it is perhaps a more fitting title than it at first appears!

Once again, I hope you will find the opening quotations an inspiring way to begin unpacking the inevitably somewhat heavy material. A moment's additional reflection can only be a blessing!

P   - *The Pitfalls of Perfectionism*
R   - *Repression*
A   - *Addictions*
I   - *Identification and Idolatry*
S   - *Shame and Suppression*
E   - *Extremes*

C   - *Compensation*
A   - *Avoidance*
R   - *Rationalisation*
T   - *Tensions (The Neurosis of Grief)*
S   - *Substitution and Sublimination*

Grief that never seems to fade, and conflicts that never resolve may be pointers to the fact that we have developed strongly entrenched protective mechanisms. When trouble threatens, or someone comes too close, these spring into action, causing us to react in ways that enable us to cope, but that others might consider inappropriate, because they distort the "reality" of the situation.

This begs a difficult question. Is it better, in absolute terms, to be somewhat eccentric but emotionally secure, or to be so acutely aware of all the dynamics involved in a situation that we live on an emotional cliff-edge? The answer lies, perhaps, in the degree to which these "protective" mechanisms skew us away from reality. A typical example would be the person (or couple) who knows deep down how serious a health issue is, but who nevertheless determines to act as though they are sure to get better.

Life is so precious that we find it hard to fully embrace the thought that everlasting life will be still more wonderful. When husbands and wives know deep down that death is imminent, yet choose to keep up the pretence that it is not going to happen in order to spare each other's feelings, it often leaves the survivor with a host of unresolved matters to deal with afterwards.

We saw earlier how the "Divine Anaesthetic" holds certain griefs at bay until we are strong enough to bear them. There is a balance to maintain here, however. As surely as some members of the medical profession are frankly brutal in the way they communicate bad news to people, others are inclined to disguise the seriousness of peoples' conditions until the very last minute – by which time their drug-induced condition may render it too late for them to face up to certain issues.

The balance favours honesty, in order to make the most of the remaining time. I came across a most moving testimony the other day of a prominent minister who declared that although thousands had been praying for his wife to recover, they had come to an assurance that she was *not* going to be healed. This has obviously been an immensely distressing time for them, but they made it their explicit aim not to look inwards – and be overwhelmed – but to focus on loving God and serving others. Testimonies like this, that are written in the midst of some great ordeal, somehow seem a great deal more authentic than those which present a neatly "finished" story because they draw the reader in to be part of the pilgrimage.

Don't all good stories do the same? My seven-year-old son and I recently watched *Because of Winn-Dixie*. The film is a sensitive demonstration of how the power of love can pierce people's protective mechanisms and bring their hearts to life again.

Newly arrived in the small township of Naomi, a preacher and his ten-year-old daughter find it a far more dispiriting place than its pleasant name suggests. The names are ironically chosen. The landlord of the home they rent in "Friendly" Corner is far from friendly, and the "Open Arms Fellowship" by no means lives up to its name. Everyone, in fact, leads miserable and lonely lives in Naomi. No wonder, then, that the girl prays to make some friends. The answers start when she persuades her reluctant father to adopt a stray dog, who she came across wreaking havoc in the local supermarket.

As the girl reaches out into the steely-hearted community to overcome people's sense of isolation, the turning point comes when she organises a party for the community. Friendships are formed and the village is transformed. Best of all, her father, who his daughter had consistently referred to until now as "the preacher," once again becomes her "daddy."

Keep the tissues handy but take heart from the truths this film is pointing to: God sees our helplessness and hears our prayers – and the power of love can reach through our protective mechanisms to make new beginnings possible.

The Pitfalls of Perfectionism

> *Once you accept the fact that you're not perfect, then you develop some confidence.*   Rosalynn Carter

Someone once wrote, "that which is written without effort is usually read without pleasure." High standards and hard work are essential for turning promising starts into something truly worthwhile. If grief hooks into perfectionist tendencies in the wrong way, however, we can end up ensnared in an entirely false model, striving to achieve higher standards than God is actually asking of us. This is not only a certain recipe for frustration, it stops us from being able to enjoy what we already have.[1] It can also cause us to project onto others our dislike of things that we despise in ourselves. As Bill Lemley reminds us,

> When nobody around you seems to measure up, it's time to check your yardstick.

The following excerpt, taken from Wikipedia under *Perfectionism (Psychology)*, will help us to make the all-important distinction between "normal" and "neurotic" perfectionism.

> Normal perfectionists derive a very real sense of pleasure from the labours of a painstaking effort, while neurotic perfectionists are unable to feel satisfaction because in their own eyes they never seem to do things well enough to warrant that feeling . . . ["Neurotic"] perfectionists are people who strain compulsively and unremittingly toward impossible goals, and who measure their own worth entirely in terms of productivity and accomplishment. ["Normal"] perfectionism can drive people to great accomplishments and provide the motivation to persevere in the face of discouragement and obstacles . . .

> The meticulous attention to detail necessary for scientific investigation, the commitment which pushes composers to keep working until the music realises the glorious sounds playing in the imagination, and the persistence which keeps great artists at their easels until their creation matches their conception all result from perfectionism.

> High-achieving athletes, scientists, and artists often show signs of perfectionism. For example, Michaelangelo's perfectionism spurred him to create masterpieces such as the statue David and the [ceiling of] the Sistine Chapel.

As surely as we should praise God for the skill and persistence which enable us to keep going until our work is fully formed, it is as well to be aware that neurotic perfectionism can lead to procrastination – that is, putting things off because our efforts never feel quite good enough to risk showing to others. This is especially likely to be the case if our self esteem is already on the low side, in which case we may be gripped by the fear of failure and the need to earn approval.[2] These are issues that require specific prayer. You may find these insights a helpful starting point.

> *Striving for excellence motivates you;*
> *striving for perfection is demoralizing.*
> *Harrriet Braiker*

> *A man would do nothing if he waited*
> *until he could do it so well*
> *that no one could find fault.*
> *John Newman*

> *Ring the bells that still can ring*
> *forget your perfect offering,*
> *there is a crack in everything,*
> *that's how the light gets in.*
> *Leonard Cohen*

Repression

> *The little screaming fact that sounds through all history:*
> *repression works only to strengthen and knit the repressed.*
> *John Steinbeck*

Think of repression and we normally associate it with the forcible subjugation of others. Here, however, we are concerned with the specific defence mechanism whereby people push anxious thoughts and desires down into the depths of their subconscious.

We saw in the section on "Resisting excessive self consciousness" that most of us are skilful at projecting the image of themselves that we wish to convey. When enough people mock our aspirations, however, we may choose to bury our hurt and put on some form of a mask to keep up appearances – rather like the actors in ancient Greek plays, who wore masks to indicate the type of role that they were playing.

Since our quest throughout this book has been to reach a place of greater emotional honesty, a major part of our efforts need to be directed towards bringing these repressed hurts and hopes into the light of the Lord's loving gaze – if possible, in the company of someone with whom we feel free to take off our mask.

One telling indication that repeated repression has caused something to go profoundly wrong in our subconscious is when we find ourselves deflecting attention away from ourselves by becoming increasingly critical of others.

In acute cases, the harrowing traumas we have pushed down resurface in our dreams, or when we are away from our usual routines and are hence more vulnerable. So far from fearing these "exposing" times, we are wise if we welcome them as an opportunity to do serious business with the Lord. Human nature being what it is, we are often tempted to skim over issues that we find too painful to address – but specific prayer for these situations may be required to enable us to live an integrated life.[3]

It is worth being aware that the source of some people's grief may not lie where we expect it to. For example, the person who sheds bitter tears in the aftermath of a divorce or bereavement may be lamenting what had been missing in the relationship (particularly if it had been a violent or abusive one) rather than just missing the person who is no longer there.

If these people had been keeping most of the knowledge of this abuse to themselves, it is only to be expected that they experience a sharp reaction now that there is no longer any time left in which to put things right. To avoid descending into depression (and to risk repeating this pattern in future relationships) it is important to recognise what is going on. This is all part of taking the mask off in order to get to the root of issues that have long been repressed.

Addictions

Every form of addiction is bad, no matter whether the narcotic be alcohol or morphine or idealism.

Carl Jung

With the levels of gambling and alcoholism ever on the rise, who could even begin to estimate the grief these addictions cause? Addictions incline people to crave for love, and to feel abandoned when life gets tough. But where someone indulges an addiction, it often induces a "co-dependent" reaction in other people (usually family members) who try to "manage" the problem. In the long run, this rarely makes it easier for the person affected to take responsibility for their problem.

When people become over-dependent on each other, they often begin to have considerable difficulty in considering their own feelings in isolation from each other. Where people constantly have to make adjustments and allowances to work around the mood of someone with addictive tendencies, they are sure to suppress a large measure of their own personality in their quest to hold the family together.

This is true not only for wives and husbands, but also for their children, who are highly likely to become ultra sensitive in such an unpredictable and volatile atmosphere. Deprived of anything approaching a "normal" childhood, whilst all the time absorbing harmful influences, a large percentage of the young people who work so hard to mitigate the effects of alcoholic parents end up drinking too much themselves – or indulging in what at first appears to be "safer" options, such as an addiction to sex, shopping or online gambling.

When people are tempted to conceal their activities, it is often a warning sign that something is more seriously out of balance than they may have wished to acknowledge. The first safeguard is to be aware of the quantity of alcohol they are consuming, the money they are spending, or the time they are devoting to certain pursuits.

As we saw "Fallout for Children", this may have left them filling roles that children should not be expected to be responsible for: maintaining the home and caring for the other siblings, as well as covering up for the behaviour of the addicted one. There is every possibility that these victims of parental inversion may become what John Sandford calls "peacemakers in the flesh," – their profound insecurity compelling them to try to make peace at any cost.

Addressing addictive behaviour is too big an issue for us to be able to do anything here but scratch the surface. One simple but essential safeguard for those who are caring for people with addictive tendencies is to be sure that they recognise their *own* needs, as we saw in the section "Caring for the Carers".

Identification and Idolatry

Men should be what they seem.

Shakespeare

One of the stock situations that great comic genius P.G. Wodehouse used in his writings is when people impersonate someone else in order to intrude into the hallowed portals of the fictional mansion he created in Shropshire: Blandings Castle. Wodehouse uses this for comic effect, and in order to further promising liasions. In real life it nearly always causes grief when people pretend to be other than who they really are.

I have witnessed men and women acting one way in courtship, only to reveal entirely different aspects to their personality once they consider themselves to be within a "safe" and established relationship. The heartache and disappointment this causes is one reason the more to pray to avoid becoming a hypocrite!

Identifying with what other people are going through is fundamental to going deeper with the Lord in prayer, but the flip side of such identification is when people seek to bolster their own sense of well being by living vicariously through others. This nearly always involves a degree of idolisation – typically parents, Christian leaders, or someone else whom they have placed on an unrealistic pedestal.

When something happens to lower this excessively high regard, nothing good comes from pushing these fallen idols off the pedestal we made the mistake of mounting them on. Beware what I call the pedestal back flip! A much healthier response is to respond, as one dear friend did twenty five years ago when she said, "I'm determined not to put you on a pedestal so that we can be friends!"

Dysfunctional and controlling people do not always have a scowl on their face. Certain people may seem only too willing to take care of us – but the "fruit" of their so-called concern is to suffocate and restrict us.[4] There is a time for insisting on proper boundaries. May the Lord keep us on the right side of the boundaries between freedom and friendship on the one hand and idolatry and co-dependency on the other.

Shame and Suppression

A man should never be ashamed to own that he has been in the wrong – which is but saying that he is wiser today than yesterday.   Jonathan Swift

Whereas many people may not know what they are doing when they repress certain emotions, some people choose to suppress them as a deliberate attempt to keep unacceptable feelings in check. For example, if somebody has caused you grief, you may, in turn, be disinclined to show them any kindness. You may also choose to not think through the implications of certain things which are sure to have unfortunate consequences for them.

When people go a long way out of their way to avoid a particular person or topic, it is often because a root of shame has taken hold in their lives. Shame ("Pride's cloak" as William Blake tellingly termed it) is a crippling and intimidating emotion, and whose wiles we need to be alert to. I have written about it in more detail elsewhere, and it is available on our web site.[5] Look out in particular for the three D's that it can engender: Denial, Deferral and Dismissing things that really do need facing up to.

Shame is a profoundly negative influence that we need setting free from, but one person, at least, found a way to see something positive about certain aspects of it:

The shame that arises from praise which we do not deserve often makes us do things we should otherwise never have attempted.

La Rochefoucauld

On another, and altogether more dangerous level, Islamic militants regard shame and humiliation as legitimate justification for resorting to violence. Patrick Sookdheo shows in *Global Jihad* that "gaining dignity is placed on a par with spreading Islamic power as fuel for the *spirit of jihad.*"[6] The whole world is reeling under the impact of militants who are attempting to take revenge for the real or imagined humiliation perpetrated against them.

At a personal level, however, we are wise if we ask the Lord to show us where shame has caused us to "swallow" emotions that would be much better brought out into the open and confessed, so that we can respond to present challenges without being crippled by influences from the past. You may wish to pray into these matters right away, for your soul and spirit to be washed clean of the taint of suppressed shame.

Extremes

Anyone desperate enough for suicide should also be desperate enough to go to extremes to find solutions to their problems.   *Richard Bach*

One way in which the subconscious adapts to lessen the pain of grief and loss is to adopt various coping mechanisms that involve constant repetition. Typical examples of what is commonly known as "obsessive-compulsive behaviour" include feeling the need to constantly wash hands, or to check that the cooker is turned off before leaving the house.

The roots of these compulsions – which tend to make life miserable for all concerned – often lie in an extreme form of perfectionism. As surely as being conscientious is a good thing, *over*-conscientiousness can lead to depression and anxiety. People may be prone to such things not only through genetic inheritance and childhood experiences, but also as a consequence of shock (in which case it may be temporary) or as the onset of a mental illness (in which case clinical treatment may well be appropriate).

Mountaineers expect to experience extreme weather on high places, and when we come across strange behavioural tendencies – in ourselves or others – we need considerable skill as well as courage to negotiate the descent from Mount Extremism. Whilst fervent prayer and counsel may occasionally set people free at one fell swoop from certain "excesses", the following are possible indicators that grief has become a neurological and chemical imbalance for which professional treatment is required.

- Excessive elation in the aftermath of loss, alternating with major downward spirals into an agitated depressive state. (This is entirely different from the authentic grace that the Lord pours out during the initial "divine anaesthetic" phase).

- A prolonged listlessness that causes relationships with friends and relatives to deteriorate, and risks turning into serious depression.

- A continuing sense of hollowness that makes people feel as though they are acting a part rather than really "living."

- A pronounced tendency to blame other people for everything that is going wrong in their lives. This often stems from having lost all confidence in themselves. The ensuing suspiciousness, and even hostility, can as easily be directed against themselves as others. This, of course, inclines them to say or do things that cause people to reject and isolate them still more.

- A strong tendency to harm themselves, sometimes as the result of self hatred, but sometimes as a complicated attempt to punish others.

- Other forms of unpredictable behaviour that range from the mildly eccentric to the genuinely unacceptable. This may sometimes manifest itself in acts of disproportionate generosity, or, alternatively, extreme miserliness.
- Taking on the symptoms or characteristics of people they are closely identified with.
- Exhibiting a constant desire for sympathy, but being unable or unwilling to accept it.
- An increased likelihood of developing diseases such as colitis and diabetes.

Compensation

Since we are exposed to inevitable sorrows, wisdom is the art of finding compensation.

Duc le Levis

We looked earlier at some of the ways in which people compensate against grief. To some extent, this is a normal part of the give and take of life. All of us can also probably think of times when, having done something wrong, we went to great lengths to make amends. Where this was offered out of a genuine desire to restore relationships, all well and good. If fear is the driving force, however, we need to be careful. Our desire to compensate can lead us into attitudes of flattery and inappropriate actions. Our goal, as always, is to act prophetically, as wisdom dictates and the Lord leads us, rather than to *react* defensively. Is this not something we should pray for?

Avoidance

Cats are dangerous companions for writers because cat watching is a near-perfect method of writing avoidance.

Dan Greenburg

Those who are in denial often put off attending to real commitments and responsibilities in favour of either the self-preservedly mundane or the seemingly more exciting, A man who is late with his mortgage payments may end up gambling, initially perhaps in the hope of winning enough to cover his debts, only to find himself falling ever further behind. Such is the lure of gambling – and the in-built bias in all gambling machines!

God honours those who shun delusory quick fixes and stick to the path of duty. We dare not allow either grief or our human reluctance to deter us from attending to matters that really do need dealing with. Giving in to "short cuts" and temptations merely yields ground to destructive forces that will make it still harder for us to recover.

Rationalisation

> *Rationalisation kills the beauty and charm of things. They are to be enjoyed, experienced, loved and felt. If you rationalise them, you will miss the beauty and charm and the feelings they evoke.*

> *Sit by the seashore. Look at it. Feel its vastness. Feel the rising up and down of the waves. Feel and be amazed at the creation and the creator of such magnificence. What good will it do you to rationalise about the ocean?*

>   *Amma*

What do we find immediately beyond the co-dependency we looked at in "Addictions", and the tendency to avoid facing up to certain things that we have also just considered? Often, the tendency to rationalise – that is, to come up with plausible reasons to explain behaviour for which one's real motives are either different or unconscious."[6]

In other words, we make excuses for ourselves in order to cover up for behaviour which might otherwise appear abnormal or even threatening. Anything that inclines towards an opposing point of view we are likely to systematically oppose or shut down.

When a woman continues to live with the demands of an abusive husband, for example, her decision may owe less to loyalty than to fear of the consequences were she to leave or report him. She therefore goes to great lengths to justify things that others would regard as being unacceptable.

For the well being of our soul, may the Lord show us where we are in danger of "papering over cracks" when the "wall" itself (the fabric of how we approach difficulties and rationalise problems) needs serious overhaul.

Tension – The Neurosis of Grief

Everything we think of as great has come to us from neurotics. It is they and they alone . . . who create great works of art.

Marcel Proust

"Neurotic" is the right word to describe perhaps fifteen to twenty percent of the population. The word frightens us, but we need not let it do so. Neurotic people simply experience an above average degree of inner restlessness that leaves them prone to anxiety.

Since grief has many ways of flushing such sensitivities to the surface, it is helpful to realize that there are usually entirely logical reasons why neurotic people are as they are. In her PhD thesis, *The Highly Sensitive Person,*[8] Elaine Aron explains that specific *physical* differences can be observed amongst the way that those who might rightly be described as neurotic are "wired."

Typical indicators of neurosis include an above average tendency to worry combined with an increased inability to control impatience and irritability. Fear of illness may be another pointer, although it must be stressed that most neurotics are surprisingly well able to cope with life, despite being unusually prone to inner conflicts, doubts and depressions, as well as absorbing a high degree of hurts and "bruises" along life's way.

Apart from any congenital tendencies towards neurosis, it can develop as the result of overly critical parents – teachers or others imposing their control on them as children. (In many cases, this pattern continues in later life too). People who have experienced much of this may come to feel "on edge" whenever they find themselves caught up in stressful arguments. This becomes so tiring that it can seriously weaken their ability to handle challenging situations. This is where more serious forms of neurosis can set in, which, in turn, greatly increase the chances of them pressing self-destruct buttons at some later stage.

Throughout this book I have encouraged prayer as a key solution for any and every situation. Those with neurotic tendencies make exceptional intercessors, their sensitivity enabling them first to pick up and then to reflect back to God burdens that others ave failed altogether to pick up.

This is precious to the Lord, but it does carry with it the risk of "overloading" that we looked at in the section of "Burden bearing in the Spirit." When those of us with neurotic tendencies pray about inner compulsions, there is a risk that it can make us still more obsessive.

A simple technique that has helped many is to wear some sort of simple wristband, twanging it sharply each time we realise that our thoughts have gone into an unhelpful spiral. This can help to jolt our mind out of its obsession and to restore the flow of faith – providing this does not become a form of obsession itself of course. Maybe this would make a novel use for a 'What would Jesus do' band!

Substitution and Sublimination

> *I believe the single most significant decision I can make on a day-to-day basis is my choice of attitude. It is more important than my past, my education, my bankroll, my successes or failures, fame or pain, what other people think of me or say about me, my circumstances, or my position.*

> *Attitude keeps me going or cripples my progress. It alone fuels my fire or assaults my hope. When my attitudes are right, there is no barrier too high, no valley too deep, no dream too extreme, no challenge too great for me.*

> *Charles Swindoll*

Most people find grief disconcerting because they do not know how long some particular phase of it is going to last. We considered in "The Sacrament of the Present Moment" the importance of trusting the Lord from day to day to give us the necessary grace to emerge beyond our grief and wistfulness into renewed inner freedom.

I discovered the other day that to "sublimate" means not only "to chemically extract a substance," but also to "refine and purify it". Often when we find ourselves going through times of great difficulty I pray, "Lord let there be interest on the trouble. Bring more glory through it than if it had never occurred!"

Many who have experienced serious loss often succeed in channelling their energies into public campaigns in order that others may be spared unnecessary grief. For example, a mother whose daughter had been killed by a drunk driver launched what has now become a highly influential organisation: *Mothers Against Drink Driving* (MADD). What better response can there be than to redirect our energies towards nobler and more ethical goals?

Discovering where the Lord would have us redirect our creativity is important both for gaining a new focus in life, and to avoid focusing our love and attention in inappropriate places. We looked at positive examples of this at the start of Part Six, but some men take refuge in their minds by endowing inanimate objects with erotic qualities. The technical term for this is fetishism. The word is most commonly associated in people's minds with tabloid revelations of extreme sexual practices, but the roots by which fetishism acquires a pathological hold in the mind usually predate any one specific loss.

Psychologists tell us that most of these foci provide a safe outlet for hostile and depressive emotions, but it is as well to take into account that once intense and obsessional yearnings acquire a prominent a place in our hearts, they are capable of dominating and enslaving our whole way of thinking.

Bearing in mind our tendency to become like the thing we worship, if we allow a substitute image to become more important to us than "real" relationships, how can this fail to develop a barrier between the free flow of God's Spirit and our inmost heart?

Some bereaved people chide themselves for thinking too much about the physical act of love, not realising how normal this is.

> When one is happily married, the physical act of marriage falls into place as a part of one's total life. That is as it should be. But the soldier lost in the desert can think only of water . . . What we must not do is to assume that the only right way to handle the problem of physical longing is to somehow get rid of it altogether. Such repression can be a carry-over from an abnormal Puritanism. . . The solution, at least for a given period of an individual's life, may lie in the re-channelling of the creativity that is sexual energy.[9]

Some, however, fuelled by the twin desires of avoiding loneliness, and proving that they can still initiate and maintain a relationship, plunge into intense new liaisons before they have recovered enough to be able to sustain it. Though this is by no means always the case, this longing to be remarried can, in the first instance, be a "mental concept" rather than a profound longing to spend the rest of their life with a specific person. If left unchecked, these powerful desires can lead to a trail of short-term relationships that cause more harm than good – a cycle that is likely to repeat itself until areas of weakness and woundedness are brought to the Cross.

Reflect and Pray

The following passage highlights the finest examples of substitution we could ever hope to experience: qualities of joy and life replacing the things that weighed us down.

> *The Spirit of the Sovereign Lord is upon me . . .*
> *to bind up the broken-hearted . . .*
> *and to appoint unto them that mourn in Zion,*
> *to give unto them beauty for ashes,*
> *the oil of joy for mourning,*
> *the garment of praise for the spirit of heaviness;*
> *that they might be called trees of righteousness,*
> *the planting of the Lord, that He might be glorified.*
> *Isaiah 61:1-3*

Lord, as we draw this section to a close,
thank You for the grace You give us,
and all the griefs You keep us from.
Purify the longings of our hearts
so that grief may take no wayward path —
and You can have the joy
of walking with us
and working powerfully through our lives.
In Jesus' Name, Amen.

References

1 See www.ruachministries.org/valeoftears/refs.htm
   "Perfection is achieved, not when there is nothing more to add,
   but when there is nothing left to take away." (Antoine de Saint-
   Exupéry)

2 The University of Dundee have prepared a helpful paper on the
   subject. See www.ruachministries.org/valeoftears/refs.htm

3 Understanding our dreams can help in this respect. See Russ
   Parker books *Healing Dreams* and *Dream Stories*:
   www.acornchristian.org and search 'Bookshop'

4 See the teaching about transference in *Is this Grief contagious?*

5 See www.ruachministries.org/valeoftears/refs.htm

6 Sookdheo, P. Global Jihad. *The Future in the Face of Militant
   Islam.* www.barnabasfund.org

7 Merriam-Webster's Medical Dictionary.

8 Broadway Books. (1997) New York

9 Catherine Marshall. "They walk in wistfulness" in *To Live Again.*
   Chosen Books. (2001)

Appendix Three

Practical Considerations

NOTHING IS PREDICTABLE when it comes to bereavement – but most people are emerging from the grief tunnel by the third year. For some, however, this third year may also prove hard to bear, as the full weight of their loss continues to bear down on them.[1] Responsibilities that had been apportioned between partners fall exclusively on one set of shoulders now, and those already stooped by grief. Although we are primarily concerned in this book with our spiritual and emotional journey, it is impossible to ignore the fact loss of financial security is likely to compound an already troubled situation.

Almost all grief episodes accelerate the timescale for attending to inevitably stressful business arrangements. Whilst some need goading into getting on with these, others need restraining from making long-term decisions too hastily. It is not without cause that the old truism reminds us that "Where there is a will, there are relatives." There are plenty of people around who are eager to make a fast buck out of someone else's misery.

Since unfamiliar tasks, such as handling complex financial details are bound to place an additional strain on those who had been content to leave such matters to their partners, this is another way of saying that it makes good sense for the living to do all they can to prepare their families for such an occurrence.[2]

Living Wills

Our days are numbered. One of the primary goals in our lives should be to prepare for our last day. The legacy we leave is not just in our possessions, but in the quality of our lives. What preparations should we be making now? The greatest waste in all of our Earth, which cannot be recycled or reclaimed, is our waste of the time that God has given us each day

Billy Graham

We have mentioned before that in many western societies, death is an all but "taboo" subject. In *The Old Folks*, Tove Ditlevsen, the Danish poetess, put it like this:

> *If they mention Death*
> *everyone cheerfully protests –*
> *which makes them more alone,*
> *with no one they can talk about*
> *this great at-birth ordained event.*

Perhaps the best way to overcome our natural reluctance to think about death is to start backwards. Since all of us are sure to die one day,[3] it is only common sense to make whatever preparations we can for it now. These will hopefully not be needed for a good long time, but it would be foolish to be caught unprepared. Catherine Marshall relates in *To Live Again* how unprepared she was for widowhood. She had naively assumed that it wouldn't happen to her – or that if it did, God would provide for her as He did for George Mueller.

There are certainly many Scriptural promises for widows and orphans, but that does not mean that we should not make sensible precautions. It is wise to draw up your will as specifically as possible, using percentages instead of fixed sums of money, since values change with the passing of time. Above all, don't forget to make sure that someone knows how to find it!

Lasting Powers of Attorney are essential but "Living wills" are becoming an increasingly popular way of indicating how you would wish to be treated if you were no longer in a position to discuss these things for yourself. Here is an example that someone sent me:

> I wish to live a full and fulfilling life, but not to prolong life at all costs. If I have lost the ability to interact with others and have no reasonable chance of regaining this ability, or if my suffering is intense and irreversible, I would not wish to be subjected to surgery or resuscitation, or have the life support of mechanical ventilations or other life prolonging procedures, *provided that refusing this treatment will not cause me to expire from severe hunger or thirst.* I wish,

rather, to have care which provides comfort and support, and which facilitates my interaction with others to the extent that this is possible.

In order to carry out these instructions and to interpret them, I authorise . . . to accept, plan and refuse treatment on my behalf in cooperation with attending physicians and health personnel. This person knows how much I value life, and how I would wish to respond in the face of suffering and dying. Should it be impossible to reach this person, I authorise . . . to make such choices for me. I have discussed my desires for care during terminal illness with them, and I trust their judgement on my behalf. In addition I have discussed with them the following specific instructions: . . Signed and Dated
Witness(es) (and their addresses).

We saw earlier how Moses and David did all they could to pave the path for their successors, who themselves received God's help and leading. Rather than tiptoeing around the thought of dying, why not plan an occasional Contingency Day to discuss financial affairs and other practical matters with the appropriate people? Far from being morbid, this may actually *help* you to appreciate the life you have together, and to make the most of every day that is given to you. After all, it would hardly be a kindness to leave someone you love (and who is likely to be in a state of emotional shock) the additional problem of having to contend with a raft of unknown financial details. Even Jesus made arrangements for the care of His mother when He was on the cross.[4]

Living Compliments

Shortly after we moved north to embark on our sojourn in Shetland, without our daughter, Ruth, who was then sixteen, we received an exquisite letter from her in which she detailed all the things that she had learned from us about life and godliness. That letter went straight into Ros's treasure box! Why risk leaving it till too late to express our appreciation for the people we love? Gillian Warren found this a wonderful undertaking.

> *We put the magnifying glass over each (good point we appreciated about them) in order to see more clearly, and then told them, as best we could, what great people we thought they were.*

> *The joy of doing it was immense . . . Now at least, should anything happen, our children know that we think the world of them . . . The result was quite unexpected. In due course, each one wrote back to us a letter in similar terms, and the bonds between us have been greatly strengthened. The whole episode released enormous joy amongst us as a family.*

Gillian recommends writing such a letter to each emerging adult, ideally when they are between seventeen and nineteen. Your children may well be a great deal older than that, but it is never too late.

As you put pen to paper, you may well find yourself recalling episodes that at the time you took for granted but which you look back on now with real pleasure and delight. Such recollections are precious, and – who knows – your loving encouragement may do more than you will ever know to help launch another generation on its way.

References

1 Janice Lord, (1988) *No Time for Goodbyes: Coping with Sorrow, Anger and Injustice after a tragic Death.* Pathfinder Publishing.

2 For further details about these practical arrangements, see www.ruachministries.org/valeoftears/refs.htm

3 Isaiah 40:6-8, Job 14:1-2, 5; James 4:14

4 John 19:26-27

Appendix Four

Antidotes to Grief

When you are feeling overwhelmed:

> *Don't be bewildered or surprised when you go through the fiery trials . . . The more we undergo sufferings for Christ, the more He will shower us with His comfort and encouragement.*
>
> *1 Peter 4:12, 1 Corinthians 1:8-9, 2 Corinthians 1:5 LB*

> *Have no fear of sudden disaster or of the ruin that overtakes the wicked, for the Lord will be your confidence and will keep your foot from being snared.*
>
> *Proverbs 3:25-26*

> *You heard my plea: "Do not close your ears to my cry for relief." You came near when I called you, and you said, "Do not fear."*
>
> *Lamentations 3:5-7*

> *You will be secure because there is hope; you will look about you and take your rest in safety. You will lie down, with no one to make you afraid.*
>
> *Job 11:18-19*

When you are feeling weak and insignificant:

> *Whether we are here in this body or away from this body, our goal is to please Him.*
>
> *2 Corinthians 5:9*
>
> *His Divine power has given us everything we need for life and godliness through our knowledge of Him who called us by His own glory and goodness.*
>
> *2 Peter 1:3*

> *Your strength will equal your days.*
>
> *Deuteronomy 33:25*
>
> *Therefore, my dear brothers, stand firm. Let nothing move you. Always give yourselves fully to the work of the Lord, because you know that your labour in the Lord is not in vain.*
>
> *1 Corinthians 15:58*

When you feel your work is bearing no fruit:

And now the prize awaits me – the crown of righteousness, which the Lord, the righteous Judge, will give me on the day of His return. And the prize is not just for me but for all who eagerly look forwards to His appearing.

2 Timothy 4:6-8

Be strong and courageous, and do the work. Do not be afraid or discouraged, for the Lord my God, is with you. He will not fail or forsake you until all the work for the service of the temple of the Lord is finished.

1 Chronicles 28:20

When you need to focus your gaze beyond the here and now:

Behold, I will create new heavens and a new earth. The former things will not be remembered, nor will they come to mind.

Isaiah 65:18-19

The Lamb at the centre of the throne will be their shepherd; He will lead them to springs of living water. And God will wipe away every tear from their eyes .

Revelation 7:17

Look, He is coming with the clouds, and every eye will see Him, even those who pierced Him; and all the peoples of the earth will mourn because of Him. So shall it be! Amen. "I am the Alpha and the Omega", says the Lord God, "who is, and who was, and who is to come, the Almighty."

Revelation 1:7-8

I am coming soon. Hold on to what you have, so that no one will take your crown. I heard a loud voice from the throne saying, "Now the dwelling of God is with men, and He will live with them. They will be His people, and God Himself will be with them and be their God. He will wipe every tear from their eyes. There will be no more death or mourning or crying or pain, for the old order of things has passed away."

Revelation 3:11, 21:3-4

On the Threshold

Today I have stood in spirit with those on the threshold:
  friends and families emerging from profound upheaval,
    flexing their wings to venture out beyond their loss.

My spirit prays for those who wait in fear or trepidation:
  the call to hospital, war, or exile from their land –
    for presidents and rulers
      who are poised to make
      the decisions that determine nations' fate.
      and church leaders as they contemplate
    the changes that they must make,
  and their flocks who debate if they will flow
    with the leaders God has sent.

For those for whom the way ahead is clear –
  the grace to pass through journey's dawn,
but for those who see no door but only walls:
  the courage to push until iron bars yield.

Father, You stand on the threshold
  of each new beginning;
    You take Your counsel and make Your plans,
      Since nothing takes You by surprise
    nothing then shall hinder Your loving purposes,
  not even our own fickleness,
so long as we surrender to Your leading,
  and allow Your peace to replace our tension.

In this sacred place,
  and at this threshold time,
    I seek Your leading now.
      Let Your praise fill my emptiness,
    and Your Spirit inspire the prayers
  that shape both lives and nations,
as Your presence rests on this journey
  that You have called me to.

A Final Prayer

As you fill in the blanks in this prayer, may the Lord melt away remaining grief and strengthen you to bring His love and grace to many, despite the many challenges that you face. Nothing you have been through is ever in vain.

Lord, I give you now the matter of . . .
as well as the comments that . . . made.
I turn from them all,
but ask You to bless all concerned,
so that together, or apart, we may experience
more of Your blessings in our lives.
Wherever the real rights and wrongs lie,
be Lord of the process
and Lord of the outcome.
In Jesus' name,

272

Index